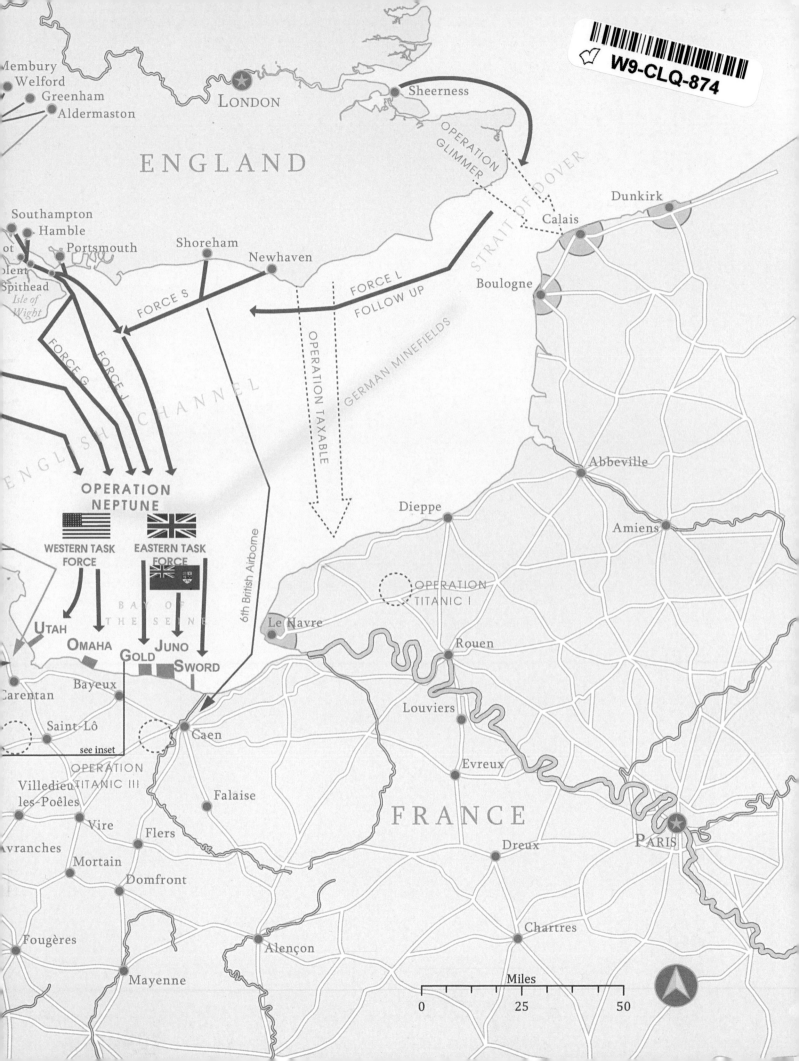

"EVERYTHING WE HAVE"
D-DAY
6.6.44

**THE NATIONAL
WWII MUSEUM**
NEW ORLEANS

"EVERYTHING WE HAVE"
D-DAY
6.6.44

The American story of the Normandy landings
told through personal accounts, images and artifacts
from the collections of The National WWII Museum

GORDON H. "NICK" MUELLER

FOREWORD BY TOM BROKAW

ANDRE
DEUTSCH

KEY TO MAPS

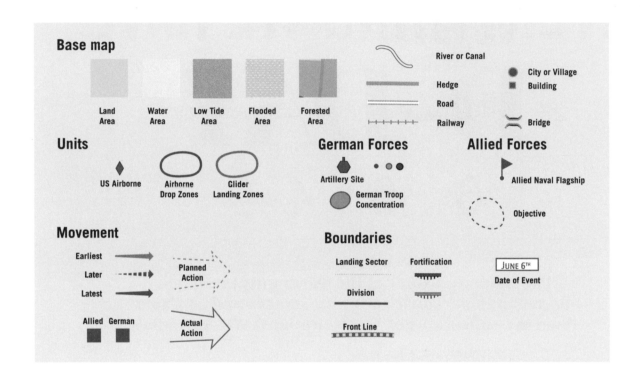

Base map

- Land Area
- Water Area
- Low Tide Area
- Flooded Area
- Forested Area
- River or Canal
- Hedge
- Road
- Railway
- City or Village
- Building
- Bridge

Units

- US Airborne
- Airborne Drop Zones
- Glider Landing Zones

German Forces

- Artillery Site
- German Troop Concentration

Allied Forces

- Allied Naval Flagship
- Objective

Movement

- Earliest
- Later
- Latest
- Planned Action
- Allied German
- Actual Action

Boundaries

- Landing Sector
- Division
- Front Line
- Fortification
- JUNE 6TH Date of Event

NOTE ON USE OF PERSONAL ACCOUNTS

Oral histories and other personal accounts in this work represent excerpts from far more lengthy accounts. Museum historians included excerpts that are especially revealing about the D-Day experience, and employed minor edits to improve clarity. Consequently, selections in this work differ from complete versions of accounts found on the Museum's Digital Collections website, or in The Eisenhower Center Peter Kalikow World War II Collection, University of New Orleans, preserved by the Museum. Care was taken to preserve the meaning of each testimonial. Also, oral histories are by nature subject to the hazards of memory and must be considered in concert with other documentary records.

This icon signals that additional archival material related to this personal account or introduction can be found on the Museum's website link **ddaybook.com**, under the appropriate chapter heading. These materials may include video clips, photographs, documents or other details.

CONTENTS

"The English language does not provide a multifaceted, exact word that alone can describe what surely must have been surging through each man's mind and body. Were such a word to be coined, it would include meanings embodied in such interrelated words as: bravery, weakness, trust, toughness, uncertainty, love, tenacity, determination, despair, fearlessness, fright, faith, assurance, doubt, hate, loyalty, distrust, resolution, seriousness, prayerfulness, bravado, and hope."

Howard Vander Beek

US Navy, Executive Officer, *Landing Craft Control 60*

FOREWORD

The greatest military invasion in history which was the beginning of the end for the greatest threat to western civilization the world had known.

That is the succinct summary of D-Day, the audacious Allied invasion of France on June 6, 1944, a massive armada of ships, planes, landing craft, armor and men from the sea and the air determined to bring to an end the ruthless power and immoral appetite of Nazi Germany and its crazed Führer, Adolf Hitler.

To contemporary audiences D-Day now is a grainy black and white screen shot from the sea of landing craft, the ingenious Higgins boats, unloading young American, British and Canadian men onto killing fields called Omaha, Utah, Sword, Gold, Juno— beaches where the Germans commanded the high ground.

Who were these bravest of the brave, not just from the landing craft but in fighter and bomber planes above, the paratroopers who jumped in the night before? The men just offshore in destroyers and battleships, laying down fields of fire on the German positions?

The engineers who struggled to get the heavy stuff onto the beaches—the tanks and armored personnel carriers?

The medics and casualty recovery and identification teams, ministering to the wounded and slipping the dead into body bags with their dog tags attached?

Not that many months before, the green troops had been farm boys and city kids, school teachers and shop clerks. They were alongside veterans their age who had already been through North Africa, Italy and Anzio.

Now we meet them in this very welcome and majestic new book from Nick Mueller who, with his fellow historian and great friend Steven Ambrose, founded The National WWII Museum in New Orleans.

The book is the perfect complement to a stunning cluster of Museum galleries paying tribute to the military genius and personal sacrifices of those who prevailed in World War II.

Here you will read the story of Harold Baumgarten, wounded five times as he came ashore and fought his way to higher ground. To the end of his life he recited the names of comrades who didn't make it and remembered his pledge to become a physician and heal, not kill, if he survived. He returned home, became a physician, and kept his battlefield promise until he died at the age of 91.

Walt Ehlers was a strapping Kansas farm boy when he answered the call to arms with his brother, Roland. By the time he hit Omaha Beach, Walt was a sergeant and a veteran of North Africa and Sicily. What he learned in those battles served him well on D-Day. Keep moving and take the fight to the enemy.

He attacked entrenched German machine-gun positions, at one point killing four enemy soldiers before they had time to react. Although wounded himself, he fought on and rallied his squad again and again. For his heroics he was awarded the Congressional Medal of Honor, but it could not replace a great loss: His brother was killed when his landing craft was hit by a mortar at the water's edge.

So much of the accounts of D-Day understandably concentrate on the sacrifices and heroics of the men who fought their way ashore or climbed the cliffs at Pointe du Hoc to knock out the German guns trained on Utah beach.

But here you'll also learn of the heroics of medics; combat engineers who blew up German barriers; artillery forward observers; tank drivers; navy pharmacists; navigators; nurses treating wounded when they were evacuated; French families struggling to survive.

Every soldier, sailor, civilian—whatever their rank or job— experienced the horrors, the heroics, the sacrifices of D-Day. A thousand years from now, historians will look back in wonder on what was accomplished by ordinary citizens.

Those who survived those days can rightly claim pride as well as humility.

In these pages you'll come to understand: this is who they were, the elite and the ordinary who stopped the spreading Nazi bloody stain at the water's edge.

It was a generation that learned at an early age that no nation is immune to history's cycles of ruthless abuse of power by immoral despots.

The World War II generation returned home to a new reality: in a world where distance was no longer a protective barrier and vigilance took on massive new meaning.

The state of political and military readiness became permanent. Alliances were formed and reflected political, economic and cultural values.

They weren't always correct or effective but they were successful in heading off another world war.

The men and women in this book, that is their legacy, equal to what they accomplished on D-Day and beyond.

Tom Brokaw
July 2018

Tom Brokaw is the author of _The Greatest Generation_. As a broadcast journalist and writer he has been on the front lines covering seismic change around the world for half a century, and was an early patron of The National WWII Museum. In 2016, Brokaw, Tom Hanks and then-Museum President and CEO Gordon "Nick" Mueller received France's Legion of Honor in recognition of their advocacy in the field of World War II history.

PREFACE

D-Day in Normandy, the monumental Allied operation of June 6, 1944, set the stage for the final destruction of the Third Reich eleven months later. The amphibious invasion and how it impacted the lives of the combatants were foundational to the writings of my longtime friend and colleague Dr. Stephen Ambrose, and to the creation of The National WWII Museum in New Orleans.

The voluminous stories of courage and sacrifice among the soldiers, airmen and sailors of D-Day inspired Steve Ambrose throughout his career. As a military and political historian, Ambrose believed D-Day offered a powerful demonstration of the American spirit and the values of the American citizen soldier. In the mid-1980s he began intensive research into the events and veterans of D-Day. At the time we both taught in the University of New Orleans History Department before I transitioned into university administration roles.

Our university overlooked the very lakefront site where, early in the WWII era, the entrepreneur Andrew Jackson Higgins tested the innovative landing craft that would play a major role in Normandy and other Allied invasions around the globe. General Eisenhower himself, during an interview with Ambrose, called Higgins "the man who built the boats that won the war for us."

In 1985, as a UNO Vice Chancellor, I was able to help Ambrose establish the Eisenhower Center for Leadership Studies to provide the staff support he needed to collect hundreds of first-hand accounts from American veterans, as well as from selected British, French, Canadian and German survivors of the climactic battles of D-Day. Ambrose began his research, in part, by showing up at veteran reunions, tape recorder and lists of questions in hand.

By the early 1990s he and his associates had collected more than 1,200 personal accounts along with a diverse mix of artifacts sent to him by the veterans. The recorded interviews and testimonials were then transcribed for his research. These recollections deepened Ambrose's appreciation of the magnitude of the D-Day story. He admired the Americans who rallied during this time of crisis, striking a tone similar to Tom Brokaw's in *The Greatest Generation*. While Ambrose—along with many of us born just prior to World War II—regarded that generation of Americans as exceptional, he also believed passionately that every future generation would respond to any comparable challenge. He was confident that they too, if called upon, would defend our freedoms and our democracy.

This conviction led Ambrose to propose two ideas to me in the backyard of his home one afternoon in 1990, ideas that would dramatically change his life and mine. The first was his commitment to use his oral histories and other research to write what would become his best-selling book, *D-Day, June 6, 1944: The Climactic Battle of World War II*. The book was written for the occasion of the 50th anniversary of the battle in 1994. His second idea was to ask me to join him in a bold venture to build a National D-Day Museum in the new Research and Technology Park that I was charged with developing adjacent to the UNO campus. Ambrose enthusiastically proposed that he donate his oral histories and artifacts and that I raise the funds to get the D-Day Museum built and opened—all in time for the '94 anniversary. We envisioned a modest project at the very site where Higgins had tested his famous landing craft.

Ambrose and I immediately agreed that a National D-Day Museum in New Orleans made perfect sense: It would honor the legacy of Higgins Industries while making the D-Day stories accessible to millions. New Orleans, an important port and military center during the war, would be honored to become the place where the personal stories and artifacts of those who fought on D-Day would be preserved and displayed. That day in the backyard, Ambrose predicted: "It will only cost about $1 million to build!" I immediately countered that he was naïve and it would cost at least $4 million, but added, "We'll raise it together; I'm in, that's the best idea you've ever had!"

Nick Mueller (left) with Stephen Ambrose at the June 6, 2000, grand opening of The National WWII Museum, known then as The National D-Day Museum.

Despite myriad challenges that came with research and writing, Ambrose did meet his goal to publish his D-Day book in time for the 50th anniversary. In contrast, the D-Day Museum became a story of fundraising challenges, plan changes, rising costs and delays. The Board of Directors wisely decided to abandon the lakefront site in favor of a downtown location which was proximate to millions of tourists. In the end, the effort required ten years and $20 million, and we finally opened on June 6, 2000. It was a day to remember! Hundreds of thousands of veterans, active military and residents of New Orleans filled downtown, and trucks carried more than 1,500 D-Day veterans in a parade that will never be forgotten.

The D-Day Museum was an instant national attraction and media favorite. Within a few years, in response to urgings from veterans and visitors, Congress designated our institution as America's National WWII Museum with an expanded mission to portray the entire American experience in the war.

Retiring from academia after the 2000 opening, I also stepped down as Chairman of the Board, then served seventeen years as the Museum's founding President & CEO. Now, nearly three decades after that conversation in Steve's backyard, I am completing *Everything We Have* as yet another tribute to those who served on D-Day.

The Ambrose-Mueller commitment to building a national museum consumed both of us until Steve died in 2002. By then he had passed the torch to me and witnessed the early progress in our expansion. Today, we are nearing completion of the Museum's $400 million capital drive and the campus fills three city blocks, offering dramatic exhibits and media experiences, conferences and education programs. High TripAdvisor ratings and millions of visitors give testimony to the power of the idea conceived by Ambrose and elevated by many others.

I will always be grateful to Steve, to our national Board of Trustees (successor to the early board) and staff, as well as to all the veterans, charter members and donors who gave life to the dream of two historians. Congress and the state of Louisiana, along with high-profile friends such as Tom Brokaw, Tom Hanks, Steven Spielberg and Gary Sinise, have also been vital to the Museum's development and success. On the institutional level, this Museum would never have been possible without unflagging encouragement from the UNO History Department and former university Chancellor Gregory O'Brien

Many individuals came together to make *Everything We Have* possible. My successor as President and CEO, Stephen Watson, provided critical backing at every stage. Several D-Day veterans who are featured in the book also advanced the Museum's mission in other significant ways; they include Walt Ehlers and Dr. Harold Baumgarten, infantrymen at Omaha Beach, and Major General John Raaen Jr., US Army (ret.), who as a Rangers captain was a key figure in the assaults at Omaha and Pointe du Hoc. Special acknowledgement must go to the Peter Kalikow Collection of oral histories owned by UNO and preserved by our Museum. All students of World War II history are indebted to Kalikow, a business leader and philanthropist, for providing the Museum's opening financial contribution in 1990, and for his support ever since.

Our staff historians collected many of the oral histories included in this work. The interviews are just a small part of an archive now holding more than 10,000 personal accounts from WWII veterans. Emeritus Office researchers Coleman Warner and Kali Martin collaborated with other historians and curators in assembling and editing book material; I owe them a deep debt of gratitude for their tireless efforts. Rowan Technology developed a detail-rich collection of maps to provide context to the personal stories. Photographer Frank Aymami III and Adept Word Management also played important roles, respectively, capturing artifact images and transcribing oral histories. And in Normandy licensed tour guide Sylvain Kast generously shared his intimate knowledge of D-Day battlefields and steered us to additional map and image resources. Finally, a heartfelt thanks to my friends and historian colleagues Dr. Julian Pleasants and Dr. Robert Citino, who made helpful suggestions in editing this work, and of course to my wife Beth, who was always patient and supportive.

Gordon "Nick" Mueller, PhD
President & CEO Emeritus,
The National WWII Museum, New Orleans

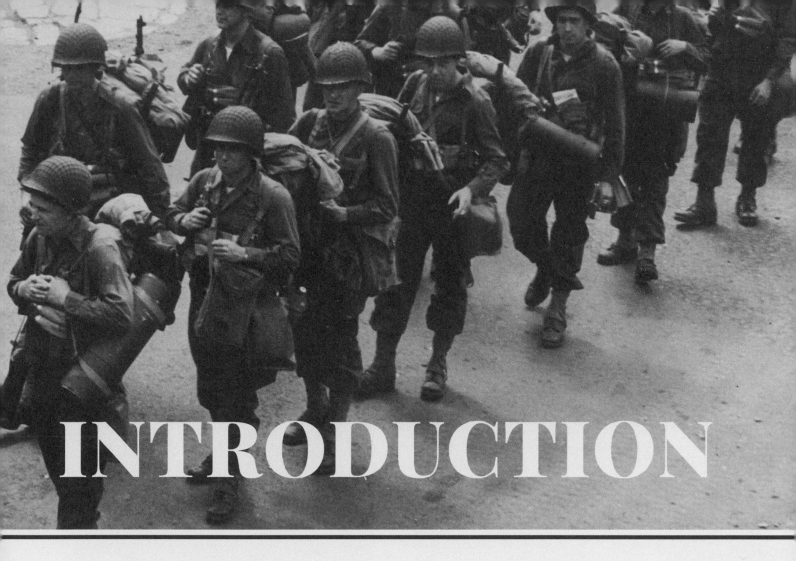

INTRODUCTION

6.6.44

"OK, let's go!" General Dwight David Eisenhower spoke those words early on the morning of June 5, 1944, and this simple directive from the Supreme Allied Commander unleashed the largest amphibious invasion in world history. Eisenhower put into motion a force of 6,000 ships and landing craft, 11,000 planes, and 160,000 Allied troops, all united in the mission of piercing Hitler's Atlantic Wall in Normandy the next day, D-Day, June 6. It would be an epic test.

Planning for Operation Overlord had been underway for years and was among the war's most tightly guarded secrets, with massive logistical and training efforts required in both Great Britain and America. Adolf Hitler knew an invasion was coming on his western front, but did not know when or where. The Nazi leader knew what was at stake and declared: "The destruction of the enemy's landing is the sole decisive factor in the conduct of the whole war and hence its final results."

Hitler put a brilliant and battle-tested commander, the "Desert Fox" Field Marshal Erwin Rommel, in charge of coastal defenses in the Normandy sector of his Atlantic Wall. Rommel believed that "the war will be won or lost on the beaches … with only one chance to stop the enemy, and that's while he's still in the water struggling to get ashore. The first 24 hours of the invasion will be decisive." In the months prior to the invasion, Rommel pushed his troops and conscripted laborers to strengthen fortifications, increase beach obstacles and lay mines that would destroy or delay Allied forces.

The Normandy invasion qualified as one of the greatest gambles in military history, ushering in a fight to the finish between the forces of freedom and democracy and the visions of world conquest refined by Hitler's fascist and racist regime. Many years hence, historian Stephen Ambrose would depict Overlord as the pivot point not only of the war, but of the twentieth century. Winston Churchill called the invasion "the most difficult and complicated operation ever to take place." And Joseph Stalin, who had long pressed for such an operation to relieve pressure on the Eastern Front, concluded at the time: "The history of the war does not know of an undertaking comparable to it for breadth of conception, grandeur of scale, and mastery of execution."

The stakes could not have been higher. Eisenhower and his top commanders knew that defeat on the beaches of Normandy would delay another broad assault for a year or more, allowing Hitler time

Eisenhower (far left) in Haunville, France in July 1944 with Lieutenant General Omar Bradley (back left), Commanding General 1st Army. They are being shown around the 79th Infantry Division Headquarters by Major General Ira Wyche (front right), Commanding General 79th Division and Brigadier General Frank U. Greer (rear right), Assistant Commander of the 79th Division.

to gather strength while putting pressure on America's support for the war on the home front. The cloak of secrecy would be gone, and with victory delayed in Europe, the Allies would be unable to transfer ships, planes and men en masse to the Pacific to join the fight against the Japanese empire. Eisenhower's commanders also knew that while their troops were well trained and equipped, most of these young men had yet to be tested in combat.

Everything depended on the assault from the sea. Amphibious invasions have always been perilous due to the uncertainties of weather and the vulnerabilities of beach landings—men attacking out of water with heavy gear, and the necessity of supplying out of water—against entrenched defenders. As far back as the fifth century BC, the mighty Persian Empire attacked fledgling Greek democracies from the sea with the benefit of overwhelming odds at the battle of Marathon, and Persia lost. In World War I the failure of combined British, French and Australian amphibious forces at Gallipoli badly discredited the doctrine of amphibious warfare. With the exception of the US Marine Corps and the Japanese, armed forces around the world believed in the 1920s and 1930s that any amphibious assault against a well-defended front was doomed.

Memories of the disaster at Gallipoli were heavy on the minds of Overlord planners, as were more recent lessons from World War II. Landings in Tarawa in the Pacific and then the invasions in North Africa, Sicily, Salerno and Anzio were all plagued by mistakes and confusion. Yet if Hitler's "Fortress Europe" were to be breached, paving the way for a drive into Germany, there seemed no viable alternative to the cross-channel invasion plan developed by General Eisenhower and his commanders.

Eisenhower's responsibilities for the D-Day landings began on December 7, 1943, when President Roosevelt appointed him Supreme Commander of the Allied Expeditionary Force. Following a brief leave in the United States, Eisenhower assumed full command in Great Britain in mid-January 1944. Exhaustive planning had long been underway, involving legions of non-combatants engaged in transporting and supplying the Allied force. By early 1944, more than a million US personnel were scattered across England, training and waiting.

Some US divisions like the 29th Infantry Division had been there since 1942 while the 1st Infantry Division, the famed "Big Red One," had seen combat in North Africa and Sicily before returning to England in November 1943. The 101st Airborne Division arrived in England in August/September of 1943, followed by the 82nd Airborne Division in December. The 2nd and 5th Ranger Battalions arrived in December and January, respectively. Signs of the impending assault by air, sea and land were everywhere, with planes, guns, tanks, vehicles and supplies of every sort stockpiled in enormous quantities.

Overlord preparations intensified at the Supreme Headquarters Allied Expeditionary Forces (SHAEF) as soon as General Eisenhower took up residence in London. Plans to that point included only three beaches for the invasion, but British General Bernard Montgomery, backed by Eisenhower, convinced the Overlord planning team of the need to expand the landing area to five beaches. This was a dramatic change at a very late date. For the

Shoulder patch for the Supreme Headquarters Allied Expeditionary Force. The flaming "sword of freedom" over the black background represents cutting the black Nazi night over Europe and points the way to the rainbow of peace and liberty. The colors of the rainbow represent the Allied nations.

Americans, the new plan called for sending an additional division to a new landing beach, code-named Utah, and for two airborne divisions parachuting in a few miles beyond the beachhead onto the Cotentin Peninsula. A significant increase in materiel, ships and planes would be required to support the changes. Eisenhower and Montgomery agreed that these simultaneous assaults were critical to blocking German counter-attacks against Allied Forces landing to the east. The expanded scale of the Overlord plan also caused Eisenhower to make urgent requests for additional Higgins landing craft to support the landings on Utah Beach, a request that delayed the planned invasion date from May to early June.

In its final form, Operation Overlord targeted an invasion front spread out over 50 miles of the Normandy coastline. In overall command was General Montgomery, the hero of El Alamein. His 21st Army Group contained two armies: US First Army, commanded by General Omar Bradley, and the British Second Army under General Miles Dempsey. Each army, in turn, had a huge naval force in support.

Bradley's operations are the focus of this book. The American general oversaw two simultaneous amphibious assaults: a landing on Omaha Beach by the 1st and 29th Infantry Divisions and one against Utah Beach by the 4th Infantry Division. While simple in conception, both of these landings also contained considerable supporting operations. Just west of Omaha, elements of the 2nd and 5th Ranger Battalions were to scale the cliffs at Pointe du Hoc and destroy a battery of 155mm German guns that posed a lethal threat to landing forces and ships alike. At Utah, the 101st and 82nd Airborne Divisions would parachute into the interior of the Cotentin Peninsula. The combined airborne and infantry units had the mission of cutting across the Cotentin, then driving north to seize the vital port of Cherbourg. Without a port the Allies could never ensure the continuous flow of supplies critical to a breakout beyond Normandy.

As Overlord gathered momentum in February 1944, US Army Chief of Staff General George Marshall sent Eisenhower the official directive that would guide him to the end of the war: "You will enter the continent of Europe and, in conjunction with the other United Nations, undertake operations aimed at the heart of Germany and the destruction of her armed forces."

The pace of training now quickened for soldiers, sailors and airmen. Dress rehearsals put the men through the challenges of loading ships, assaulting beach defenses, scaling cliffs and fighting at night. Training at rifle and artillery ranges, strenuous hiking, crawling through barbed wire, and practice in takeoffs and landings for glider craft were all part of the daily regimen.

Despite the rigors of training, the success of Overlord and Operation Neptune, the invasion's initial seaborne phase, still hinged on factors difficult to control. Secrecy was the first imperative. SHAEF planners took extraordinary steps to keep the Germans guessing. An elaborate deception campaign, Operation Fortitude, aimed to deceive Hitler on the time and location of the impending attack. A "ghost army" employed dummy trucks, tanks and jeeps under the very public command of the military figure that Germans respected and feared most, General George Patton. Additional deceptions included double agents and false intelligence, suggesting to Hitler and his generals that the invasion would come at Calais, just 22 miles across the Channel from England. Other misleading clues tried to fool the Germans into believing that Norway or southern France would be the site of the invasion. These multiple deceptions continued to have an effect even weeks after D-Day, when many in the German High Command still refused to believe that Normandy was the primary Allied target.

Another critical factor was the weather and the tides on D-Day. Since the decision had been made to land at low tide, when the water would be below the obstacles and mines placed on the landing beaches, the invasion would have to come on one of the rare dates when a low tide coincided with the first light. A landing just before dawn was essential to allow the half-light to conceal the massive attack force as it sailed toward Normandy. Another major concern of the Allied commanders was the prospect of stormy seas and high winds over the English Channel. Not surprisingly, the weather and tides were also important to the German defenders' projections as to the timing of the expected invasion.

In the final months leading up to D-Day naval vessels of every stripe filled the ports and harbors of England, Ireland and Scotland. Meanwhile, Allied bombers and fighter planes carried out daily missions to decimate the Luftwaffe—and ensure air superiority—while also damaging the transportation infrastructure that the German Wehrmacht needed to move reinforcements toward the coast. As D-Day drew near, Eisenhower placed the Allied expeditionary forces on standby in anticipation of his final invasion order. He was unshakable in his message to his commanders: "This operation is planned as a victory … We're going down there, and we're throwing everything we have into it, and we're going to make it a success."

In early June, Eisenhower moved the SHAEF command to Southwick House, near to one of Britain's principal naval ports at Portsmouth, where final decisions would be made. D-Day was set for June 5, so the invasion fleet was already on the move on the evening of June 4 when a storm with driving rain, high winds and heavy seas struck England and the Channel. Overlord seemed, more than ever, at the mercy of the elements. Ike ordered a one-day delay in the invasion, adding to the anxieties of the hundreds of thousands of soldiers and seamen aboard ships that had already left their harbors for the June 5 landings.

Prospects for the invasion looked bleak because of the poor conditions. Then, in meetings with SHAEF commanders on the evening of June 4, and again at 3:30 a.m. on June 5, Eisenhower's weather forecaster, Group Captain James Martin Stagg, offered promising news of a slight clearing in weather over the Channel for 36 hours starting on June 6. This was Eisenhower's last

American troops aboard an LCT (Landing Craft, Tank) in southern England, waiting for the invasion to begin.

In ports across southern England, tens of thousands of American troops boarded Higgins boats that took them to troop transports for the trip across the English Channel.

chance to postpone and recall the ships already underway. For a few moments, the Supreme Commander was the most powerful man on earth as he weighed his momentous decision. He polled his commanders and they were divided on whether to proceed or pull the fleet back. After a few moments of pacing the room, Eisenhower gave the long-awaited order: "OK, let's go!" A cheer broke out from those in the room as they raced to their Overlord commands. The invasion was on.

In the next hours, everyone under Eisenhower had a job to do. The Supreme Commander was left to his own thoughts, ceding to others the control of battle operations. Expecting the paratroopers to suffer horrific casualties as the first to land—behind enemy lines—in Normandy, Eisenhower made an impromptu visit to the 101st Airborne troops at the Greenham Common airfield on the evening of June 5. He bantered with the paratroopers, thanked them, and asked if they were ready. He found them in fighting spirit.

Eisenhower carried this note accepting responsibility should the invasion fail. In error, he dated it July 5.

But shortly thereafter, Eisenhower privately wrote a statement that he placed in his wallet. In the message, he accepted responsibility for failure in the event that the Germans prevailed: "Our landings in the Cherbourg-Havre area have failed to gain a satisfactory foothold and I have withdrawn the troops. My decision to attack at this time and place was based on the best information available. The troops, the air and the navy did all that bravery and devotion to duty could do. If any blame or fault attaches to the attempt it is mine alone." For emphasis, he had drawn a line under the words "mine alone." Eisenhower knew the risks and the stakes were extraordinarily high.

Even as he privately weighed the possibilities of failure on the eve of battle, the Supreme Commander publicly exuded confidence and inspiration. In the final hours before the invasion, Eisenhower sent out his Order of the Day to every member of the Allied invasion force:

SUPREME HEADQUARTERS
ALLIED EXPEDITIONARY FORCE
Soldiers, Sailors and Airmen of the Allied Expeditionary Force!
You are about to embark upon the Great Crusade, toward which we have striven these many months. The eyes of the world are upon you. The hopes and prayers of liberty-loving people everywhere march with you … you will bring about the destruction of the German war machine, the elimination of Nazi tyranny over the oppressed peoples of Europe, and security for ourselves in a free world…
I have full confidence in your devotion to duty and skill in battle. We will accept nothing less than full Victory!

Eisenhower's stirring words could not still the anxieties of those of thousands of young Americans who faced battle, not knowing what their fate would be. But the bravery and devotion to duty of which Eisenhower spoke were at work in grand measure among armed forces members. Even before the explosions began and smoke shrouded the rugged shoreline of Normandy, the Americans were confident that, together, they would carry the day. As one P-47 fighter pilot who enjoyed a lofty vantage point on D-Day later recalled, "Ships and boats of every nature and size churned the rough Channel surface; seemingly in a mass so solid one could have walked from shore to shore."

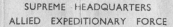

SUPREME HEADQUARTERS
ALLIED EXPEDITIONARY FORCE

Soldiers, Sailors and Airmen of the Allied Expeditionary Force!

You are about to embark upon the Great Crusade, toward which we have striven these many months. The eyes of the world are upon you. The hopes and prayers of liberty-loving people everywhere march with you. In company with our brave Allies and brothers-in-arms on other Fronts, you will bring about the destruction of the German war machine, the elimination of Nazi tyranny over the oppressed peoples of Europe, and security for ourselves in a free world.

Your task will not be an easy one. Your enemy is well trained, well equipped and battle-hardened. He will fight savagely.

But this is the year 1944 ! Much has happened since the Nazi triumphs of 1940-41. The United Nations have inflicted upon the Germans great defeats, in open battle, man-to-man. Our air offensive has seriously reduced their strength in the air and their capacity to wage war on the ground. Our Home Fronts have given us an overwhelming superiority in weapons and munitions of war, and placed at our disposal great reserves of trained fighting men. The tide has turned ! The free men of the world are marching together to Victory !

I have full confidence in your courage, devotion to duty and skill in battle. We will accept nothing less than full Victory !

Good Luck ! And let us all beseech the blessing of Almighty God upon this great and noble undertaking.

Dwight D Eisenhower

Above: Eisenhower's message to the invasion force. This copy belonged to US Navy Corpsman C. Ed Nelson.

Right: American soldiers prepare to board US Navy ships that will carry them to the invasion coast.

The National WWII Museum is proud to share, in this work, a rich mix of individual narratives, artifacts and related images that provide fresh perspectives on the American battle experience on D-Day and beyond. These selected oral history excerpts and other accounts, drawn almost exclusively from the Museum's collections, are subject to the hazards and ambiguities of memory but offer vital details and reflections that, in concert with documentary evidence, round out the picture of an epic struggle. With few exceptions, American veterans of World War II say they were simply doing their jobs when called to defend their country, that the "real heroes" are those who gave their lives. The Museum pays tribute to them all, those who came home—many forever changed—and those who did not, as it preserves and passes on their collective story. For their ideals, for the greater good, these young Americans gave everything they had, and they will be remembered always.

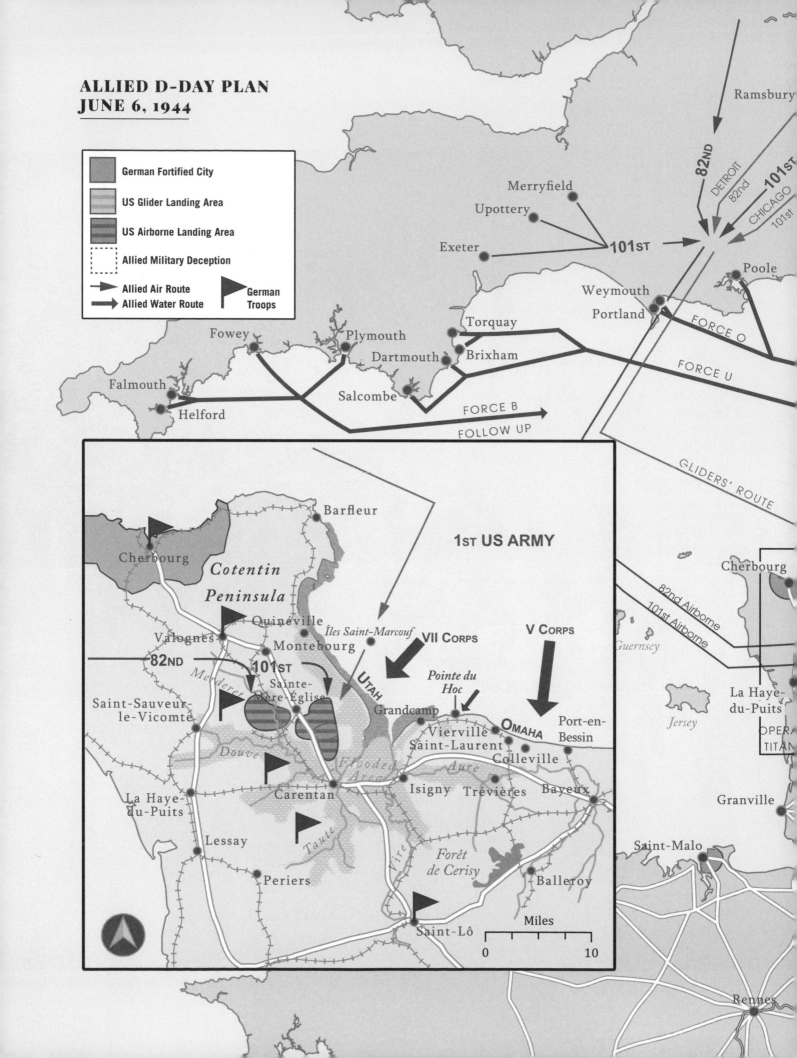

ALLIED D-DAY PLAN
JUNE 6, 1944

Legend:
- German Fortified City
- US Glider Landing Area
- US Airborne Landing Area
- Allied Military Deception
- Allied Air Route
- Allied Water Route
- German Troops

Ramsbury

82ND

DETROIT 82nd

101ST CHICAGO 101st

Merryfield

Upottery

101ST

Exeter

Poole

Weymouth

Portland

FORCE O

FORCE U

Fowey

Plymouth

Torquay

Dartmouth

Brixham

Falmouth

Helford

Salcombe

FORCE B

FOLLOW UP

GLIDERS' ROUTE

1ST US ARMY

Barfleur

Cherbourg

*Cotentin
Peninsula*

Quinéville

Îles Saint-Marcouf

VII CORPS

V CORPS

Valognes

Montebourg

82ND

101ST

Merderet

UTAH

*Pointe du
Hoc*

OMAHA

Port-en-
Bessin

Saint-Sauveur-
le-Vicomte

Sainte-
Mère-Église

Grandcamp

Vierville

Saint-Laurent

Colleville

Bayeux

Douve

*Flooded
Area*

Aure

La Haye-
du-Puits

Carentan

Isigny

Trévières

Lessay

Taute

Vire

*Forêt
de Cerisy*

Balleroy

Periers

Saint-Lô

Cherbourg

82nd Airborne

101st Airborne

Guernsey

Jersey

La Haye-
du-Puits

OPERA
TITAN

Granville

Saint-Malo

Rennes

Miles

0   10

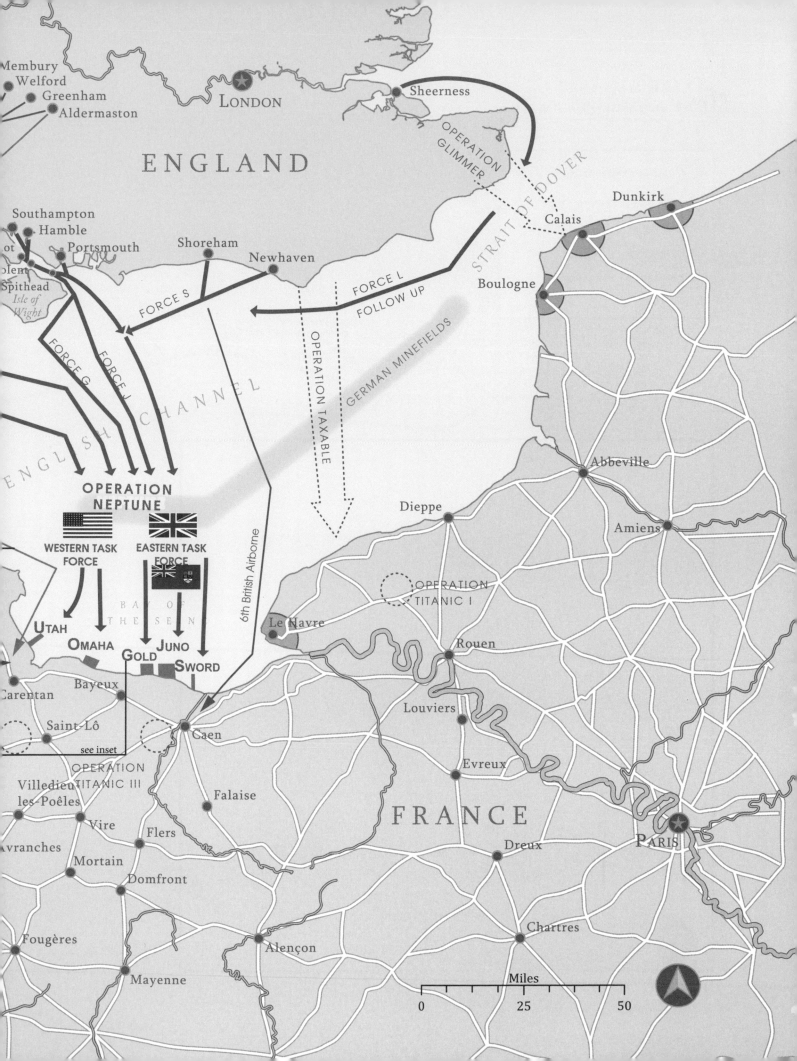

Membury
Welford
Greenham
Aldermaston

LONDON

ENGLAND

Southampton
Hamble
ot
Portsmouth
olent
Spithead
Isle of Wight

Shoreham
Newhaven

Sheerness

OPERATION
GLIMMER

STRAIT OF DOVER

Calais

Dunkirk

Boulogne

FORCE S

FORCE L
FOLLOW UP

GERMAN MINEFIELDS

OPERATION TAXABLE

FORCE G

FORCE J

ENGLISH CHANNEL

Abbeville

Dieppe

Amiens

OPERATION NEPTUNE

WESTERN TASK FORCE

EASTERN TASK FORCE

BAY OF THE SEINE

6th British Airborne

OPERATION
TITANIC I

Le Havre

Rouen

UTAH

OMAHA

GOLD

JUNO

SWORD

Carentan

Bayeux

Saint-Lô

see inset

Caen

Louviers

OPERATION
Villedieu TITANIC III
les-Poêles

Falaise

FRANCE

Evreux

Vire

Flers

Dreux

PARIS

vranches

Mortain

Domfront

Fougères

Mayenne

Alençon

Chartres

Miles

0   25   50

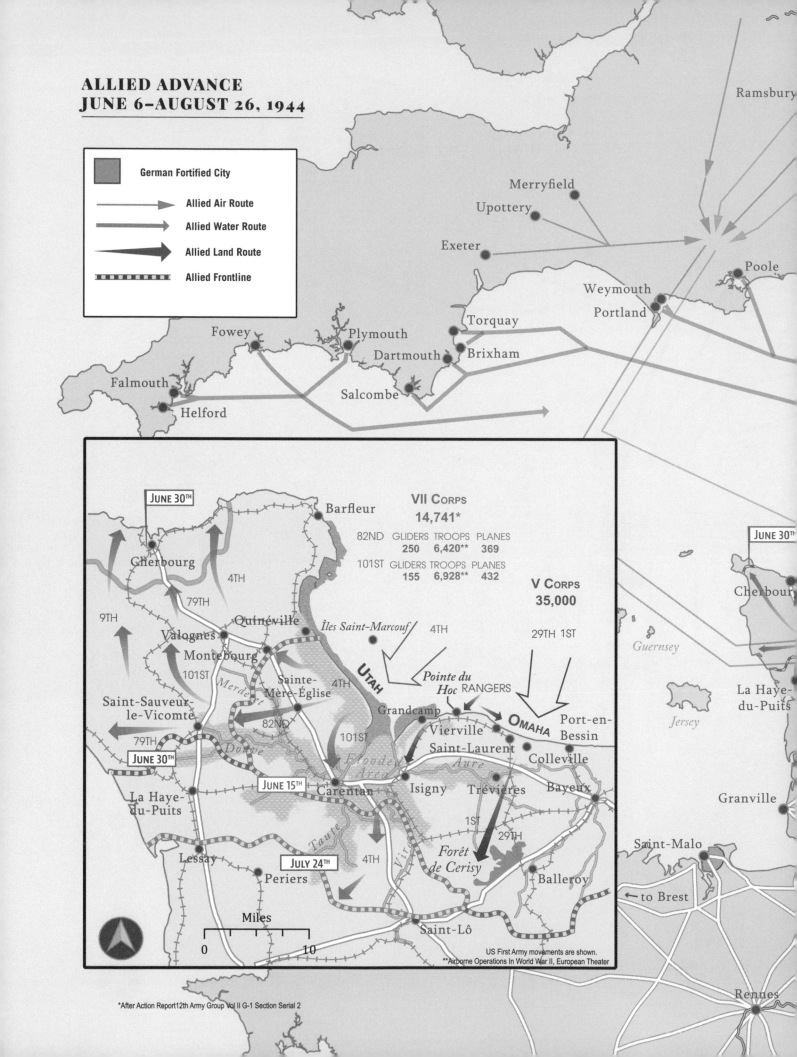

ALLIED ADVANCE
JUNE 6–AUGUST 26, 1944

Legend:
- German Fortified City
- Allied Air Route
- Allied Water Route
- Allied Land Route
- Allied Frontline

Ramsbury

Merryfield

Upottery

Exeter

Poole

Weymouth
Portland

Fowey
Plymouth
Torquay
Dartmouth
Brixham

Falmouth
Helford

Salcombe

JUNE 30TH

Barfleur

VII CORPS
14,741*

82ND	GLIDERS	TROOPS	PLANES
	250	6,420**	369

101ST	GLIDERS	TROOPS	PLANES
	155	6,928**	432

V CORPS
35,000

JUNE 30TH

Cherbourg

4TH

79TH

9TH

Quinéville

Valognes
Montebourg

101ST

Saint-Sauveur-
le-Vicomte

79TH

JUNE 30TH

Merderet

Sainte-
Mère-Église

82ND

Douve

La Haye-
du-Puits

JUNE 15TH

Carentan

Lessay

Periers

JULY 24TH

Taute

Vire

4TH

Îles Saint-Marcouf

4TH

UTAH

4TH

Pointe du
Hoc RANGERS

Grandcamp

101ST

Flooded
Area

Isigny

Vierville
Saint-Laurent

Aure

OMAHA

Port-en-
Bessin

Colleville

Trévières

Bayeux

1ST

29TH

Forêt
de Cerisy

Balleroy

Saint-Lô

Guernsey

Jersey

JUNE 30TH

Cherbourg

La Haye-
du-Puits

Granville

Saint-Malo

← to Brest

29TH 1ST

US First Army movements are shown.
**Airborne Operations In World War II, European Theater

Miles
0   10

Rennes

*After Action Report 12th Army Group Vol II G-1 Section Serial 2

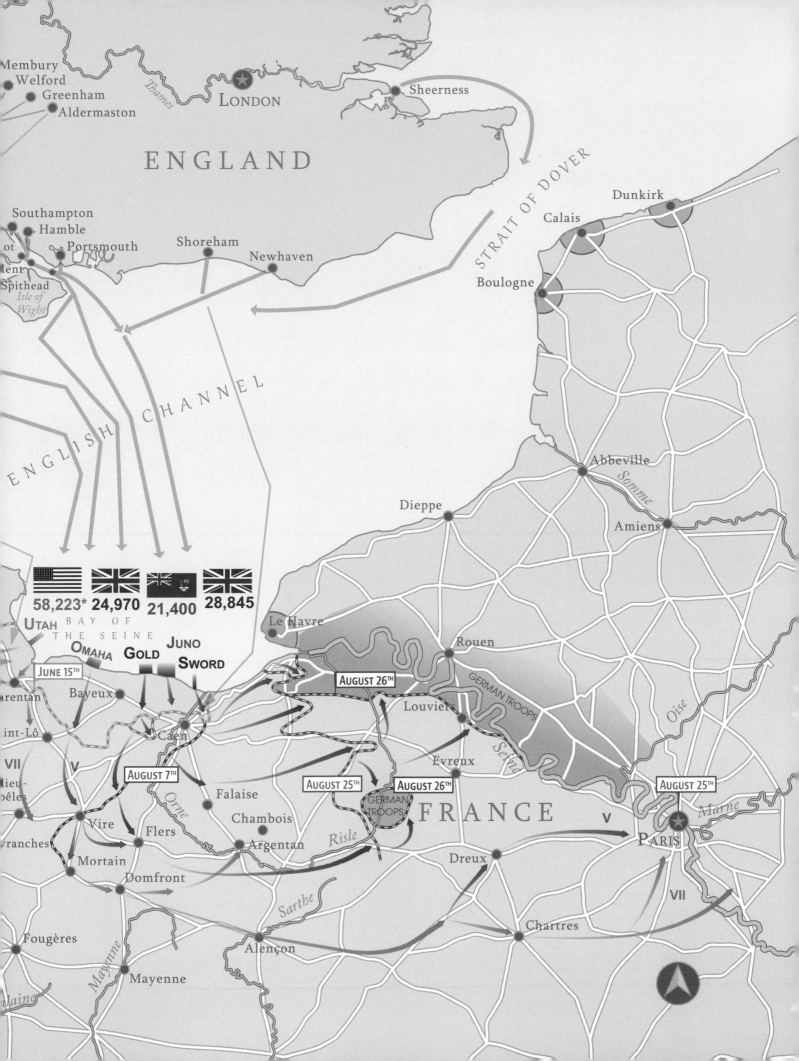

ENGLAND

London

Membury
Welford
Greenham
Aldermaston

Thames

Sheerness

STRAIT OF DOVER

Dunkirk
Calais

Boulogne

Southampton
Hamble
Portsmouth
Shoreham
Newhaven

Spithead
Isle of
Wight

ENGLISH CHANNEL

Abbeville
Somme

Dieppe

Amiens

58,223*   24,970   21,400   28,845

Le Havre

Rouen

Utah   BAY OF
        THE SEINE

Omaha   Gold   Juno   Sword

June 15th

Bayeux

Caen

August 26th

Louviers

GERMAN TROOPS

Oise

Evreux

Seine

arentan

int-Lô

VII   V

lieu-
êles

August 7th

August 25th   August 26th

Falaise
Chambois

GERMAN
TROOPS

FRANCE

August 25th

Marne

Paris

Orne

Vire   Flers

Argentan

Risle

V

Avranches

Mortain

Domfront

Dreux

VII

Fougères

Sarthe

Chartres

Mayenne

Alençon

Mayenne

aine

AIRBORNE
OPERATIONS

CHAPTER ONE

6.6.44

"Mount up!" The order arrived at bustling airfields across England as the last light faded on the evening of June 5, 1944. The command went out to the 82nd and 101st Airborne Divisions, signaling the start of the invasion of Normandy. Tension mounted as engines roared to life in more than 900 C-47 Skytrain troop transports and over 13,000 paratroopers climbed aboard the aircraft bound for the French coast. During earlier frenzied activity at the bases, the planes were painted with black and white stripes to aid Allied ground and ship personnel in identifying them as "friendlies."

Soldiers had to be helped into planes, as each was loaded with 100-150 pounds of extra gear—ammunition, radios, fragment grenades, K-rations and more. Some carried items in British-made canvas leg bags designed for release just before landing. A "stick" of sixteen to eighteen paratroopers, a designated group jumping at the same time, was packed into each C-47. Shortly after midnight on June 6, planes carrying the infantry units of the 82nd and 101st lifted off. The first units would be followed hours later by elements of the 325th and 327th Glider Infantry Regiments (GIR). The fate of the airborne soldiers on D-Day would be decided in fighting behind enemy lines in the hedgerows and country lanes of Normandy's Cotentin Peninsula. The paratroopers were trained and ready, and the confidence in their mission found voice in one soldier who cried, "Look out, Hitler, here we come!"

Paratroopers who looked out over the English Channel that night were awed by the moonlit scene below: an armada of thousands of ships and landing craft, steaming toward the Normandy beaches for a climactic battle with entrenched German forces. Inside the planes, restless men were mostly silent in their thoughts. Some worked their rosaries and prayed; most wondered if they would survive the night and worried about letting buddies down. Some slept; others got airsick as the C-47s passed over the Channel Islands of Guernsey and Jersey. As they approached the coast and enemy flak began pounding their planes or bursting nearby, it was abundantly clear that this mission would bear little resemblance to their practice jumps. The soldiers knew they were the tip of the spear of an Allied invasion in planning for several years, and they knew the operation was high risk.

Left: First Lieutenant Wallace Strobel, with blackened face and in combat dress, was immortalized in a photograph taken during his conversation with Supreme Allied Commander, General Dwight D. Eisenhower on the eve of the invasion. He carried this M1911A1 pistol (above) with him on D-Day.

Opposite: Glider Infantry Regiment personnel loading up for the drop into Normandy.

THE AIRBORNE PLANS FOR D-DAY

The airborne troops began the assault on Hitler's Fortress Europe using controversial tactics questioned by many army leaders. The United States was the world's last major military power to develop airborne capabilities, with only a fledgling paratrooper force as late as 1940—a single test platoon. But when German airborne units demonstrated the potential of paratroop operations by capturing Crete from the air in May 1941, US Army leaders scrambled to build up their own paratrooper force. The first American airborne battalion, the 501st, was established in October 1941, followed in the fall of 1942 with the formation of two complete airborne divisions, the 82nd and 101st, at Fort Bragg, North Carolina.

These new paratrooper regiments were all-volunteer, unlike their attached glider regiments. Training troops to drop by parachute into the heart of enemy defenses was demanding. Those who completed a rigorous, months-long course, including five successful jumps from a C-47, earned the coveted jump wings. Paratroopers enjoyed elite status and took immense pride in their skills and training. They looked the part: uniforms included bloused trousers over tall and spit-shined jump boots. Qualified paratroopers earned jump pay, an extra fifty dollars a month. For a number of young men shaped by Depression woes, the added income was incentive enough to sign up. Many others joined

because of the challenges of becoming jump-qualified and a desire to fight with the best-trained men in the army.

The 82nd, the first American airborne division to face combat in the war, fought with mixed results at the start of the Italian campaign. Landing first in Sicily in July 1943, the division suffered a tragic mix of confusion and friendly fire that brought the loss of aircraft and troops. The incidents caused many high-ranking American officers to believe the use of airborne and glider regiments in support of amphibious assaults was too risky. Despite these worries and near disastrous drops in Sicily and Salerno, General Omar Bradley believed the airborne troops were essential to the success of the invasion force at Normandy's Utah Beach. If American troops could not get behind enemy lines and disrupt German troop movements, Bradley feared the Allies could not hold the beachhead. Paratroopers had to secure roads that the Germans needed to get Wehrmacht forces to the beaches. Both Bradley and British planner General Sir Bernard Law Montgomery argued that the Allies had to go "all in" with airborne forces to have a chance at success.

Early plans for the invasion of Europe, code-named Operation Overlord, called for only one Allied airborne division for the invasion. The division would have to be British because in early 1944 the US Army Air Forces had only 100 C-47 aircraft available in England—not nearly enough transport aircraft to drop even one airborne division. Bradley and Montgomery agreed that even an unproven American airborne force was better than none at all, and advocated fiercely to Supreme Commander Dwight Eisenhower for getting the aircraft needed to transport the 82nd and 101st Airborne Divisions. Eisenhower then challenged Allied planners to accelerate the delivery of C-47 aircraft in sufficient numbers to drop the two divisions simultaneously. Generals Bradley and Montgomery would need nearly 1,000 aircraft to drop 13,000 men in the two divisions in a single bold stroke. With the aircraft crews standing by in the United States, the Army Air Forces raced to expedite the delivery of C-47s to England, increasing the number there from 100 to 1,000 in a matter of months. By April 1944, Bradley had the airborne divisions and transport aircraft he needed to support the landings at Utah Beach.

Training intensified for airborne units in England in the months prior to D-Day. Planners created elaborate sand tables to convey details of the terrain in the targeted drop zones. However, less than two weeks before the invasion, the American airborne divisions got bad news: the battle plans they had memorized had been compromised and had to be rewritten. The Allied high command decrypted German messages revealing that the German Army had moved a new division directly into the 82nd drop zone near Saint-Sauveur-le-Vicomte. In addition, "Rommel's asparagus," ten-foot wooden poles designed to wreak havoc on paratrooper and glider landings, had been installed quickly and extensively at the planned landing zones. Just ten days before the invasion, objectives had to be changed, shifting drop zones for the 82nd nearly fifteen miles to the east. The change meant the 82nd had to take over the 101st objective of Sainte-Mère-Église, allowing the 101st to focus on seizing the critical causeways leading to the Utah landing zone.

Fears that airborne divisions would suffer high fatalities loomed large in the minds of planners at the Supreme Headquarters Allied Expeditionary Force. Dropping in at night, surrounded by the enemy, and with only small arms to begin the fight, the airborne troops faced extreme risk. Late in the planning, strident criticism of the American tactics came from Eisenhower's senior air officer, Royal Air Force Chief Marshal Sir Trafford Leigh-Mallory. He was convinced that the airborne drop would result in the slaughter of the two divisions and argued the western flank of the invasion would fare just as well without airborne forces. Leigh-Mallory's vocal opposition eventually prompted Eisenhower to direct him to submit

Technician Fourth Grade Joseph F. Gorenc of Headquarters Company, 3rd Battalion, 506th Parachute Infantry Regiment, 101st Airborne Division boards a C-47 at an airfield in Devon in preparation for the night drop on Normandy.

his position in writing. Eisenhower considered the issue a "soul-racking problem." If he cancelled the airborne drop, Eisenhower felt he would likely have to cancel the landings at Utah. If he overruled his chief technical expert and Leigh-Mallory's fears became reality, the Supreme Commander would be blamed for the failure. In the end, Eisenhower decided the risk had to be taken, that Leigh-Mallory's projected losses of 50 percent for the airborne regiments were only estimates, and that the drop would proceed as planned.

In the early morning hours of June 5/6, six regiments of the 82nd and 101st Airborne Divisions were to drop into the Normandy fields behind enemy lines, inland from Utah Beach. The paratroopers would be joined by elements of the 325th and 327th Glider Infantry Regiments. The combined mission was to secure major towns, crossroads and causeways, blocking German reinforcements from access to Utah and Omaha Beaches to the east. Eventually the landing forces had to link Utah and Omaha, securing beachheads and protecting further landings from the English Channel.

Major General Maxwell Taylor commanded the 101st Airborne, nicknamed the "Screaming Eagles." The division included the 501st, 502nd and 506th Parachute Infantry Regiments (PIR), and the 327th Glider Infantry Regiment. The three parachute regiments were to land to the eastern end of Utah Beach and seize four causeways, or elevated roadways. If the Germans still held the causeways by mid-morning, troops of the American 4th Infantry Division could be decimated as they attempted to move inland. The first mission of the 502nd was to secure causeways 3 and 4 near St. Martin. Causeways 1 and 2, along with the village of Sainte-Marie-du-Mont, were to be taken by the 506th. The 501st would be held in reserve, awaiting orders to assist as needed. Meanwhile, the 327th would land by glider and by sea. This meant that 155 men of the 327th would land by glider in the early hours of June 6 and the remaining men of the regiment would land on Utah Beach with the 4th Infantry Division. Together, the 327th Regiment and 4th Infantry Division were to support parachute regiments as they moved toward their final objective: the city of Carentan.

The 82nd Airborne, dubbed the "All American" Division, was led by Major General Matthew Ridgway. For the Normandy campaign, the 82nd was comprised of the 505th, 507th and 508th Parachute Infantry Regiments and the 325th Glider Infantry Regiment. Plans called for the 505th to capture Sainte-Mère-Église and a small bridge over the Merderet River known as La Fière. The village of Sainte-Mère-Église was a major objective because

of its location at the intersection of six major roadways. German forces to the north or west of Utah Beach had to pass through the town to launch a counter-attack on American forces landing on the beaches. The 507th had to move west of La Fière and take the nearby towns of Cauquigny and Amfreville, thereby gaining control of the La Fière causeway to Utah Beach. The task of seizing and holding bridges over the Douve River at Beuzeville-la-Bastille and Étienville, southwest of Sainte-Mère-Église and La Fière, fell to the 508th. The 325th was to come in later, on June 6 and 7, to support the parachute regiments in taking their objectives.

For the most part, the American airborne troops were untested: of the eight parachute and glider regiments slated to land in the invasion's opening two days, only the 505th and 325th had seen combat. While most of the soldiers had not yet faced the enemy, the young men who dropped from the sky in parachutes and gliders were well prepared. Many of the unit members had been together for two years. Trained to work as teams in night-time maneuvers, these men could recognize one another in the dark. They would need each other and all of their training as they faced the enemy in Normandy.

As one of more than 900 planes carrying the 82nd and 101st Divisions reached the French coastline, they encountered an unexpected cloudbank. Flying wingtip to wingtip in "Vee" formations without lights, pilots struggled to maintain their positions. Some pulled up or down to avoid the cloudbank, causing formations to scatter. The start of intense anti-aircraft fire from the ground made matters worse. As the C-47s crossed the coastline, German flak filled the sky, hitting or jolting the American planes. Despite the intensity of the barrage, only 21 aircraft were shot down, a far lower number than Leigh-Mallory had projected.

C-47 pilots courageously flew through the heavy flak and attempted to follow radio signals as they searched for ground signal lights set up earlier by "pathfinders" to mark drop targets. Inside the planes, men were bounced around as their aircraft descended and lowered airspeed for the jump, though not all reached the planned speed or altitude. As red lights switched on, signaling the moment had come to stand and hook up, aircraft continued to veer off course due to clouds and flak bursts, moving away from designated drop zones. Even amid the explosions, many paratroopers were anxious to see the red light switch to green, indicating it was time to jump. They believed their chances would be better jumping into the flak than staying in the plane a minute longer.

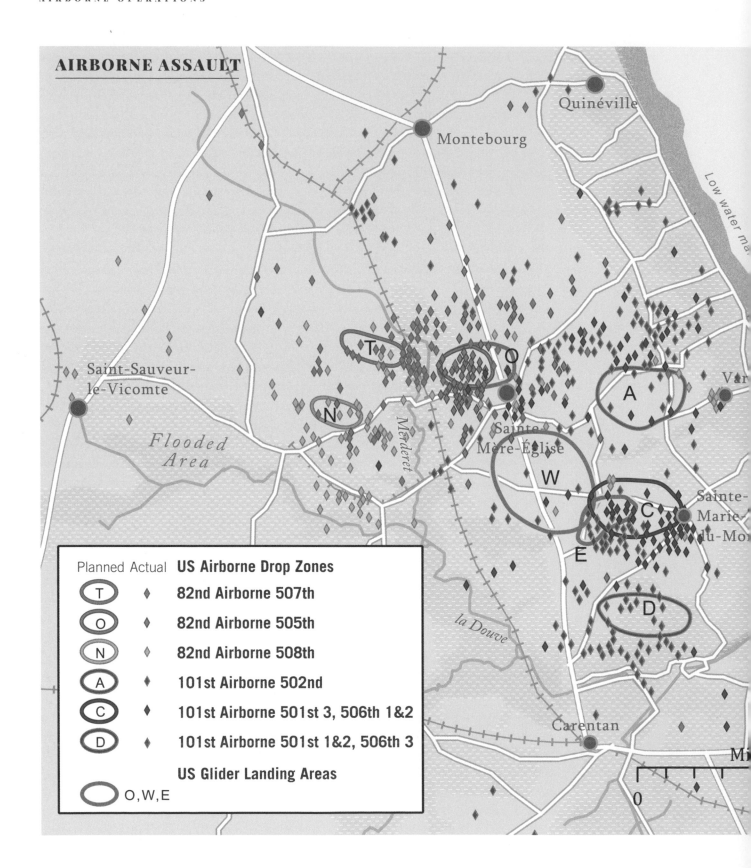

AIRBORNE ASSAULT

Quinéville

Montebourg

Saint-Sauveur-
le-Vicomte

*Flooded
Area*

Merderet

T

O

N

A

Var

Sainte-
Mère-Église

W

C

Sainte-
Marie-
du-Mo

E

D

la Douve

Carentan

M

Planned **Actual** **US Airborne Drop Zones**

T	♦	**82nd Airborne 507th**
O	♦	**82nd Airborne 505th**
N	♦	**82nd Airborne 508th**
A	♦	**101st Airborne 502nd**
C	♦	**101st Airborne 501st 3, 506th 1&2**
D	♦	**101st Airborne 501st 1&2, 506th 3**

US Glider Landing Areas

O, W, E

Îles Saint-Marcouf

UTAH BEACH
LANDING ZONE

Isigny

5

Above: Illustration of the D-Day paratrooper drop drawn by Captain Raymond Creekmore, US Army Air Forces.

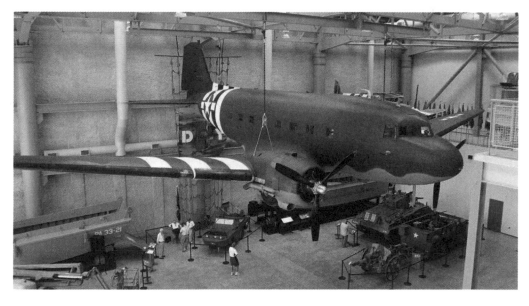

Above: Immediately after arriving in England on May 28, 1944, the C-47 designated 42-93096 was transferred to the Ninth Air Force. One week after arriving in England, "096" carried pathfinders from the 82nd Airborne Division into the Normandy Invasion.

AIRBORNE OPERATIONS

Charles Moore

C-47 Squadron Navigator, 95th Troop Carrier Squadron

440th Troop Carrier Group

Charles Moore, one of millions impacted by the Selective Training and Service Act, was drafted in April 1941. He had graduated from Virginia Tech and expected to complete a compulsory year of service and return to his work as a mechanical engineer. After the December 7, 1941 Japanese attack on Pearl Harbor, Moore knew he would remain in service "for the long haul." Married with a young son, needing extra pay, he applied to Officer Candidate School. Moore had always wanted to fly and got his wish at the Army Air Forces Navigation School at Selman Army Airfield in Monroe, Louisiana. From there he became a C-47 navigator and joined Allied forces preparing for the invasion in England.

I was supposed to go into Exeter one day, and all of a sudden, we go down and the gate's closed. So we knew something was up. Then for about a week, we began the briefings and the whatnot for the flight for the D-Day operation. I had gone with the colonel outside of London somewhere, to a big briefing. I don't know why I went along. I guess I went because I was a squadron navigator. I remember they laid it all out for us. I wasn't supposed to tell anybody.

I remember the paratroopers moving in through the base. That night, June 5, I guess 10 o'clock, we started to get assembled, load up the airplanes. I can't remember what time we took off. Probably 11- something. We were transporting the 506 Regiment of the 101st Airborne. They had a lot of equipment. That took up a lot of space. I can remember taking off. It was night. We had a prescribed route to follow: we went up the coast of England for a while, and then we headed southwest, out across the Channel. They had what they call beacon lights or occult lights out in the Channel which marked our check points and turning points. I remember when we turned to cross the Cherbourg Peninsula, our group commander and his squadron were ahead of us, with some other squadrons. I could see the flak come up. It looked like it was real slow.

I remember we picked up (Le Mont-)Saint-Michel, that little island castle off the coast of the Cherbourg Peninsula. When we turned to go across the peninsula we could see the flak coming up. As each group passed, you could see the flak come up. Then it would die down. And it got closer and closer and, uh oh, we're next.

(As the navigator) I was to take charge of the route, make sure that we followed the proper route, the altitude, the times, and guiding the airplane, really, because it was black night, and we had no other lights. We were supposed to have the guidance beacons that the pathfinders had dropped, but apparently they got screwed up somehow or other.

We dropped near a little town, Vierville, in France. It was behind Utah Beach. But back to the flight itself, I can remember looking back from my position. I could get up and move around in the airplane, which I did. A lot of times I would get up and stand between the copilot and the pilot, looking out the front so that

The M-227 Signal Lamp was used by airborne signalmen during the Normandy Campaign. It could be operated from the shoulder or remotely from the tripod by a Morse-style key attached to several feet of wire.

I could see where we were and what was going on. That's when I saw the flak. I looked back, and just before we made a turn to go across the peninsula there was a lot of talk in the airplane. But as soon as we turned and started across the peninsula, everybody went quiet. You could tell they were probably praying. We were scared. But we did our job and we got back safely.

According to the records, we did have a good drop. We took a few hits, but nothing serious. We only lost like three planes in our squadron. One of them was my good buddy, but we returned home and returned back to base. The first thing when we got off the airplane, they gave us a shot of booze (laughs). That settled us down. We went into interrogation and, after that, it was back to more training.

....

Charles Moore continued to fly missions in Europe through 1944, dropping supplies to American troops in Normandy, and carrying elements of the 82nd Airborne during Operation Market Garden in September 1944.

Moore's flight crew was fortunate to get their "stick" close to its designated drop zone. Others fared worse. A bank of clouds mixed with flak caused confusion for many aircrews, leading to massive mis-drops that often put paratroopers miles from their designated drop zones. Scattered units of 82nd and 101st paratroopers formed up with whomever they could find in the dark. Others found themselves alone and without weapons in the early hours of June 6, surrounded by German forces, trying to evade capture. On balance, the C-47 aircrews got the job done on D-Day, flying in harrowing conditions—in the midst of heavy flak, close formations, poor visibility and turbulence. Most of the 13,000 paratroopers made it into Normandy and rallied to complete their mission in a historic battle.

Above: Prospective paratroopers practice manipulating risers in suspended harnesses at Fort Benning, Georgia.

Right: Worn with trousers bloused over the tops, these jump boots were designed specifically for paratroopers. Laced high and tight, they protected ankles when landing. Jump boots became an iconic part of paratrooper uniforms.

Top: A patch worn by the 101st Airborne "Screaming Eagles." This variation has a white tongue instead of the traditional red.

Above: Corporal Louis E. Laird of Elyria, Ohio, with a full equipment load, boards a C-47 for a dress rehearsal drop for D-Day.

AIRBORNE OPERATIONS

Robert Williams

Sergeant, Headquarters Company, 2nd Battalion

506th Parachute Infantry Regiment, 101st Airborne Division

Robert Williams worked at Wright Aeronautical in Cincinnati, Ohio, which qualified him for a draft deferment in the early years of the war. But at age 20, Williams wanted excitement, and he found it in August 1942, when he enlisted in the US Army and volunteered for the paratroops. Williams credited his time as a Boy Scout in his younger years as excellent preparation for army service. Williams and his fellow paratroopers trained with the 101st Airborne at Toccoa, Georgia, to fight behind enemy lines. On the morning of June 6, Williams, like many American paratroopers, found himself alone and surrounded by the enemy in Normandy.

I know when I went out I wasn't in a very good position. I lost my balance because I just fell out the door and the chute opened. I talked to the pilots years later—we were supposed to jump out at about 850 feet and he told me we would have been lucky if we were 650 feet because they had really got down on the deck to get out of that anti-aircraft fire. And it (the drop) wasn't but just a few seconds. I landed, and I couldn't see on this dark moonlit night. It was a good moon but white clouds caused a lot of shadows, and we couldn't really see the ground. I landed and found out I was in three feet of water. I actually didn't know how deep it was until I stood up and my head popped out of it; it was a great relief to find the water was only three feet deep. It was pretty tough getting out of that chute. Actually, it was a better landing than a lot of my friends because when they hit the ground with all the equipment, some of them got sprained ankles and I think some of our officers had broken legs. So, I had a pretty nice landing even if I did get all wet.

I stood there taking my chute off, and parachutes got a little tighter because of all that water. Somebody off about ten, fifteen feet away was clicking one of those crickets. So, I quit worrying about the chute and was trying to find the string on my wrist that had the cricket tied on, so I could click back at him. I remember I said something to him in English. I couldn't find the cricket right away. He did give me the password, I forget what the password was. Thunder, lightning or something like that. I got the chute off and eventually he and I started walking through the water trying to find our way out of this thing.

This marsh area had been flooded by the Germans weeks before, where they had poles set up in each corner of each hedgerow with barbed wire strung between it to catch the parachutists as they came down. Where they didn't do that, they flooded it; they opened the gates there at Carentan and let the water in from the Channel. I think we lost 33 men that night because some

of them landed in deeper water than I did. Some of the planes overshot and went out into the Channel. And some of the guys landed out in the Channel and drowned with all that equipment on them. Even if you had a life jacket on, you'd have to get your equipment off before you could use a life jacket.

So we started off in the dark, trying to find out which was the best way to get out of there. We ran into two more guys, and none of these were from my outfit. I was in the 506th Parachute Infantry and I think they were from the 82nd Airborne. But that made four of us together. One of them found a hard surface under the water that we figured was a road. So, we headed in the direction where it seemed like the road was going to lead to. Then we started getting into shallow water, it was two feet deep, one foot deep and, finally, we did come out on dry land.

We hadn't gone twenty feet before we ran right into a German machine-gun nest. The two guys in the middle were killed and the one on the left side, he went into the water and I got twelve machine-gun bullets in my left pants pocket. I had three or four K-rations in there and a couple of hand grenades. But they didn't hit the hand grenades; they went through the K-rations and tore the whole pocket off, the flap on there. I was sure I was hit because of the way it spun me around, and I fell down. While I'm on the ground I'm going to roll back in that water to get out of that machine-gun fire. And they just kept shooting right over my head. I got down to where just my nose and my eyes were above the water. I stayed there for about fifteen, twenty minutes. I put my hand down besides my pants to see how bad I was hit. I was sure my hand was going to come out with blood on it, and I couldn't believe it, I just kept feeling around, feeling around, and there wasn't anything there. They had missed me, they just hit my pants pocket. So, I didn't try to hook up with the guy on the other side of the road, I just stayed in the water on my side and started moving away from that machine gun. There was a

A "Cricket" of the style issued to American airborne divisions. Hastily issued just prior to Operation Neptune, this child's toy was used as a quick recognition signaling device for airborne forces who parachuted into the Normandy countryside during the pre-dawn hours of the invasion. If challenged with one click, a response of two clicks identified a "friendly," fellow trooper.

machine gun that opened up on the other side. The machine-gun crews have a pattern, they triangulate, and they have a set pattern. I don't think they even saw us, they just heard us, and they opened up on us.

I must have gone a quarter of a mile in that water; it didn't get any better, it was still waist deep. About that time, the B-26s came over. I was facing the beach; I could see the ridgeline of the coast. The B-26s came from the north and came down across the beach dropping bombs and I stood there and I saw a couple of those B-26s blow up that were hit with anti-aircraft fire. They went the whole length of the beach. They weren't that high, I would say maybe 1,500 feet, 1,000 feet. The whole length they were bombing, pillboxes and gun emplacements.

It was quite a show; the sun was coming up, I was looking toward the sun. I can still remember today, those B-26s with the sun shining on the belly of those airplanes. If I'd had a camera, that would have made a terrific picture with that sun coming up. It (the sun) was still down below the horizon but it was showing on the bottom of the airplanes. Of course, there was a lot of noise, and the ships were opening up on the beach. The invasion had started. It was 6:30 when they hit the beaches.

I did find my way out of that water. I was near a farmhouse, and ten or fifteen other guys had gathered there and were talking to the French people. They were getting our bearings and we all had objectives. So, we started down the road towards Sainte-Marie-du-Mont, which is at the lower end of Utah Beach. Along the way we would see what had happened. We passed a big hole where one of our fighter planes had dropped a bomb and there were two Germans that were coming down the road on a motorcycle, and it was a direct hit and the Germans were laying way over there in the field. That was my first experience with what was *really* going on besides hearing all the noise.

....

In the week after D-Day, Robert Williams peered through a hedgerow with binoculars during fighting with the 506th outside Carentan. As he attempted to discern enemy movements, two 88mm German shells landed close to him. The explosion left Williams in a daze. "I wandered around and the medics caught me and put a tag on me," he recalled. "You're disoriented and your nerves are shocked." They sent Williams back to England with combat exhaustion. He never returned to the fighting.

Robert Williams during training at Fort Bragg.

Opposite: American paratroopers perform a practice jump in Europe.

AIRBORNE OPERATIONS

John Marr

First Lieutenant, Platoon Leader, G Company

507th Parachute Infantry Regiment, 82nd Airborne Division

John Marr, a Missouri native, was drafted into the US Army in the spring of 1941 after holding a series of odd jobs during the Great Depression. He was prepared to serve the mandatory year of service until hearing a speech by Colonel Robert Sink about an elite unit that was being formed—the airborne. Marr volunteered and headed to Fort Benning, Georgia, for training. There, he was surprised to find that his new battalion commander was none other than Colonel Sink. In late 1942, Marr was assigned to command a platoon in G Company of the new 507th Parachute Infantry Regiment. When the 507th shipped out for England, Marr left his fiancée with the promise of marriage at war's end, but there was no guarantee that Marr would survive his drop into enemy-controlled Normandy.

Paratroopers of the 506th Parachute Infantry Regiment began to find their way towards their first objective, Sainte-Marie-du-Mont, while paratroopers of the 82nd Airborne gathered to move on their objective. The 82nd was tasked with taking the town of Sainte-Mère-Église and securing bridgeheads across the Merderet River, and then with holding the American line at the Douve River. On June 6, elements of the 507th Parachute Infantry Regiment were to seize the small hamlet of Cauquigny, west of the La Fière bridge, then continue west to Amfreville to hold the line on territory secured by paratroopers. The 507th was a new addition to the 82nd Airborne, and unlike their battle-hardened comrades in the 505th, the men of the 507th did not yet have combat experience.

As we moved down the railroad Schwartzwalder (Captain Floyd Benjamin "Ben," commanding officer, G Company) said to me several times, "John we've got to get onto Amfreville. That's on the other side of that swamp out there." And he said, "The first opportunity that we get I want you to get up off of this railroad and head toward Amfreville and the rest of us will follow." So I took up lead of our group within the larger group and, when we came to the overpass of the Sainte-Mère-Église–Amfreville road, I saw the opportunity to get up on that road which was about 30 feet above the rail band (line). So I appointed two individuals to start scrambling up the bank to the road. I followed and the rest of the group followed behind. It was coming very close to dawn at that time and as we got up, we decided to cross the road and continue on the south side of it in a westerly direction toward the farmstead called the Manoir La Fière, which was adjacent to the bridge across the Merderet River.

The Manoir was then under attack by the 505, A Company of the 505, whose job it was to seize and hold the eastern approach to the causeway across the Merderet River to the churchyard on the western side of the crossing. They were fighting to seize the Manoir. They had landed north of it fairly intact. In fact, the 1st Battalion of the 505 had landed there and A Company's job was to lead the attack on the Manoir and seize the eastern end of the causeway.

We proceeded down through this rather large field that was east of the Manoir. Schwartzwalder had told me to take up the advance party of our group and move along to skirt the Manoir to the south. So we moved our little party—there were five of us—down the hedgerow which led to the southern hedgerow along the Manoir, beyond which was a more inundated area and the river which ran under the bridge, proceeding on south toward Chef-du-Pont.

As we approached a cattle gate at the southeast corner of the Manoir, a machine gun opened up and we all hit the ground and reached for a grenade at the same time. We were perhaps 30 yards away from the machine gun, and how he didn't kill us all it's hard to explain. We all got out grenades and threw the grenades at this gun emplacement by the cattle gate and two Germans came up out of there. The opening blast of their machine gun had hit two of our people, Private Escobar and Corporal Lawton.

Opposite: Second Lieutenant John Marr after attending Officer Candidate School in 1942.

Left: A group of paratroopers during training jumps at Fort Benning, Georgia. Marr is second from the left in the back row.

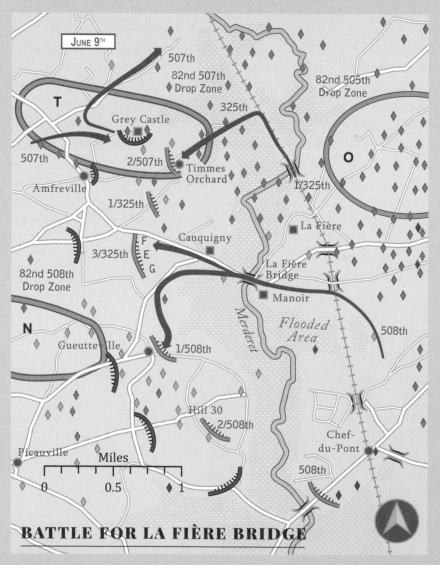

JUNE 9TH

507th

82nd 507th
Drop Zone

82nd 505th
Drop Zone

325th

T

Grey Castle

O

507th

2/507th

Timmes
Orchard

Amfreville

1/325th

1/325th

La Fière

Cauquigny

F
E
G

3/325th

La Fière
Bridge

82nd 508th
Drop Zone

Manoir

N

Gueutteville

1/508th

508th

Merderet

Flooded
Area

Hill 30

2/508th

Chef-
du-Pont

Picauville

Miles

508th

0   0.5   1

BATTLE FOR LA FIÈRE BRIDGE

As these two Germans jumped up Escobar mistook them for wanting to continue the attack and he rolled over with his Tommy gun and killed the two Germans. That was the end of the machine-gun emplacement at the southeast corner of the Manoir.

We stopped our movement at that point to get our wounded back to where Schwartzwalder had the main body of our group. It was at that time, as we were moving back towards Schwartzwalder, that I ran into Red Dolan (First Lieutenant John, J. "Red Dog") who was commander of A Company of the 505 and that's where I learned that Major McGinty (James E.), whom I had known of the 1st Battalion of the 505, had been killed just prior to our movement up there.

So we got on back to Schwartzwalder's group, got the two wounded people taken care of, we got them evacuated back to safety. Colonel Lindquist (Roy E., commanding officer, 508th) showed up in the field behind us and it had been our understanding, or at least this was the prevailing thought, that Lindquist was going down the railroad with a whole host of his regiment heading to Chef-du-Pont, but he came up in that field. He was talking with Schwartzwalder when General Ridgway (Matthew B., commanding general, 82nd Airborne) showed up in the field. General Ridgway said to Lindquist,

A ground-level view of the causeway and bridge over the Merderet River at La Fière.

"Lindquist, I want that bridge down there and I want it right away." Lindquist turned around (to head to the bridge) and Red Dolan had come up from the attack (on the Manoir) with A Company apparently thinking that all the Manoir was pretty well under control. So we had a representative of the 505 and Schwartzwalder representing the 507 and Lindquist himself representing the 508. He (Lindquist) turned and gave one of the shortest field orders I've ever—(laughs)—experienced in my life! He said, "The 505 you go down the right, 507 you go down the left, and the 508 is going to go down the center. Move out." And that was how the attack was formulated for the Manoir.

We had to go back down where we had knocked that machine gun out. Schwartzwalder placed me in the advance party again. So I put two scouts out and went around the south side of the Manoir. We had already knocked out the only resistance on the south side, so we went around the south side while the Manoir was under fire by the 505 and the 508. It was a very short, noisy battle and they took the Manoir. There weren't that many Germans in there.

Schwartzwalder halted our group at the highway, at the road that went across the bridge. The wall around the Manoir was very close to the bridge, so we had come to the road at the junction of a small wall that ran around the southwest corner of the Manoir. We were waiting for further direction and Schwartzwalder had been called to go see Lindquist, who was then on the grounds of the Manoir. He came back and indicated to me that he wanted me to go on across the bridge and go to the other side (towards the Cauquigny Church). And he indicated to me that the 508 people under Lindquist's command were going to follow up.

So off we started westward across the causeway. I had two scouts, one was John Ward and the other one was Jim Mattingly. Ward was in the lead and he crossed over the bridge and was about a hundred yards down the roadway along the causeway and Mattingly crossed the bridge. I got to the bridge behind Mattingly, when a German rose up out of the machine-gun emplacement on the north side of the causeway and took aim at Mattingly, who saw the movement out of the corner of his eye and whirled and fired his M1 rifle. Emptied the clip, fired eight rounds. And the German fell back into the gun emplacement.

Mattingly then dropped his empty rifle to the roadway and reached for a grenade and tossed it over into the emplacement, whereupon four Germans rose up and threw their hands up. One of them was severely wounded and the others had minor wounds, I presume from the grenade explosion. Then Mattingly picked up his empty rifle—(laughs)—stood up and covered these individuals and ordered them out of the emplacement. All of this happened perhaps in the space of fifteen seconds, twenty at the most.

As Mattingly was motioning the Germans to come forward out of the gun emplacement on the north side of the road, five Germans rose up out of a concealed—(laughs)—gun emplacement on the south side of the road behind him. And here he had captured nine Germans and two machine guns in the space of about fifteen or twenty seconds. I was absolutely amazed at how he conducted himself. It was almost as if he was a robot. He was decorated with a Silver Star for that.

Well, after he had collected these Germans and we had sent them back under control, we continued on across the causeway. When we were about halfway across we witnessed a smoke bomb, a smoke grenade actually. It was set off in the churchyard at Cauquigny and that signified to us that there were friendly troops up there. That was one of the signals that we had. Yellow smoke meant friendly troops.

So we continued quickly across there, Schwartzwalder bringing up the main body of our group, which I say is about 70, 75 people and we got to the crossroads—actually it was more of a Y in the road where the main road from Sainte-Mère-Église turned southwestward to go to Picauville. Then another road went straight by the churchyard and on to Amfreville.

A German ambulance came up the road from Picauville, made a turn to the west and they had the rear doors of the

Paratroopers march to C-47s in preparation for the invasion of France at an undisclosed airfield in England, June 5.

ambulance open. We could see that there were some American uniforms, casualties aboard that ambulance and also German casualties, German uniforms. People were laying on the floor of the ambulance. The ambulance made the turn toward Amfreville and halted for about two or three minutes. Of course, we did not bother the ambulance because it was headed for an aid station and had American soldiers in it or American uniformed bodies in it.

As we were deliberating on what our next move was going to be we heard the rumble of tanks and we also began to receive artillery at this Picauville–Amfreville junction, which was just across the road from the churchyard. When we approached the churchyard we met up with Lieutenant Levy of the 2nd Battalion, who was out posting the churchyard under the control of Colonel Timmes (Lieutenant Colonel Charles J., commanding officer, 2nd Battalion, 507th). It was his (Timmes') mission and the 2nd Battalion of the 507th to take and hold the west approach to the La Fière crossing.

With this, we heard the rumble of tanks, and artillery began to fall on the road junction. The ambulance moved on out of sight and we concluded that the ambulance halted there to send a message to the German force coming up from Picauville. So we

evaded to the north and went around two coves of the inundated area and came to Timmes' orchard, which is where he had come to rest with his folks after having tried to attack Amfreville.

As we joined Timmes' group we then comprised about 150 folks all together in the surrounding area of the orchard. And of course, the outpost remained until they were driven off from Cauquigny back into Timmes' orchard. The Germans had moved in, in force. It was later concluded that the force that moved in there was a reinforced German regiment or equivalent to what would be a US regiment, so it was a sizeable force.

Schwartzwalder, in talking with Levy, first wanted to know where Timmes was (in the orchard northwest of the bridge) and Levy told him. Schwartzwalder had been saying to me all along, "John, we got to get over there and take up our defense positions on the airhead line over there." It was south of Amfreville where G Company was to take up positions. I believe it's fair to say we all understood that the main thing that the 507 had to do was to seize and hold that crossing (on the Merderet River) because we knew that the landing divisions at the beach were going to have to have those crossings to cut off the peninsula.

We understood the bare outlines of the overall plan, so you could easily conclude what was the most important thing for you to do in the mission. But then when the Germans were coming up the road there with sizable strength, we knew that we were not going to be enough to defend that bridgehead. So we just moved on around to go in, we just didn't have enough people. We may have had a chance if we linked up with Timmes instead of going to our place in the airhead line, which we likely would not have been able to do because the Germans were in there (in strength) in Amfreville.

Well, he (Schwartzwalder) actually was moving on toward the objective (holding the line south of Amfreville). He decided to move and join ranks with Timmes' position, which Levy had described to him. All Levy could say is, "we're here outposting the bridge". Of course, understanding what outposting meant—when the enemy showed up, you weren't the main fighting unit, you were supposed to pull back to the main fighting unit and join ranks for the defense of your area.

When Schwartzwalder found out where Timmes was and the Germans were coming up the Picauville road to the Cauquigny junction, he decided the best thing to do at that point was to go and join Timmes and strengthen his ranks because we would probably be able to do more. Timmes probably had at the most 80 people. So we had about 150 people when we all got together back in Timmes' orchard.

It was clear by then that we didn't have enough troops to establish the airhead line, to make a defense of it there. We just didn't have the troops. So Schwartzwalder placed us under Timmes' control. We were going to do whatever Timmes wanted us to do. Timmes wanted to take the town of Amfreville because that was one of his objectives. He also had the objective of holding the western approaches to the La Fière crossing, so he had a big job to do and he was sitting right in the middle between them (objectives) with not enough troops to do either one.

Lieutenant John Marr continued to lead G Company through fierce fighting in Normandy until he was wounded in early July. When he recovered he took command of B Company of the 507th during the Battle of the Bulge.

John Marr during jump training in 1942.

The standard sub-machine gun of the German Army, the MP 40 fired a 9mm pistol cartridge. It had limited range, but its high rate of fire made it an excellent weapon in close-range fighting.

AIRBORNE OPERATIONS

Robert Murphy

Sergeant, A Company, 505th Parachute Infantry Regiment

82nd Airborne Division

Robert Murphy was only seventeen when he joined the US Army. A star track athlete at a Boston-area high school, Murphy left before graduation to begin serving his country, volunteering for the parachute infantry. In 1943, at the age of eighteen, he fought against German forces in the Allied invasion of Sicily. Murphy trained to become a "pathfinder," a select group who jumped prior to the main airborne drop in order to mark drop zones with lights and radio beacons. He was among the first to land in Normandy on D-Day, and after playing the pathfinder role rejoined his regular infantry unit, A Company.

The task of capturing the vital two causeways across the Merderet River west of Sainte-Mère-Église fell to combat-tested paratroopers of the 505th. Their 1st Battalion, including A Company, was given the mission of taking the causeways and holding the bridgeheads. But German forces were determined to hold the causeways. The battle at La Fière Bridge would become a defining moment for the 82nd Airborne in Normandy.

In the afternoon of the first day, we went through a very heavy attack by (German) tanks trying to get across (the bridge at La Fière) up through to Sainte-Mère-Église. They had a lot of mortars, a lot of artillery, because they knew that their men were captured and that we owned the La Fière Manoir and were in control of the La Fière bridge, which is a small bridge. I think a regular huge trailer truck would have difficulty getting across

it. If you got a sixteen-wheeler truck, it may get across but very slowly with somebody watching both sides. It's not a large bridge.

In the afternoon, when the Manoir had been taken and things were quiet, we got their prisoners. We were then setting out battle defenses. So the Germans attacked. That morning, Captain Schwartzwalder and his men went across the causeway over to the other (western) side of the causeway. After a few men went over, there were still Germans on the causeway and they captured the Germans and got across.

Schwartzwalder's forces were trying to locate Colonel Timmes, who was in an orchard on the northwest side across the causeway. At one point now, the Germans started an attack with tanks. They had three tanks coming. We could see one tank coming and then another tank behind it. As they approached, the bazooka men, Lenold Peterson and John D. Bolderson, and their

Opposite: Robert Murphy in Italy, 1943.

Above: Pathfinders of the 505th PIR before the jump into Normandy. Robert Murphy is in the back row, third from the right.

assistants set up. Marcus Heim was with Peterson, a combat soldier in Sicily and Italy. Gordan Pryne was the assistant to Bolderson, who fought in Sicily and Italy, and was very familiar with combat.

When the first tank came up, the commander of the first tank opened the hatch of the tank and looked out. I think there must have been 50 guys firing at him. The Germans that were around the tank just disappeared in the thickly treed area. The Germans are waiting for the tank to come and crush our defense and get across. So that tank came forward a lot more. It was knocked out by Bolderson and Peterson's bazookas. A second tank came up and knocked off a cement telephone pole, knocking that in half, shooting at Lenold Peterson and Marcus Heim.

Then the two tanks hit by Bolderson and Peterson's bazookas were knocked out. And the 57-millimeter was firing at the third tank and the second tank because the first tank was completely knocked out. Then the German infantry were still trying to come at us, but we had superior fire force. We were up on a hill so we had the altitude to fire and look down. But they had machine guns from across the causeway and they were firing at us. Then all that afternoon and evening, they fired all kinds of artillery and mortar rounds. You really had to dig in. A tremendous amount of artillery. But we had knocked out their three tanks.

There were a lot of our men killed. My good pathfinder friend, Currin (Private James J.), was killed during these attacks. There were a lot of men killed on both sides; it was difficult. We didn't have any American artillery. All we had was mortars. Prentice Murray in my platoon was the 60-millimeter mortar man, and

he fired mortars on the causeway in the direction of the tank.

German infantrymen that were coming were attacking with the tanks because tanks don't go out alone. They always have infantrymen with them. So that attack ended and the Germans backed off. That night, we had tremendous artillery coming in until the next day. The enemy came with tremendous force, and artillery, and more tanks. And at this point in the battle, we had tanks. General Ridgway was there trying to get the tanks to fire on the attacking force.

The Germans were coming at us in tremendous force with artillery. It was difficult to stand up out of your hole. There was so much shrapnel going on and so much of their machine gun firing at us. Even though they might have been across the causeway,

The standard light mortar for US forces. With a range of approximately 2,000 yards and firing a 3-pound projectile, the M2 mortar was very effective in placing fire beyond the range of most infantry portable weapons.

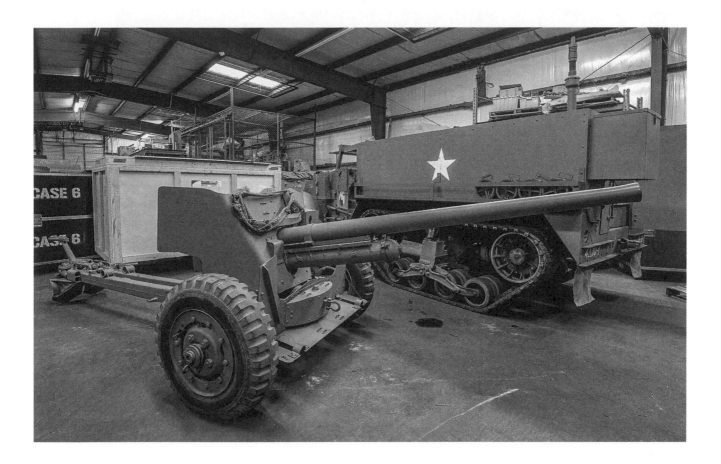

Top: The US Army entered the war with a 37mm anti-tank gun, which proved inadequate during the North African Campaign. The 57mm anti-tank gun design (shown here) was acquired from England and quickly put into production. Light enough to be delivered by glider, one 57mm anti-tank gun participated in the battle for the La Fière causeway.

Above: The M1A1 Rocket Launcher was the second version of the famous M1 "Bazooka." The M1A1 gave infantry the ability to knock out tanks and other armored vehicles. Using the M6 fin-stabilized high explosive anti-tank rocket, it could penetrate up to 3.5 inches of armor.

501st PIR Chaplain Francis Sampson provides last rites to paratroopers who died on D-Day. Sampson was captured by German forces during the Battle of the Bulge and spent the rest of the war as a prisoner of war. Sampson went on to serve as a chaplain with the army through the Vietnam War.

those guns and rounds certainly reached out. About this time during the battle we were practically out of ammunition—this was on day two. This is when Sergeant Owens (William D.) stepped up. He was now the platoon sergeant, and before that, my squad sergeant and my good friend. He was much older than me. And he looked after me like a son. I think he was about thirty-three or thirty-four, maybe even thirty-six. A very brave man. A man that should've got the Medal of Honor for his defense force and for what he did.

Sergeant Owens told me to go over to Lieutenant Dolan and tell him we have no ammunition here and many of our men are dead and wounded, that we got to get out of here. We can't hold this position. We've got to go back up over the hills and either get some ammunition or get some help here or we're all going to get killed. We can't defend ourselves. So I went over to Lieutenant Dolan to tell him that. Lieutenant Dolan, who was a very tough, red-headed officer and a good officer, one of the best, took a note out of his pocket and he wrote something on it, and he says, "You give this to Owens. We stay. You give this to Owens. We stay."

And I took the message. I ran back across the road, missed a round of bullets. I made it. And I said, "Here, sergeant." He read it. And he says, "There's no better place to die. We stay." That was the note. And we did.

At this point in time, because of the American artillery coming from behind, we had killed so many Germans. I mean, you could see them in the trees. You could see the blaze of their fire from their guns coming at us. And we just fired into that area. The Germans raised a red and white flag like a Red Cross flag on a pole.

We stopped firing and they stopped firing. A German waving this flag came across the bridge, talked to Dolan and said that they would like to have peace for about a half an hour and could we stop the battle while they pick up the wounded men or the dead men and get out of there. Being out of ammunition and with not much support, Captain Dolan was very gracious, of course, said to give them the truce. So the truce was allowed, and the Germans picked up their men. That night we had no attacks. No further attacks but a lot of artillery. That never ceased.

Robert Murphy fought with the 82nd Airborne until they returned to England in July 1944. He jumped again in September as part of Operation Market Garden. Though injured while fighting in Holland, he recovered and rejoined his unit in time to fight again in the Battle of the Bulge.

Reinforced M1942 Jump Jacket and Trousers of Alphonse Czekanski

After losing his job at a Cleveland area steel mill, Alphonse Czekanski joined the US Army in March 1940. Upon completion of basic training, Czekanski was assigned to the 11th Field Artillery Battalion, 24th Infantry Division, based in Schofield Barracks, Hawaii. Czekanski's peacetime army experience abruptly ended on December 7, 1941, when attacking Japanese aircraft strafed the mess hall where he was eating breakfast. For the next few months Czekanski manned defensive positions in Hawaii until he was granted a transfer back to the United States to attend Officer Candidate School. After receiving a commission as a Second Lieutenant, Czekanski attended Airborne School, where he was assigned to the 376th Parachute Field Artillery Battalion, 82nd Airborne.

By June 1944, Czekanski was the commander of Battery D, 376th Parachute Field Artillery Battalion, 504th Regimental Combat Team, 82nd Airborne. His unit had jumped in two invasions and was fighting in its third, at Anzio, Italy, when they were redeployed to England for the Invasion of Normandy. As the planned invasion date approached, the 504th Regimental Combat Team was ordered to remain in England as reserve due to a lack of replacements and limited time to reequip before the invasion was launched. Instead of sitting out the invasion of Normandy, Czekanski volunteered to fill an open spot and jumped with the 82nd into occupied France. He wore this reinforced M1942 jump jacket and trousers when he landed in the vicinity of Sainte-Mère-Église and took part in the battle for La Fière Bridge. Preferring to fire his Thompson submachine gun from the hip, Czekanski had his jump jacket specially modified with an olive drab arm patch to reinforce the sleeve where it made contact with the gun.

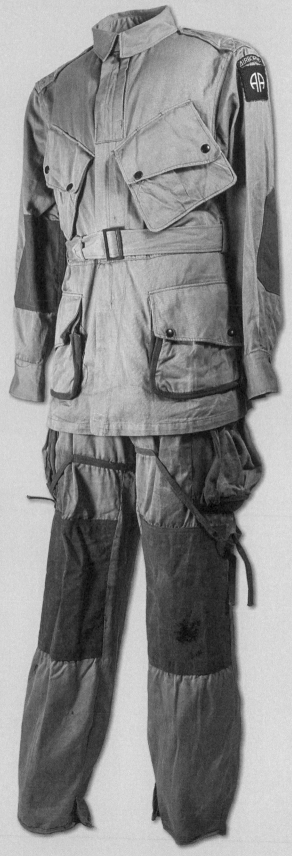

AIRBORNE OPERATIONS

Elmo Bell

C Company, 505th Parachute Infantry Regiment

82nd Airborne Division

Elmo Bell grew up in Mississippi and before the war worked as a carpenter on army bases, a role that qualified him for a draft deferment. His early interactions with soldiers as a civilian carpenter left him with a negative view of the army. But he did not want to be seen as a draft dodger, and decided to enlist in the US Marine Corps. Just prior to enlistment, he had a cup of coffee with an army recruiter who changed his life, convincing him to join one of the paratroop units that were being created. Missions would be difficult and dangerous, but it was an elite force with high standards and the promise of extra pay. Bell changed his mind and signed up for the 82nd Airborne.

After a dangerously low drop, the men of C Company, 505th joined in the fight for the causeways at La Fière. Limited to weapons they could carry in a parachute drop, paratroopers were outmatched by German armored units, but they improvised, waged a fierce fight, and held their ground.

As we approached Normandy, the jumpmaster was watching the doors and, as soon as he could see landfall, he ordered the troops to stand up and hook up. While we were in the process of doing that, the plane was hit by anti-aircraft fire. The engine on the right side was knocked out, and the plane winged over sharply. Just a few of the troopers had hooked their static lines up, and the others were in the process. And they dumped everybody onto the floor.

I was number two man in the stick, and I was able to get to the door first. I crawled to the door, intending just to crawl on out. But when I got to the door we were down at treetop level, much too low to drop. Then Sergeant Zeitner (Herman R.), who was the jumpmaster, crawled up and the two of us stood together in the door and locked arms to hold the others back. Everyone had one thought in mind: to get out of that crippled plane. And I was

yelling, "No! We're too low!" The push continued, and I finally realized that "no" and "low" sounded like "go." And they were trying very hard to do that.

The first sergeant leaned over and shouted in my ear, telling me to watch the ground and to tell him if we gained enough altitude to drop. It was still cloudy but, through the intermittent cloud cover, I could see the ground. I visualized a football field,

Above: When the red light of this jump signal illuminated, paratroopers were given the command to "Stand up, hook up!" Once over the drop zone, the green light would illuminate, signaling to the jumpmaster that it was time to jump.

Below: In England, paratroopers check equipment bundles for the jump into Normandy.

thinking of one pair of goalposts on the ground and the other one as the plane. After a while, I could tell that we were gaining altitude. I thought we were still too low to jump, but I wanted to let the jumpmaster know at least we were gaining altitude. I leaned over to tell him that. And when I called his name, he jumped. Realizing that I had triggered his premature jump, I went out too. Going out the door, I realized that the rest of the stick was going to follow me. So I had just compounded a small problem.

But anyway, we landed safely. And the jumpmaster said later that he thought I intended him to jump. He didn't realize I was just telling him that we were gaining altitude. He said the timing was absolutely perfect. He said his chute popped open and his butt hit the ground at the same instant. But we had no injuries and we landed extremely close together. We rolled up the stick and were ready to go in a matter of minutes. So the drop turned out ideal.

After we assembled, we immediately started toward Sainte-Mère-Église. Then we reached the river and realized that it was flooded. So the commander decided that we needed to go and reinforce the batteries to defend that bridge. We started moving in that direction. Short of the bridge, there was a German strongpoint on a little ridge on the edge of the woods. The woods that we were in were separated from the German strongpoint by 500 or 600 yards of flat, bare ground. The Germans had that covered with automatic weapons. We were held up there, and everyone that showed themself out of the woods was picked off.

I climbed a beech tree and had a good view of the German strongpoint. I climbed down then and gathered two or three mortars that I could find and placed them near the tree, so I could climb the tree and give them corrections and adjust on the strongpoint. I succeeded in doing that. When we delivered fire for effect on the strongpoint, the Germans put down their

Above: John H. Capehart had his comrades sign this parachute from a signal flare. The souvenir was created by members of the 505th Regimental Combat Team, comprised of the 505th Parachute Infantry Regiment and the 456th Parachute Field Artillery Battalion.

weapons and came out with white flags. I gave the command to cease fire. The mission was at an end. The lieutenant immediately countermanded the order. He announced that, "I countermand that order. Repeat range. Repeat fire for effect." And I argued with him. I climbed down out of the tree and said, "Climb up there and look and see. It's over there. They're putting down their weapons and coming out." He repeated his command. And of course, when they started firing with the mortar, the Germans took up their weapons and got back in their holes and resumed the conflict. I was extremely perturbed, because we had ten,

Below: Created by B Company, 660th Engineer Topographic Battalion in early 1944, this map shows the area where the 82nd engaged in some of its fiercest fighting around Sainte-Mère-Église. The map also includes Chef-du-Pont, La Fière and Amfreville.

fifteen men killed before we overcame the strongpoint. That was not necessary.

When I criticized the lieutenant, he said, well, we had no choice. We knew that we were needed at the bridge, and we didn't know how much resistance we'd have in getting there. We didn't have any way to control the prisoners once they were captured. My argument was that these ten or fifteen people that were killed could have guarded the prisoners, and they would have lived to fight another day. But it didn't work out that way.

As we approached the bridge, we began to get sporadic fire from the built-up area that was on the Sainte-Mère-Église side of the river and on the up-current side of the bridge we called the "mound." This mound consisted of a large, two-story stone house and numerous outbuildings behind the wall. After we occupied positions along the river, there were still 25 or 30 Germans in

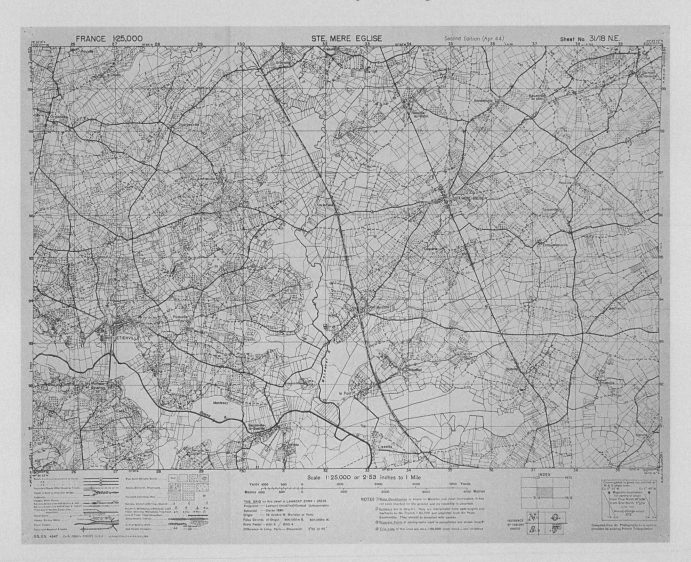

the mound. But our primary concern was setting up a defense to defend the bridge, and we were not concerned. Several times, they fired on us sporadically. It was late in the afternoon by the time we cleared the buildings there. We captured another 25 or so Germans. But they didn't cause any real concern.

We set up along the river. A Company had already arrived and they had occupied positions right along the river flank. So the later arrivals occupied the river in greater depth, further back from the river's edge. This floodplain we could see across the river, and there was water on both sides of the causeway. The causeway extended about 600 yards, and then the road gradually turned back to the left and disappeared around the curve and some timber. We could hear the sound of vehicles, both track and wheel vehicles, back around the curve. So we knew that they were assembling for an attack. We rushed to get our defense set up there.

Sometime about noon, three tanks pulled out in sight, followed by about a battalion of infantry. They came on towards the bridge, and they had ten or twelve paratroopers who had been captured. They were marching ahead of the tanks with their hands behind their heads. The tank commander of the lead tank was carrying a submachine gun, and he was directing these paratroopers to pick up the mines, you know, and throw them off the road. As they approached they got closer and closer and still.

Not a shot had been fired. I was apprehensive. I had a mortar laid on the foot of the bridge there, and I had a shell in hand in a tube, just waiting for the command to fire to drop that shell in the tube. The command didn't come.

When the lead tank got to the bridge I was afraid that no one had assumed command, that no one was going to give the command to fire. I was ready to start the show by dropping that mortar round. But about this time, there was a little 57-millimeter anti-tank gun back down the road a hundred and fifty or two hundred yards that I didn't even know was there. This little anti-tank gun had been recovered from a wrecked glider by some engineer crew, and it was in position. They fired a shot. And whether it was by design or accident I don't know, but it knocked the tread off of the tank. The tank immediately turned crossways across the bridge. The second tank was following close behind the first, using the first for a shield. It was following so closely that it climbed up on the rear of the tank that had the tread knocked off. The bazooka gunners were down dug in on the riverbank under the bridge. They fired into the belly of the

A crashed invasion glider. The infamous Normandy hedgerows created deadly landing zones for the gliders on D-Day.

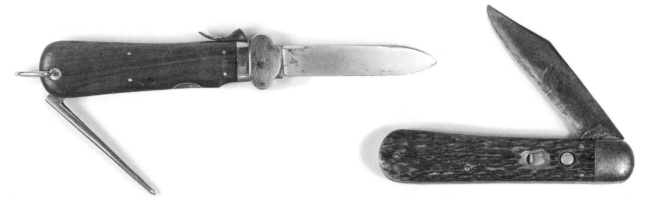

Easy Company 506th PIR soldier Paul Rogers recovered this German gravity knife during the Normandy Campaign. German aircrew and *Fallschirmjäger* (paratroopers) were issued this knife to cut themselves out of their parachute harnesses if the need arose. Paratroops of the 101st and 82nd Airborne Divisions faced their German counterparts of the 6th *Fallschirmjäger* regiment in numerous engagements in Normandy.

Sergeant George Leidenheimer, B Company 507th PIR 82nd Airborne Division, carried this switchblade during the Normandy Campaign. Issued to every American paratrooper, the switchblade was intended to help the paratrooper get free of his parachute, especially if he landed in a tree. The knife was carried in a special pocket in the placket of the jump jacket. Paratroopers who lost their equipment in the jump found this was the only weapon they had when they landed in France.

tank that was climbed up on the other, and it caught fire. That effectively blocked the bridge, and the third tank started back down the road.

The infantry started running for cover. They realized that the bridge was blocked, that they were not going to get across. As the infantry pulled back down the road it was really a slaughter because they had no protection. The causeway was up a foot or two above water level, but it only protected them from one direction. If they were on the upper side, they were exposed to troopers defending on the upper side of the river bridge, and vice versa. The little 57-millimeter anti-tank gun was firing and was hitting that tank back and down the road. These were little, light tanks. They were French Renault. But even that small, little tank had enough armor on the front that that little 57-millimeter gun wouldn't knock it out. He backed away, all the way down the road to the curve. And they were shooting continuous to there. The rounds were popping like pinned balloons on the front of the tank, but did no damage.

Then sometime after the German forces had withdrawn out of sight, a motorcycle with a sidecar and also with a white flag came out. He came down near the bridge, and he had a megaphone. He asked for a truce of thirty or forty minutes to recover the dead and wounded. That truce was granted, and he called back on the radio. A number of cargo trucks then rode down the causeway, and they started loading up the dead and wounded. We were

surprised, because there was no ambulance. There was nothing but cargo trucks. We couldn't tell that (they were alive or dead)— they seemed to be handling them all the same. They'd pick up a soldier by the feet and the arms and toss him over in the back of a truck. Several other people were trying to count the number they picked up, and the counts all ran around two hundred. If they were all dead, that would account for their handling, because they didn't handle any of them as though they were wounded. They just threw them in the back of a cargo truck and hauled them away. And that was the end of their first counter-attack.

After that, we stayed in position. We were constantly battered by artillery and mortar fire. We had many, many casualties from mortar and artillery, because we couldn't move. We were there on the riverbank. We just had to hunker down there in a foxhole and take it. That was the extent of the first attack. And the other attacks, I don't remember all of the details, and it's difficult for me to separate the two. They were pretty much alike. But all of the attacks failed, and we held the bridge until the amphibious forces arrived and the bridge was open for their disposal.

Elmo Bell stayed with the 82nd Airborne for the duration of the war. He later joined the Mississippi National Guard, retiring as a Brigadier General.

Wayne Pierce

First Lieutenant, Executive Officer, B Company, 325th Glider

Infantry Regiment, 82nd Airborne Division

Executive Officer Wayne Pierce was older than most of his fellow glidermen at the age of 26. Pierce was drafted in 1941 and attended Officer Candidate School in 1942 before training for the glider forces. He married in September 1942 just after his commissioning as a lieutenant. Pierce missed the fighting in Italy when a jeep his team was loading into a glider broke loose and pinned him to the back of the glider, dislocating his wrist. He believed the accident saved his life after learning of heavy casualties during the fighting in Italy. Pierce would see an abundance of combat and death in Normandy.

Above: Wayne Pierce after his promotion to Captain.

Above: C-47s towing gliders over the invasion armada.

In the early morning hours of June 7, 100 C-47s took to the air in England. They were towing a mix of American Waco and British Horsa gliders, packed beyond their limits with ammunition, vehicles, artillery and men of the 325th Glider Infantry Regiment. Their mission called for three waves of gliders to land on D+1, bringing in the 325th along with a battalion of the 401st Glider Infantry Regiment as reinforcements for the parachute regiments dropped on D-Day. The gliders were critical to providing much-needed supplies to the invasion forces. The contributions of glider troops were considered so valuable to their paratroop counterparts that after the fighting in Normandy they were allowed to wear the iconic paratrooper jump boots and were given the same hazard pay as paratroopers.

We moved through Sainte-Marie-du-Mont, and out toward the La Fière causeways. We ended up that night behind the railroad at La Fière. In that position, we were a reserve for Taskforce A, which was commanded by General Gavin (James M., Assistant Division Commander, 82nd Airborne), and was manned by 507th, 508th and 505th, the little group of men there. That night, or that evening, probably about six o'clock, General Gavin came by with a jeep. He wanted someone to go with him, back to where (Major General) Ridgway was, so Major Sanford (Teddy H., executive officer, 1st Battalion, 325th Glider Infantry Regiment) and I went with him.

We got in his jeep and rode back to the house where Ridgway was. There, I cooled my heels out in the orchard, and had a little bit of a rest. Sanford was briefed by the division staff, and Gavin went in and had a conference with Ridgway. When we got ready to leave it was probably eleven o'clock at night and it was dark. We got back on the jeep and walked up the road till Gavin decided that we didn't want to go any further, and we found a little orchard

Inset: The 82nd Airborne patch bears two As, for "All American," the nickname first bestowed upon the unit at its formation due to its unique makeup of men from all 48 states. Formed in 1917 as an infantry division, the 82nd was reorganized and designated an airborne division in August 1942.

M-1 Helmet used by Private First Class Edward Sabo, Easy Company, 2nd Battalion, 506th Parachute Infantry Regiment, 101st Airborne Division. The helmet shell has a white spade painted on both sides with a tick mark at the 6 o'clock position. Each of the four infantry regiments in the 101st Airborne used a suit from a deck of cards as its identifying mark. The location of the tick mark denoted which battalion a soldier belonged to within each regiment.

path with a hedgerow around it. He pulled the jeep off the road, and we went in this little orchard path to sleep. Sanford and I huddled up close to try to keep warm.

That night, about three o'clock in the morning, probably, there was a German patrol that came wandering around, and they would fire a Schmeisser (MP 40) every once in a while. I think they were just trying to stir us up to see where we were. They didn't know where we were, either. Gavin got up, went around to the two or three enlisted men that he had with him, and he kicked them awake and put them out in the corner of this little path, then he went back and went to sleep. I'm sure that Sanford was awake, same as I was, but neither one moved. I thought it would be foolish to get out and try to find that patrol, and I didn't know the lay of the land—and they did.

The next morning at daylight, we headed back on the road. I rode on the truck bumper on the hood of the jeep. Sanford rode with Gavin, and we went on up the road to where our battalion was bivouacked. We spent the day there. Gavin, of course, went on in his duties, but we spent the day there, and that's when Lieutenant John Marr came over and found the rest of the men.

Major Sanford was our battalion commander. My situation with Sanford was that I was a helper. I helped keep the men on the road. I helped keep the column moving on along the railroad. I waited up where we turned off to the ford, to make sure everybody turned off. This was 11 o'clock at night. About 11:30, and all of a sudden, the column quit. I went running back down the railroad to find out what was the matter. I found

a man seated on the rail, asleep, and everybody else behind him was sitting on the rail, probably sleeping also. I woke him up and got him started back up, and I took him up to the place where you turned off. One of the things we used to say in training, "You will do in combat the same as you do in training." This man that I woke on the railroad that night was a man that I had awakened several times in my classes.

We crossed the ford and came into the orchard. C Company was on ahead of us, and they made the feint against the grey castle (a large house near Amfreville). The tracers were flying through the air, lighting up the area like daylight. When they moved back, the rest of us moved on around through the orchard and past the buildings and past Chambers (Lieutenant Willard E., with 507th PIR) and his men.

Chambers had about a hundred men in that area. As we moved on through the orchard behind the left platoon of Company C, we thought we would be more or less in the center of the attack, and could give guidance to Company B on the left and Company C on the right; Company A was to protect our rear. I saw Lieutenant Brewster Johnson in that area. He had been in on the attack on the grey castle. He slapped me on the back and said, "Pierce, they can't shoot worth crap," but he was killed within an hour after that. We crossed two roads, and we went down through a wheatfield, and down toward the Cauquigny Church.

I was with Sanford, and we were on the left. There was a small orchard, and then we came to a road that was somewhat sunken. There, Major Sanford, myself, and a couple of runners, and maybe a couple other guys, were all laying in the ditch when the platoon went across this road. There the firing picked up and it was daylight from the tracers that were flying through in both directions.

Then, it quieted down for a minute. Sanford moved up to the road. I was back about twenty yards, maybe. He came back to me, and he says, "The C Company is wiped out." I thought, "How can he know that? Men are still out there." He said, "We're moving back to the orchard." So, he went back, telling the other men in the little group that we were there, and they got up and followed him. I looked back, it was getting daylight by that time. I looked back to the wheatfield, and I saw them run over the knoll through the wheatfield, heading back to the orchard. I still didn't think that the C Company was wiped out, and I could find a man or two, so I ran across the orchard to the other side.

I got to the other side and looked through the bushes to see if I could see any of the C Company men. I could see no one. All

I could hear was German voices across from me. I sat there for a little while and decided that I'd better get moving too. Then, I went back through the wheatfield, over the knoll. There I found about eight or ten men from the C Company. They told me that the men had surrendered somewhere, wounded. That they had gotten back the best they could. We crossed the road back over to where we could see the orchard and farm buildings where we had gone through. I told the C Company group that, "I'm going to organize you men into a couple of squads." I had two sergeants. I divided the group, and I said, "We're going back up to B Company. They're still in there, and they're still fighting," though firing was sporadic. It was bad. Before we got started, we started receiving fire from our rear, from the direction of Amfreville.

Then I gave up. I said, "Men, we're going back to the orchard." So, we made a run back into the orchard. There, I found Sanford. He was on his radio, trying to get regimental headquarters across the river. He finally made contact and got artillery fire directed into where it would help us. We dug foxholes there and waited. About 11 o'clock, we heard that the 3rd Battalion had been ordered to attack across the causeway, so we sat tight until probably about 2 or 3 o'clock. Colonel Sanford then ordered me to take the C Company and go out, and make contact with the paratroopers, or whoever was out there—the 3rd Battalion. I did this with the group. We spread out along the road, and holed up.

There were four Germans piled up in a ditch out in front of the line that I was setting up. I took a man that could speak German, and we went out in front of our lines, and pointed our weapons at them, and this man yelled, "Get up, sergeant," and all four of them

stood up. We took their weapons and sent them back over to the orchard. That night, we held our line. There was a lot of German conversation up in the woods, but nothing had happened. The morning of June 10, the 90th (Infantry) Division came through. There was a regiment of the 90th. It went through us, and started the attack up toward Amfreville. We felt elated to have some help.

The next day, I saw the dead piled up that they were picking up from the causeway, and it was a terrible sight. I went back to my company and, about that time, the 90th Division Regiment that had gone through us started backing up. I got a hold of one of their officers, and I said, "What are you doing?" and he said, "We're backing up." He says, "I'm going to back up by a couple hundred yards, and then, somebody else is going to back up through me." I said, "What are you going to do when you reach the river?" he said, "Is there a river back there?" He didn't know that—I said, "Sit down here and help us. We can't move." So, anyway, they settled down there, and we spent the night. And the next day they took off on another attack up through Amfreville.

Wayne Pierce was promoted to captain and became commanding officer of C Company. The 325th GIR landed in Holland in September. Pierce was awarded the Silver Star for his role in the attack on the Mook Plain in Holland in October.

James Peninger, a glider pilot, took the Aeronautic First Aid Kit from his glider after he landed in Normandy. The kit was designed for use by air crews in all types of planes. Transport planes and gliders carried multiple kits during the D-Day invasion.

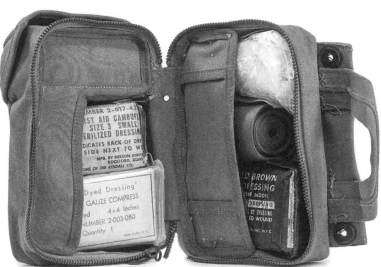

Richard Winters

First Lieutentant, Platoon Leader, E Company, 506th

Parachute Infantry Regiment

101st Airborne Division

Richard Davis "Dick" Winters, began D-Day as a Platoon Leader in Easy Company, 506th Parachute Infantry Regiment. During the drop, Easy Company's commander Lieutenant Thomas Meehan was killed when his C-47 was hit and crashed, making Winters the highest-ranking officer to survive June 6. Already a favorite with his men, Winters, as Easy Company's new commanding officer, earned further admiration for his leadership as his unit dropped into the invasion zone in the early hours of D-Day and later steadily fought its way across Europe.

The crossroads town of Carentan had to be taken. It was a major objective of the 101st Airborne as the 82nd fought to secure the area around La Fière in the first week of the Normandy campaign. Carentan lay on a major roadway connecting Omaha and Utah beaches. The town provided a strongpoint from which German forces might drive a wedge between the V Corps fighting inland from Omaha, and the VII Corps advancing from Utah, spelling disaster for American strategy. On the night of June 12, the 506th Parachute Infantry Regiment began moving south of Carentan, to participate in a coordinated attack on the city with the full strength of the division.

Winters' reputation was further enhanced by the 1992 publication of *Band of Brothers*, Stephen E. Ambrose's portrayal of Easy Company in the European Theater. Ambrose interviewed Winters in 1990 during research for the book. The interview traces Winters' memory of tense days and hours before the Normandy invasion and his intense praying during E Company's hazardous flight into the war zone; he was "praying to live through it, praying that we wouldn't fail. Every man, I think, had up in his mind, 'How will I react under fire?' You've never been tested under fire, and you hoped that you would become a soldier, you wouldn't disgrace yourself." A notable testing episode came days after Winters' drop into France as his unit fought to take a strategic intersection at the town of Carentan, near the Omaha and Utah invasion beaches. Queries arc from Ambrose (in bold), as he and Winters scanned a map, offer a glimpse into the military historian's methods.

Opposite: Captain Richard Winters in July 1944 in Aldbourne, England. (Photo from the Hershey Derry Township Historical Society Collection.)

Above: Aerial view of Carentan, France prior to the Allied invasion.

Richard Winters as a First Lieutenant, before a demonstration jump for British Prime Minister Winston Churchill in March 1944. (Photo from the Hershey Derry Township Historical Society Collection.)

Now, your assault position ended up where?
We flanked Carentan.

To the —
To the west. We came across a bridge. Then we flanked to the right.

And we came over—the railroad was our guiding (reference)—we do not go over the railroad. So we came down over the bridge through these fields, cutting over here, to come down the roadway into town (Carentan) in this fashion.

So you were coming into Carentan pretty much from the west—
That's correct.
And were you there at first light, in assault position?
We were very close to it—by 5:30 in the morning, I had received word that the attack is kicking off at 6:00, and we were just getting in position.

So is the whole regiment involved in this attack?
Oh yeah. Yeah. The division (101st).

Did the Germans know you were there? Had you encountered patrols and they had fallen back?
Oh sure, yeah.

So they knew you were coming.
Yeah, definitely. The fighting back here in the center, as you look at the map there, you can see Carentan, and you can see that the way we're coming into here and they (Germans) had to fall back to the south.

'Cause they've got pressure coming from Omaha Beach and—right.
That's correct. And they had the rest of the division (101st).

So we've just skirted along the edge of this flooded area. If the Germans are going to retreat, there's only one way for them to go. They either have to go through that flooded area, which is about impossible, or come down this road. So as we're—as the pressure's being put here by the (101st) division, we're over here, and if we take this intersection, we—

You're going to be a blocking force for the whole German—
That's right.

So that intersection that we're looking at here becomes a damn crucial point. Cut that and you're cutting off their retreat.

What do you estimate the German strength in Carentan was?
That's hard for us to say. The only thing that I have read, which doesn't make a hell of a lot of sense, was that some people said that they thought there were about 200 men. I can't help but think there'd be a whole lot more than that, baby.

There was a tremendous amount of firepower. But where they ever got 200 men from, I don't know. And what day they're talking about, I don't know. It depends what day you're talking about, because these people had been pulling out of there. As you can see, if we come down this road here, that's sloping down, and we take that intersection, we've cut the main roadway out of Carentan, and if they want to retreat, they've got to go through the flooded area, and we've got them blocked. Retreat 27, glider boys (327th Glider Infantry Regiment), they're over here on this side, and we're over here, we're cutting the men loose. We're coming down this road. E Company's in front. Right behind E Company is 2nd Battalion headquarters, Strayer, Baxter, Nixon. Which is a good position, Battalion Headquarters. Behind us is D, F is over here …

As I caught up to the company, I moved back and forth, back and forth, trying to communicate this whole plan. We have E Company on both sides of this road—the road wasn't that big or wide. There were ditches on both sides. I am up here on the right-hand side, and Harry Welsh (First Lieutenant) was down here on the left-hand side, and I looked down in there and there's Harry Welsh kicking it off —it was close to 6:00—taking about six guys out in front of him. And as he kicks it off, a German

machine gun opens up, fires right down this road, and the rest of the guys, they go face down in the ditch, head down, trying to snuggle in as close as they can to the ground. Harry has six men coming into the intersection all by themselves. It just takes one man behind Harry not to move out, and the rest of the line stops. I'm over here on the side, I'm hollering, "Move out! Move out!" Everybody's just flat.

I threw everything off, just took an M1, jumped up on the road, and ran up the road hollering like a mad man, "Get going!" I kicked ass. And I mean I was—I was furious. I was kicking them on this side of the road, kicking them, go on this other side of the road and kick them, and kept going back and forth, working to get these guys moving.

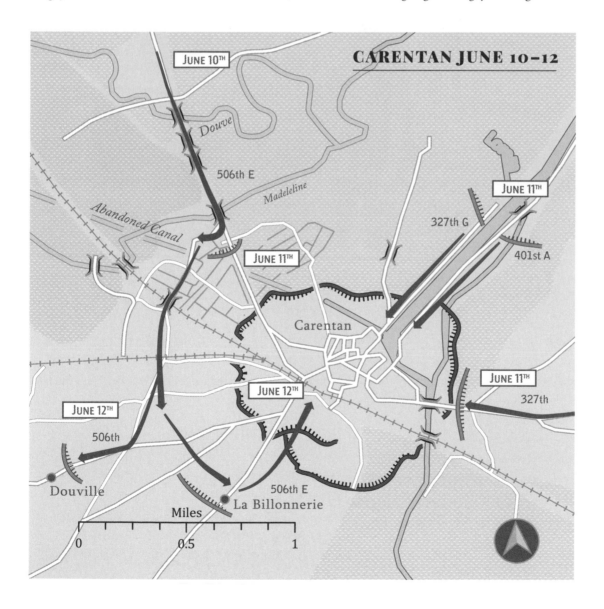

Above: American paratroopers and army medics move through Carentan, June 12.

Opposite: The *Mashinengewehr* 34, or MG 34, was the first successfully developed general purpose machine gun fielded by the German Army. Lightweight, easy to use, and with a high rate of fire, the MG34 served as the primary infantry machine gun of the German Army until it was replaced in 1942 by the MG 42.

Let me ask you this: When you say "kicking," you mean literally kicking?

I mean kicking. Nobody'd ever seen me like that. I'd never done anything like that. But I was kicking ass. As you would kick—you know, they would look up, they're scared as hell—and you'd get them up on their knees and then get going. But this machine gun was firing bursts down the road, and I'm on the road, zigzagging through.

Were you firing at all?

No, I wasn't.

As your men got up, did they start shooting from the hip?

No.

Throwing grenades?

No.

No answering fire at all, then?

Couldn't. Couldn't. Couldn't. I'm going back and forth, back and forth. Frankly at that point, I thought to myself, "My God, I'm leading a blessed life. I'm charmed." Hell, I was about to get hit.

Would it be unfair to use the word you were "possessed?"
I was possessed at that point.

OK, go ahead.
If we want to be dramatic, and it's the truth, I had just seen my friend kick off with six guys into this machine gun, and the rest of the company stopped, froze. He's a dead man if I don't do something. No question about it. But I kept going, back and forth, back and forth, back and forth. And my kicks got the company moving and they drove down in. Here is where discipline comes in—here's where it all paid off. They moved out once they got the message. Harry got down here and he was the guy with his few men that's responsible for neutralizing that machine gun.

Where was it located?
Right here at the end of the road in this building—

This was an MG34? That heavy German machine gun?
Tremendous amount of fire power.

So are you in the middle now of German positions? That is to say, are there still Germans in Carentan or have most of them already withdrawn?
The only Germans that we've seen for now have withdrawn, or the ones in here—

So you're not facing pressure now from both directions.
No. No. Just from a counter-attack.

Yeah. You yourself were now wounded.
Yes, I was wounded.

Where were you hit?
I was wounded right here at the intersection, with a ricochet. Not bad. Through the top of the boot, the left leg. I kept going. It didn't stop me. But we had quite a few casualties. We had ten casualties, to be exact, at this intersection. I can't name them all today, but I can name some of them. The aid station was right here, and when I went back there, I looked for that aid station, and it's still there. We immediately set up—and again, we were talking about a counter-attack. That was the first thing—to set up a defense for a counter-attack, and check my munition supply. Next thing I did was go to the aid station to see how many casualties I had. I found Tipper (Edward), I found Lipton (Carwood). The rest of them were there. So, we got ourselves organized, the regiment, the division.

It's an interesting point there. When Sink (Colonel Robert Sink, commanding officer 506th PIR) caught up to me in Carentan, when we went outside and got better under control—this would be three or four days later—he stopped me and he said, "I'm putting you in for the Congressional Medal of Honor." Which was very nice. But at the time, frankly, the thought that goes through you is "What the hell," because you just think, "How about all the men that were with me? Hey, they did as much if not more than I did." It's not a personal thing.

Promoted to captain in July 1944, Richard Winters continued to lead E Company until he was made the executive officer of the 2nd Battalion, 506th PIR in October 1944, much to the disappointment of the men in E Company. A favorite of his men, Winters led the battalion through the Battle of the Bulge, and on to Hitler's Eagle's Nest, high in the Bavarian Alps near Berchtesgaden. Fittingly, it was here that the 2nd Battalion celebrated its role in the destruction of the Third Reich and the end of World War II in Europe.

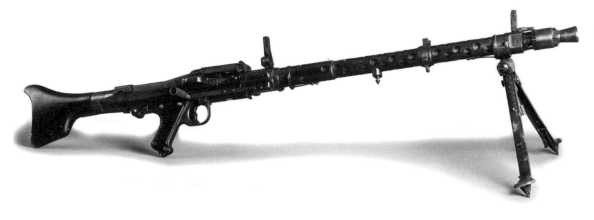

Edward Tipper

E Company, 506th Parachute Infantry Regiment

101st Airborne Division

Two weeks after the attack on Pearl Harbor, twenty-year-old Edward Tipper went to his local Marine Corps recruiting office to enlist. He was rejected due to an issue with his teeth. Initially angry at the rejection, he later recalled it as one of the most fortunate events in his life. He immediately joined the army and volunteered for the airborne. Like many, he wanted to be in an elite unit; he believed that fighting with the best would increase his chances at survival. At Camp Toccoa, Georgia, Tipper was assigned to E Company, 506th, under the infamous Captain Herbert Sobel. Under Sobel's notoriously difficult training and often arbitrary directives, Tipper and the other men of E Company became one of the best conditioned and most cohesive units destined for the invasion of Europe. Tipper said late in life that his extreme conditioning under Sobel probably saved his life after he was severely wounded.

As Easy Company fought to take the critical town of Carentan, it suffered devastating losses. The close camaraderie formed during their difficult training at Camp Toccoa made those losses even more difficult. Fighting in a village brought new challenges, as the enemy could fire from hidden positions. Clearing houses in the village was dangerous, but the paratroopers kept moving. For some, like Edward Tipper, it would be their last task of the war.

It's a testimony (taking Carentan), I think, to our training. I think a regular army infantry never could've done what we did. Somebody decided that the best place to take Carentan was from the south. There's a huge swamp to the south of Carentan. And the Germans had just decided nobody could go through that swamp, maybe one or two, but not enough to make any attack. So their south end was very lightly defended.

We spent the night moving. About 200 men with full equipment ready to fight went single file for miles. I don't know, probably 30 or 40 miles all the way around that area—around the swamp, and then through the swamp, you had to be very careful. Single file. One wrong step, one guy would ruin the whole thing. It never happened. We did it perfectly. And we attacked the Germans in a place that they didn't think anyone could attack them from. So we were very quick. We took Carentan. I was wounded before we took it, I was wounded in that action.

We had three machine guns. They had one. And we were moving them back. We came to a crossroads—a three-way crossroads. And I realized at the same time as a couple of other people, that if we kept advancing, there were houses in backwoods. Maybe there were Germans in those houses. And

American paratroopers ride through Carentan on a captured German jeep, June 14. The red markings on the photo are military censor marks.

Mark I trench knife carried during the Normandy Campaign by 505th PIR, 82nd Airborne Division trooper Arthur "Dutch" Schultz. Known as the "knuckle duster" in GI parlance, the World War I vintage Mark I was issued to the army's elite formations in the early days of World War II. By D-Day, the M-3 trench knife had replaced the Mark I as the army's standard issue fighting knife.

they could start shooting us from the back. So we said we better go clear those houses first.

Well, we didn't have any grenades. But that didn't matter. We knew how to do it with or without a grenade. And Joe Leibgott and I went out to clear a house. The first house I got to, I kicked the door in, went in, nobody was there. The house was burning. How it was burning, I don't know because it was almost all stone. But the banister was wet, there was smoke coming out of it. And I noticed there was no toilet, no bathroom. I said what kind of people are these? They don't have a bathroom. But that was a middle-class house.

So I went upstairs. I went out on the back porch, it had an outhouse, I think, kind of thing. I hollered in German in there, "Come out with your hands up!" nobody answered. I just put a couple of shots in there. No reaction. The backyard had a wall—a stone wall about five feet high. Nobody was there. I went back in the house and waited. I yelled across to Leibgott, "This one's clear!"

A big explosion happened. I thought it was a grenade. I thought a German had missed a shot and thrown a grenade. Both my legs were broken. My right eye was destroyed, I had shrapnel in my elbow and back. I did not drop my weapon. I turned around. I was ready to get this sniper, what I thought was a German who threw a grenade. He was coming and I was ready for him. Well, I was in shock. That's why I could still stand.

But it's amazing that most people in a situation like that— most regular army guys' weapon would've gone flying. All the time I was in that training, your rifle is your best friend. You cannot ever leave your rifle. You hang onto it no matter what. And that training stuck. I'm pretty sure Leibgott yelled across the street he said, "Tipper, that's a mortar shot. I'm coming." And he came running over. By that time, I was not able to stand. Two or three guys risked their lives to rescue me. But that was just the

way we all worked. What do you expect? I was not surprised that they would risk their lives. That's just the way you did things in that group.

They had an aid station very close to that intersection. There they had some Germans they were treating. The doctor was a doctor I knew. And I got pretty good treatment then. They got a jeep in from the beach. The jeep had a stretcher on either side and another stretcher crosswise on the back. And they put on the three most seriously wounded. And I was one. And that jeep driver took off through German territory just gunning it. The red flag didn't mean anything. The red cross (indicating medical personnel and vehicles)—Germans shot at us. But they were too far away. I was thinking, my God, we thought we were doing something dangerous. This guy (the driver)—his life expectancy is probably about two days. And he's not getting any extra pay or recognition. To this day, I don't have any idea how he got us into the beach hospital. Then we were okay. I got first-class medical attention. But I should've died from that wound. (Many in Easy Company thought Tipper had died of his wounds.)

One of my friends in E Company was Sergeant Floyd Talbert. And back in the States I was in the hospital in Indianapolis. I went up and had Thanksgiving dinner with his parents. And they made a big fuss over me. We had a great time. His mother wrote to him: "Talbert, we had Ed Tipper come to visit us." He wrote back right away. "You call the MPs and have that guy put in jail. He's not Ed Tipper. Ed Tipper was killed. I saw him killed in Normandy. And that guy's an imposter. Get the MPs on that."

But everything was in my favor. I was 21 years old, I had all this training, I was in the best shape of my entire life. But I probably needed an army. I was in the hospital a year before they let me out.

Like many Americans who landed in Normandy, Edward Tipper saw his war end quickly. Unlike many, he managed to recover from his wounds. Though he was never able to rejoin E Company during the war, the bonds he formed with his fellow "Screaming Eagles" lasted a lifetime.

a.

b.

c.

CONCLUSION

The entire 101st Airborne Division was thrown into the fight for Carentan, and by June 14 the town was in American hands. The success of the 101st secured a vital link between Omaha and Utah Beaches, creating a continuous beachhead which propelled the American drive inland. The gains were far from secure, as the division had to fight off German counter-attacks. The 101st continued to hold its defensive position around Carentan, even in the face of heavy shelling from German forces armed with the dreaded 88mm flak gun. In late June, the division began to move towards Cherbourg to clear out German forces in the entire peninsula. In mid-July, the division returned to England for a much needed recovery period. Their sacrifices had been great: Of the roughly 14,000 men wearing the Screaming Eagles patch in Normandy, more than 4,600 were killed, wounded, or missing in action.

The 82nd Airborne also recorded hard-won successes as it supported American troops landing on Utah Beach, adjusting to changes in objectives and drop zones and overcoming the initial confusion. Their crucial test came in the four days of combat around La Fière. German military leaders knew La Fière was key to control of the critical causeway linking the beach sectors, and fought fiercely but failed to keep it out of American hands. The 82nd Airborne continued to fight German forces in the Cotentin Peninsula, moving southwest until the division was pulled off the line on July 8. Days later, the men were given showers and new uniforms and, on July 11, after 33 days of combat, the 82nd arrived at Utah Beach to evacuate. Of the more than 11,000 men of the 82nd Airborne who landed in Normandy on June 6 and 7, just over half remained to board LSTs in July to make the trip back to England.

First Lieutenant Wallace Strobel, a platoon leader in E Company, 502nd PIR, recovered several German pistols. The brown leather holsters which accompanied the side arms suggest the former owners were Luftwaffe personnel, likely German paratroopers defending Carentan, considering the 502nd's heavy involvement in the battle for the city. German Army and SS units were generally issued black leather gear.

a. CZ27 pistol
b. P08 "Luger" pistol
c. Walther P38 pistol

UTAH BEACH

CHAPTER TWO

6.6.44

On the evening of June 5, Rear Admiral Don Moon was on his flagship, the USS *Bayfield* (APA-33), leading Force U at six knots through rough seas and weather toward Normandy. Operation Neptune was underway. Moon led a massive naval task force destined for a violent encounter with the enemy at Utah Beach the next morning, and his responsibilities weighed heavily. He knew this amphibious assault on the westernmost sector of the invasion front was among the more daring and complex of Operation Overlord. The admiral also understood that the Utah landings were critical to the entire Allied plan for liberating France.

LCIs (Landing Craft Infantry) flying barrage balloons as protection against low-flying German aircraft, move toward the Normandy coastline on D-Day.

Despite the tension of the moment, Moon took some comfort in knowing the secrecy of Overlord remained intact and that the Force U armada of 865 ships, landing craft and troop transports, was part of the largest amphibious force in history. Aboard his ships were the well-trained 4th Infantry Division and the battle-proven 70th Tank Battalion, who would lead a combined force of more than 21,000 troops in the ground assault the next morning.

The initial objective of Force U was to fight across the beaches and drive miles inland to join up with airborne troops in seizing and holding causeways crossing the flood plains. Their collective mission: prevent German counter-attacks against other Allied forces and supplies flowing onto the Normandy shore. Once the beachhead was secure, American troops were to work their way across the Cotentin Peninsula and seize the strategically vital deep-water port of Cherbourg. Capturing this port was critical to bringing in the enormous quantities of materiel needed to sustain the invasion and destroy German forces. But first, Moon had to get Force U safely through mine-infested waters and deliver his troops ashore at H-Hour—6:30 a.m. on June 6.

There were many reasons to worry. The scale and complexity of the operation was daunting. Moon and his commanders had to coordinate airborne drops, naval and Army Air Force bombardments, and the landing of the VII Corps, all at precisely the right moments. Dangers in the English Channel were not confined to mines. German discovery of the armada was a real possibility, as his task force was the closest to France. Just a few weeks earlier in the Operation Tiger training exercise at Slapton Sands, Moon was commanding a convoy of troop ships when a German *Schnellboot* (E-boat) carried out a daring raid and sank several of the ships with a loss of 749 soldiers and sailors, a tragedy and personal humiliation that still tormented the admiral. A similar surprise attack by German E-boats on the night of June 5/6 could produce another disaster and lift Overlord's essential veil of secrecy.

Moon was concerned too that early plans for the Normandy invasion had not included Utah Beach and the Cotentin Peninsula. These beaches and objectives had only recently been added to the Overlord plans at General Montgomery's insistence. Montgomery believed a foothold on the Cotentin Peninsula was vital to securing the western flank of the invasion and eventually taking Cherbourg. This new addition ushered in a host of new challenges.

Late in the evening of June 5, Moon's immediate priority was getting his armada of warships and transports through the thousands of mines the Germans had planted in the middle of the turbulent channel. Some 225 minesweepers had to clear the enemy mines and mark the lanes leading to the Normandy landing beaches. The mission had started badly a few hours earlier at just before 6 p.m. on June 5 when the one of the navy's most experienced sweepers was sunk by a mine mid-Channel with 6 dead and 29 wounded sailors. The rest of the minesweepers made it through the night without incident, allowing Force U to reach its designated anchorages by about 2:30 a.m. As the anchors of hundreds of Admiral Moon's

Rear Admiral Don P. Moon

vessels thundered through their hawse holes in the mooring area—some six miles offshore—he was relieved that the mission's first leg had been completed without further incident. That would change dramatically in the execution of the assault.

The weather was still chancy with light rain, fog and five-foot seas. Moon could hear enemy anti-aircraft fire in the distance as C-47 transports dropped 101st and 82nd Airborne paratroopers into German-held territory. By 3 a.m. more than 600 troops from the 4th Division were moving into their landing craft and other vessels. They were to be the first wave of soldiers onto the Utah beaches.

The unit was ready for battle. Among the commanders was Major General "Lightning Joe" Lawton Collins from New Orleans, Louisiana, hand-picked by General Eisenhower to lead VII Corps. Eisenhower had learned the importance of having commanders with combat experience and Collins, a graduate of the US Military Academy, had distinguished himself as a commander in the jungle battles for Guadalcanal and New Georgia in the Pacific. Within the VII Corps, the 4th Infantry Division was under Major General Raymond O. Barton, who had supervised their training for the previous three years, including amphibious exercises in the Gulf of Mexico. Although the 4th Division had not yet fired a shot in combat, its men were unusually mature with an average age of 28. Attached to the 4th were the 1st and 3rd Battalions of the 90th Infantry Division's 359th Infantry Regiment. The rest of the 90th Division, along with the 9th and 79th Infantry Divisions, was waiting in the wings, prepared to enter Normandy the week after D-Day. Vital to opening up the beachhead was the 1st Engineer Special Brigade with a mix of army and navy units, including demolition experts, beach masters for traffic control, amphibious (DUKW) truck companies and medical personnel, all specially trained to support the landing with specific tasks. Another important unit was the 70th Tank Battalion, which had proven itself in North Africa and Sicily and employed the Duplex Drive (DD), or swimming tanks.

Generals Collins and Barton had paid special attention to the Utah landing area—long, flat, sandy beaches and dunes, without high bluffs of the kind that favored the entrenched Germans on Omaha Beach to the east. They also knew that strong tides

allowed the ocean to flow inland through a system of flood gates, used by the Germans to inundate the fields with four to ten feet of water between four causeways. Failure to secure these causeways meant that troops landing later would be trapped on the beach or forced to wade through the flooded fields. They also knew that tides carried strong currents that might hamper navigation and that the H-Hour landings at low tide meant the troops would have to cover 100 to 400 yards from the water's edge to a seawall.

There were, however, advantages to the Utah landing zones. The relatively flat terrain exposed German strongpoints, or *Widerstandsnest*, as easy targets for the naval firepower scheduled to be unleashed at 5:50 a.m. This bombardment was to be followed by a "beach drenching" bombing run by 341 B-26 Marauder aircraft of the Ninth Air Force. The follow-up pounding from Marauders was set for 6:09 to 6:27 a.m., precisely timed to end just three minutes before the landings of the first wave of troops.

The "boats away" order came at 3 a.m., three and a half hours before H-Hour. The mooring area of Admiral Moon's flagship and the troop carriers placed them out of range of most German batteries. Men clambered down the nets into hundreds of LCVPs

Troops disembark from LCM-83 on June 6.

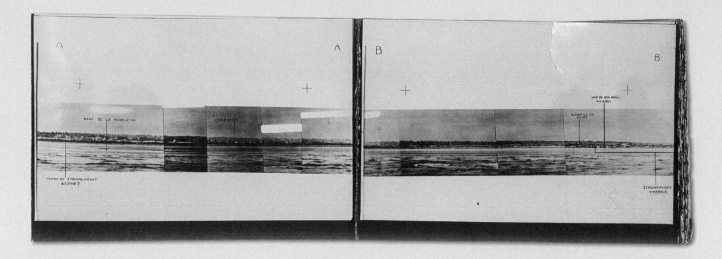

Large bound volumes of panoramic photos showing the invasion beaches were created using shots taken by reconnaissance pilots. These panoramas were used by sailors and soldiers to study the coastlines and learn landmarks, allowing them to identify their position along the coast.

(Landing Craft, Vehicle, Personnel) and joined the other small craft, LCCs (Landing Craft Control) and LCTs (Landing Craft, Tank), forming up for the assault. Soldiers in the Higgins boats were crammed in tightly, 36 to a boat. Many got seasick from the rough seas as they set out on an anxious three-hour ride to shore.

The landing force got off to a rocky start. One Patrol Craft directing the flotilla hit a mine and sank and *LCC-80* fouled a propeller on a buoy and had to turn back. As H-Hour drew closer, *LCC-60* took the place of *LCC-80* in leading the boats to the designated landing zones. Confusion gripped the troops on the passage to shore. They were stunned by an onslaught of German artillery fire on their boats and Allied ships that began about 5 a.m.

At 5:36 a.m., fourteen minutes ahead of schedule, the powerful naval bombardment began, returning fire with salvos from the battleship USS *Nevada* (BB-36) and from other American and

B-26 bomber pilot Asa Clark pictured with his flight crew. Clark is on the second row, far right

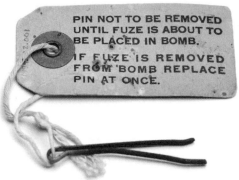

Asa Clark flew his 45th combat mission on June 6. On one of the discarded bomb-arming tags, Clark wrote: "The big show is on."

Allied warships. The big offshore guns delivered a torrent of fire on German coastal batteries, creating a deafening roar. The seasick troops were dazed by the booming guns and their shock waves. Soldiers witnessed some of their craft receiving hits, then saw dead bodies and debris floating by as they drew closer to shore.

The 300-plus B-26 Marauders arrived right as scheduled at 6:09 a.m. Flying south over the Cotentin Peninsula, the Marauder crews flew parallel to the beach, maximizing their ability to strike targets. Some bombers carried 250-pound bombs designed to leave no craters. Others carried two 2,000-pound "blockbuster" bombs, designed to knock out fortifications. As the planes neared the coast, they dropped altitude to 4,000–6,000 feet, ducking below cloud cover that hid their targets. Right on time, 293 of the aircraft dropped their payloads, unloading more than 4,000 bombs equaling more than one million pounds of ordnance onto German positions.

Smoke along the shoreline from the bombardments and shelling obscured landmarks as landing forces came within sight of the beaches. They did not immediately notice that strong

tidal currents had swept them about 1,500 yards south of their designated landing zone at Les Dunes de Varreville, between exits 3 and 4. The first wave headed to the wrong part of the beach at La Madeleine—close to exit 2. Thirty-two DD tanks, loaded onto eight LCTs, approached the shore in the first wave. *LCT-593* hit a mine, blowing four tanks almost 100 feet into the air. The remaining seven LCTs released 28 DD tanks into the ocean 3,000 yards from the

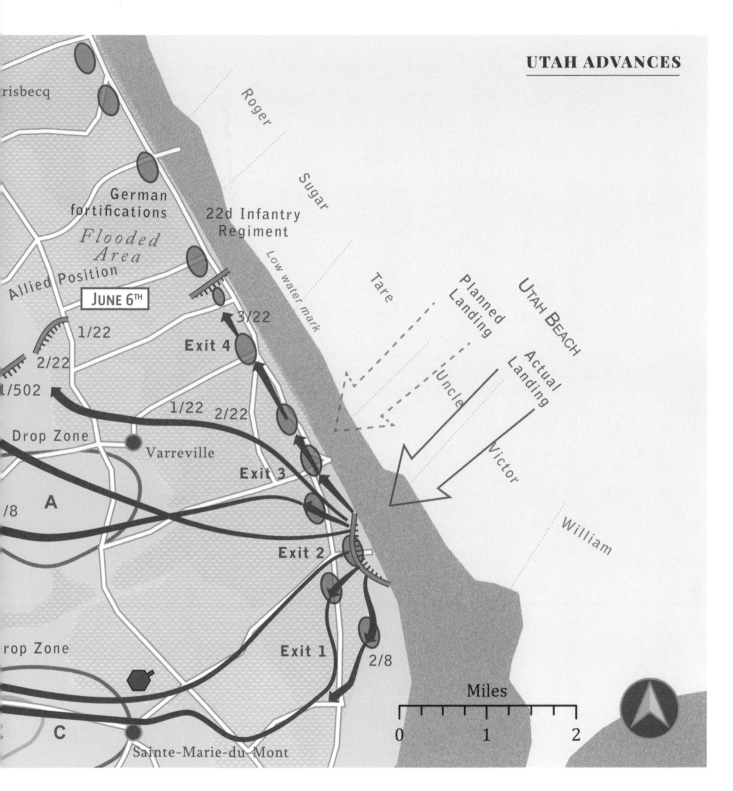

risbecq

German
fortifications

Flooded Area

Allied Position

JUNE 6TH

1/22

2/22

1/502

Drop Zone

Varreville

A

/8

rop Zone

C

Sainte-Marie-du-Mont

Roger

Sugar

22d Infantry
Regiment

Low water mark

Tare

Planned
Landing

Actual
Landing

UTAH BEACH

Uncle

Victor

William

3/22

Exit 4

1/22 2/22

Exit 3

Exit 2

Exit 1

2/8

Miles

0   1   2

beach to lead the armada of small craft. Troops were desperate to
get on solid ground when the ramps of the Higgins boats dropped.
Whether landing in waist-high surf or on dry sand, they slogged
forward through a hail of sniper and machine-gun fire, trying to
cover hundreds of yards between the water's edge and a seawall
in front of the dunes. What the soldiers did not know was that their
toughest challenges would come beyond those dunes.

Howard Vander Beek

Lieutenant (junior grade) US Navy, Executive Officer

Landing Craft Control 60

Howard Vander Beek graduated from the University of Iowa in 1938, and taught high school English. In 1942 he joined the navy and entered the United States Naval Reserve Midshipmen's School at Notre Dame, graduating in 1943. Vander Beek participated in the invasion of Sicily in July 1943 before he returned to the United States and reported aboard *Landing Craft Control 60* as the executive officer. Leading the first wave onto Utah Beach, Vander Beek had an exceptional view of the landings.

I was aboard the USS *LCC-60*, a landing craft control vessel. She located Utah Beach's Green Tare and Uncle Red Sectors, the imaginary halves of that combat area, and led DD tanks and small amphibious craft to it. LCC denoted "Landing Craft Control." She was an all-steel vessel 56 feet in length and 13 feet in beam, powered by two 255 horsepower diesels, and was capable of a maximum speed of 13.4 knots. We knew her well, but there were not many who even so much as knew of her existence. She and her purpose, for obvious reasons in wartime, were kept secret.

At about 2:00 a.m., we entered the transport area which lay about 22,000 yards off Utah Beach. It was there that our flagship, the USS *Bayfield*, with Rear Admiral Moon, high-ranking US Army officers, and troops for Uncle Red and Uncle Green beaches aboard, anchored. We continued ahead toward the assault beach, following *PC-1176* (Submarine Chaser put to use as a control vessel), our primary control vessel, through the Uncle Red approach lane. As we advanced in the darkness at about 4:30, we were struck with the realization that the silhouette of Nazi-held territory which appeared before us matched the one in our minds. And, when a voice using Germanized English came in on our radio frequency and the speaker tried to disguise himself as a British Red Cross worker wanting us to come near shore to rescue him, we felt the icy chill of the initial confrontation with the enemy.

For the next while, minutes lost their pace. The surf relentlessly tossed us about on a briny no-man's land. We felt naked, defenseless. Hundreds of friendly guns on US battleships and destroyers five to ten miles behind us waited silently to begin their onslaught, but enemy artillery hidden in the shore bunkers did not wait. They began their bursts of fire. Luckily, the missiles directed at us hissed and sizzled over and around us and pierced only the shallow water.

Ahead, on the low-silhouetted beach, we could observe little or no activity. But we knew the enemy was there: they continued to fire at us! In time we gave their barrage little more than cursory attention. Instead, we focused on a multitude of tasks, including sending, receiving and relaying messages, making sightings and ascertaining our position.

At approximately 5:40, the real horror of battle was unveiled before us. We saw *PC-1261*, primary control vessel for Red Beach, suddenly go off course to starboard. Within five minutes, dead in the water, with mainmast down and men going over the side, she sank. She had been the victim of either a chance shell hit, or she had made contact with a mine on her port bow.

Then, suddenly—still during the slowed-down minutes before H-Hour—a deafening, and thunderous roar sounded behind us, then over us, then ahead of us. Fright changed to a feeling of warmth—a blending of relief, security and gratitude, for we realized that the Ninth Air Force and the 9th Tactical Command had begun air bombardment to soften up the enemy's beach-line defenses.

Soon after the direct air attack—about twenty minutes before H-Hour—USS *Nevada* led the ships out at sea in a saturating, long-range bombing of the beach defenses. Over us—also at a terrifyingly low level—drenching streaks of fire from rocket launchers whooshed to the shore. Tons of destructive force fell upon the mist-shrouded, open-air theater only yards in front of us. Quickly, violent explosions and colossal blazes changed the scene, and bursts of smoke, dust and scurrying sand curtained our view. The heavy defense batteries that for the most part had survived pre-D-Day air bombings were being destroyed.

PC-1176 led landing craft toward the Green Tare Sector of Utah Beach.

SS *T.B.Robertson* anchored off Utah Beach. The *Robertson* served as the port control ship for the Utah Gooseberry (manmade breakwater).

This handmade green signal flag was used by Robert Maidlow aboard *PC-1176* to guide landing craft into the Green Tare Sector of Utah Beach.

Perhaps it was during this period of destruction of enemy defenses that we received a message about our sister *LCC-80*, with Ensigns Tom Glennon and Bob Davis and their crew, aboard. Before leaving the transport area, she had fouled her screw on a dan buoy and was unable to advance into the assault area. Because she was out of commission and because the primary control vessel for her beach had been sunk, we knew what was in store for us. We added the duties of the two control boats for Red Beach to those of our own for Green Beach.

I must have stood overwhelmed by the sight as I clung to the rail for a moment to take in the magnitude of the assembled fleet: several great, gray ships majestically poised in their positions; larger numbers of unwieldy landing vessels heaved by the heavy sea; and countless smaller amphibious craft tossed mercilessly by the waves. Above the armada and attached to the larger ships, anti-aircraft barrage balloons buffeted the strong Channel winds. Soon the hands of my Westclox would move to mark a historic minute in history: 6:30, the H-Hour of the Invasion of Normandy's D-Day.

At some time earlier, we had gone out to direct the LCTs—the large landing craft with troops, LCVPs with tanks aboard, and to move 2,000 yards inward to form an assembly area 3,000 yards offshore. That change, possible because enemy shellfire had not been as heavy as expected, was made to save time and traveling distance for the amphibious craft and vehicles that LCTs would discharge. It benefitted us, too. We had a shorter distance to go to direct the boat circles to get information to follow our lead to the invasion beach.

By 6:15, the primary control vessel for Green Beach had dropped a dan buoy at her station to mark the line of departure for the invasion waves. We went to that point to lead in Wave 1,

the first of the LCVPs and Wave 1A, and the DD tanks.

Once we had led the boats and tanks near the beach and we were assured that they saw their assault point, we dismissed them and reversed our course to return to bring in Wave 2. This gave us a chance to see the soldiers on the overcrowded LCVPs at closer range. We shouted cheers and gestured support and encouragement, but only a few of the men on each boat returned acknowledgment. Some, we realized, were too busy using their helmets to bail out the cold seawater sweeping over their low-set craft. Others, suffering from seasickness, were bent over the boat sides. Most of the GIs, however, stood pressed together—motionless, saltwater soaked, and dulled by fear and cold.

The English language does not provide a multifaceted, exact word that alone can describe what surely must have been surging through each man's mind and body. Were such a word to be coined, it would include meanings embodied in such interrelated words as: bravery, weakness, trust, toughness, uncertainty, love, tenacity, determination, despair, fearlessness, fright, faith, assurance, doubt, hate, loyalty, distrust, resolution, seriousness, prayerfulness, bravado and hope.

Once H-Hour had passed, we on the *LCC-60* went on with our roles—small parts in the center of the action on the stage of the huge combat theater. Looking back today, it seems that at the time there was no doubt in our minds that when the drama ended it would be an acclaimed success, not another Dunkirk. On land, at sea, and in the air, the participants carried out their parts as they had been directed to do. Their guns blazed on the beach and from their ships at sea; their explosives shattered enemy defenses and hurled debris skyward; their rockets ignited conflagrations from which heavy smoke rose and slowly moved southeasterly; and their aircraft dropped parachutes that sprang open to crowd sky space with silent, floating backup forces.

Hour trailed hour that morning as we led successive waves of men, arms and war equipage to the two sectors of Utah Beach. Our minds were so dulled and our bodies so desensitized that we were like robots steering our boat between the line of departure and the dispersal point. Even so, I am somehow still able to recapture scattered fragments of the sensations and images I had as we threaded in and through the mighty military spectacle.

A nauseating mix of diesel fumes, gun smoke and salt-laden air made my breathing difficult. Deafening blasts of Allied artillery fire, thunderous sounds of onshore explosions and plaintive whines of enemy retaliatory arms muffled my hearing. A multitude of unidentifiable rumbling, piercing and hissing noises—along with the grinding, chugging and splashing sounds of amphibious craft; the unexpected, spasmodic detonations of concealed mines; the last gasps, or the awesome silence, of sinking vessels; and the cries for help of the wounded and drowning—echoed and re-echoed in my ears.

I can re-create fairly well, too, portions of the mental snapshots I took that morning from our boat's deck: sunstreaked American planes spewing dark blobs—each a fighting man or a load of equipment or supplies—from which parachutes opened to give them safe, smooth descent to the Normandy countryside; red, white and blue-black masses of smoke on the coastline, which—losers in their attempts to rise and dissipate—were being pushed inland by the more powerful wind; orange flames consuming the dried grasses that topped the rise behind the beachhead; rusty, threatening beach barriers in a variety of grotesque forms being exposed by the receding tide; and glossy, multicolored jellyfish—presumably defenseless victims of underwater explosions—bobbing and floating on the steel-gray waves around us.

When we had taken in the third wave, we observed a greater barrage of enemy gunfire on the beach than there had been after we had led in the first waves. Later we learned that 88-millimeter Nazi guns, perhaps not fully manned earlier, had begun dropping shells among our troops and had knocked out some of our tanks. Succeeding waves that we led during the day—bringing the total from H-Hour to nineteen—encountered only sporadic shellfire.

At 2:00 p.m., we were relieved of our primary control duties for Red Beach by *PC-484*. We returned to Green Beach to act as secondary control—our original duty position before we took over for the ill-fated *PC-1261*.

On June 8, his duties aboard *LCC-60* complete for the time being, Vander Beek was temporarily attached to the Liberty Ship SS *T.B. Robertson*. The *Robertson* served as the port control ship off Utah Beach. In July Vander Beek returned to *LCC-60* in preparation for Operation Dragoon, the invasion of Southern France, scheduled for August.

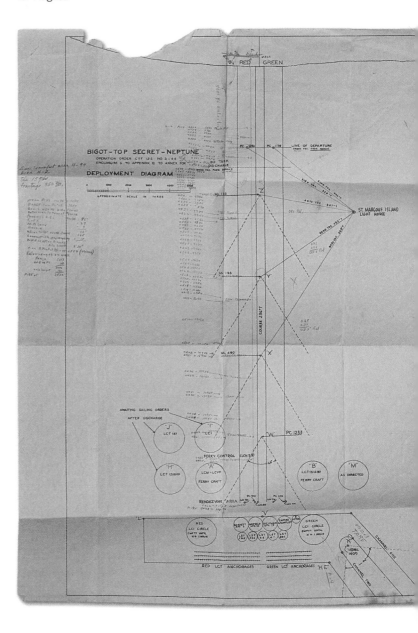

This map, used aboard *LCT(R)-439* (Landing Craft Tank, Rocket) commanded by Lieutenant Elmer H. Mahlin, lays out the assembly areas and travel lanes for Utah Beach. *LCC-60* and *PC-1176* can be seen on the far right line marking the travel lanes.

UTAH BEACH

Ross R. Olsen

Electrician's Mate First Class, US Navy, USS *Nevada*

Seattle, Washington native Ross Olsen reported aboard the USS *Nevada* in June 1942, as the battleship stricken at Pearl Harbor was being repaired at the Puget Sound Navy Yard. The *Nevada* blockaded the island of Attu, Alaska, as American forces fought to retake it, and escorted convoys across the Atlantic before assignment to bombardment duty off Utah Beach. Promoted to Electrician's Mate First Class just five days before the Normandy invasion, Olsen had a bird's-eye view of the invasion from the signal bridge of the *Nevada* as she shelled German strongpoints.

USS *Nevada* firing on German positions on D-Day.

Stationed several miles offshore, a massive bombardment force of American destroyers, cruisers, and battleships lay in wait. The US Navy had begun to perfect the art of shore fire bombardment by pinpointing predetermined targets and coordinating with Shore Fire Control Parties (SFCP) and spotter planes to hit targets of opportunity. The deadly naval guns, ranging in size from five to fourteen inches, could decimate German gun emplacements with a single salvo. One of the three American battleships in the bombardment force, and the only one stationed off Utah Beach, was the USS *Nevada*, the only American battleship to get underway during the Japanese bombing of Pearl Harbor. Nearly 30 years old by D-Day, she was considered an "old lady" in the fleet. Her 14-inch guns were manned by eager, highly trained sailors, ready to fire 1,500-pound shells toward enemy targets as far away as eleven miles.

As we neared our position in the bay, we felt like we were sneaking up on the enemy and even talked in whispers, thinking that we might be heard by the Germans on the beach, which of course was impossible as we were at least a mile off the beach. When we reached our assigned position, the order was given to drop anchor. I recall that when the anchor was cut loose it made a tremendous noise as the anchor chain went through the hawse pipe. We were sure that it had been heard on the beach. At that time, it was breaking daylight and we could see the beach and the houses near the beach. It wasn't long before we were seen by the Germans on the shore and we were being shelled. We could see the shells landing in the water around us. We were the only battleship in our group of ships; the rest were all cruisers and destroyers.

The early shelling seemed to be concentrated on us, as we were the largest ship. The ship had been turned so that the port side was parallel to the beach. We had been shelled for what seemed like ages before we saw our main battery of 14-inch guns being trained and ready to open fire. When we started shooting we felt more relief knowing that we were at least shooting back, even if we were not shooting at the guns that were shooting at us.

We continued to be fired upon. Some of the shells were landing so close to the ship that they splashed water up onto the deck and got the men manning the 20-millimeter guns wet. I don't know how some of those shells landing on the starboard side, so close, managed to get through the superstructure above without hitting something up there. I remember mentally counting the bulk heads between me and the port side where the shell would hit, if we were hit. Then I remembered that the first compartment was a magazine holding 40-millimeter shells for the anti-aircraft guns. Who knows what kind of an explosion that would make? I and the rest of the signalmen were huddled on the starboard side behind part of the superstructure housing the pilot house. We learned later that we were straddled 27 times by shells and never hit.

I did see one of the British cruisers take a hit in about the same location on that ship—the HMS *Black Prince*—as our position on the *Nevada*. It cleared a hole through the superstructure big

Aboard the USS *Nevada*, crew listen as an officer reads a letter from Admiral Alan Kirk, informing them when and where the attack on the French coast will occur.

enough to drive a truck through. That didn't make us feel any better about our chances if we got hit.

The cruisers were firing all the time at the targets, as we were. Sometime after several hours, someone must have put the gun shooting at us and the ships in our group out of commission, as we no longer seemed to be under fire, which was a tremendous relief. From my position on the signal bridge I had a pretty good view of the ships at the beachhead. I could see the landing craft heading for the beach and saw several get hit or hit a mine and they just disappeared in the water. I also saw a destroyer get hit and start to sink. It was closer into the beach than we were. I remember seeing the forward gun mount firing until it seemed to be under water. When the ship sank, the water was shallow enough that about twenty feet of the mast was sticking out of the water.

Later on during the lull in the firing we were called to shoot at a target that required our guns to be trained straight, nearly ahead with a result that the whole port side was raked by the muzzle

blast of all the guns, including 14-inch guns. The concussion was so intense that it did considerable damage to our own ship. I was sent out on the end of the bridge on the port side to take down the signal light before it was knocked to the deck below because it just kept bouncing up and down like it was going to fall off. This put me in direct line to receive the muzzle blast from the gun. I could look down and directly into the muzzle of the gun of the 5-inch gun below the signal bridge. As a result, I have lost the hearing completely in my right ear and 50 percent in the left ear and must use hearing aids. The shelling also destroyed the 26-foot whaleboat on the boat deck, knocked the door off the mess hall, peeled all of the insulation material off of the mess hall bulkhead wall, and broke almost every light bulb in the overhead fixtures on the port side of the ship.

Later during the day, I looked over the side to the outgoing tide to see what looked like coconuts floating past. After a closer look, I realized that I was seeing the backs of the heads of men floating face down in the water. I assumed that it was some of our GIs killed on the beaches or before they got to the beach.

In the afternoon, we watched the minesweeper between us and the beach, sweeping for mines. They were in real close to the beach when they came under fire from a gun emplacement on the shore. They called for help from the ships in our group and an admiral, who was on one of the cruisers, ordered them to open fire on the gun.

After several salvos, the gun was still firing at the minesweeper and they had given up their sweep and were heading toward us. Since the cruiser was unable to put the gun out of order, we were asked to fire on it. After two salvos, the spotter said that we had eliminated the gun and the men manning the gun had run into the headquarters building. So they gave us a new coordinate and the next salvo destroyed the building.

Ross Olsen remained aboard the *Nevada* for the invasion of Southern France. After a few months aboard the cruiser USS *Baltimore* (CA-68), Olsen was transferred to the USS *Tolovana* (AO-64), a fleet oiler, at her commissioning in February 1945. Olsen sailed with the *Tolovana* to the Pacific Theater in support of the invasion of Okinawa in June 1945.

Flames and smoke pour from the muzzles of two of the USS *Nevada's* 14-inch main battery guns.

Grant G. Gullickson

Chief Machinist's Mate, US Navy, USS *Corry*

At nineteen Grant Gullickson left his home state of North Dakota and joined the US Navy. First assigned to the battleship USS *Mississippi* (BB-41) in 1940, Gullickson was a seasoned sailor when he reported to the destroyer USS *Corry* (DD-463) in 1942. The *Corry* supported the Allied landing in North Africa and a British raid on Bodø, Norway, before joining the great armada assaulting the French coast. As a newly appointed chief machinist mate, Gullickson was in charge of the forward engine room of the *Corry* on D-Day.

Even a mile or two offshore, American ships were not out of range of large German shore batteries. Ship crews were on the lookout for mines missed by minesweepers and dodging lethal shells from shore batteries, all while firing their own guns in support of those landing on the beach. Aboard these ships many sailors were stationed below decks, toiling without knowledge of what was happening above. The explosion of shells from shore batteries could be felt as they landed near the hulls where sailors kept ship engines working and turrets supplied with shells and powder. Despite the best efforts of ship crews, enemy shells sometimes found their mark.

We proceeded across the Channel and the *Corry* was assigned to lead the first wave of boats into Utah Beach. I was the chief machinist mate in charge of the forward engine room in the USS *Corry*. We had dropped some depth charges on the way across the Channel on a submarine contact and we had a nipple rupture on one of our feed pumps and I had spent the whole night with my fellow crew members repairing this broken nipple because we knew that when the big thing happened the next morning all power was going to be required.

Around midnight we were close to ashore. I guess around 2:00 in the morning, we received word from smoke watch; we had a smoke watch on destroyers, to watch the stacks to make sure that we weren't leaving any smoke out that we shouldn't. He was our pipeline of information of what was going on topside. He said that it looked like the whole world had lit up. I stuck my head out of the hatch and had a breath of fresh air and the whole world was lit up. There were thousands of bombers in the air and they were dropping what we call Pathfinders, illumination flares. About that time the whole earth just shook. I immediately dogged the hatch down.

We had four boilers on the line. We were dripping wet with sweat and turbines were hissing steam. Our job was to give the skipper whatever speed was ordered, full speed ahead to emergency astern, while overhead the guns roared as they fired on the German targets on the beach. The ships would shudder as the German shells hit the water near the ship, some of them hitting the ship topside. We had only been there a few minutes, but it seemed like eternity. I imagine we fired about 400 or 500 rounds.

All of a sudden, the ship literally jumped out of the water! As the floor plates came loose, the lights went out and steam filled the space. It was total darkness with steam severely hot and choking. We figured that this was it, that our grave was to be the forward engine room in the *Corry*. At about this time, there was another rumble from underneath the ship. We felt that we would never remove ourselves from the bowels of the ship. But after this rumble, everything became real quiet and the steam that filled the space dissipated. The water was up to the upper level, up to our waist at this time, but the steam had stopped. We grappled to open the hatch, which we did, and removed our shipmates from the space. I found out later that the reason that steam dissipated was that the boilers in the forward fire room, that's where we were getting our steam from, had ruptured. Undoubtedly, the fact that these boilers ruptured and all the steam went up the stack saved our life. As I said, we did evacuate through the hatch and, by the time we got up on deck, the main deck was awash. The machine shop where the hatch that you exit from the forward engine room was located—the deck there was ruptured clean across. It was obvious that the *Corry* was dead.

A minesweeper detonates a mine off Utah Beach on D-Day. Photo taken from the USS *Quincy* (CA-71).

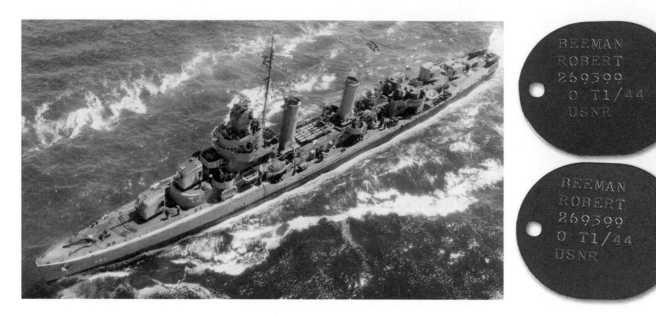

The USS *Corry* (DD-463) underway in April 1944.

Dog tags worn by Ensign Robert Beeman, an officer aboard the USS *Corry*. Beeman was on the bridge of the ship when it sank and he survived.

I noticed at this time that my life belt and shirt were missing. We wore life belts in the engineering space. They had been ripped from my body by shrapnel, but that didn't draw any blood. I knew from training that I would need a lifebelt, that I would need some type of floating device because that water out there was 54 degrees and, although I was a pretty good swimmer, I knew that I would need something to keep me afloat. My head and chest hurt, but there was no blood. I was okay. The thing now was to make sure that we had all the guys out of the engine room and to move away from the ship, because the shore batteries continued to shoot at the ship. The shells were hitting near and some were hitting the ship as it lay there dead in the water. I needed a lifebelt!

About this time Chief Bernard Peterson, who was in charge of the damage control party, was topside working with his repair party, doing what he could to save the ship. I said, "Pete, do you have any idea where I can find a life belt?" He said, "Yeah, up in the Chief's quarters. I seen it hanging on the bunk as I went through there a little bit ago." I went up to the Chief's quarters, got the life belt, and then I went to the after-engine room where Charlie Brewer, chief machinist mate, was in charge. He stuck his head out of the hatch and he said, "I got a full head of vacuum but I can't go anywheres, the screws are out of the water."

At this time, word came out to abandon ship. We were still receiving heavy fire from the shore. So I abandoned ship on the starboard side about midships. We didn't jump off the ship or anything; we literally floated off the ship because the ship was underwater. As I got in the water I noticed that out in the distance there was a floater net, a life-saving device that was cast into the water as the ship was sinking. I managed to get out and grab ahold of this floater net. I had the lifebelt on and with my swimming I could do that. This particular net I got ahold of had mostly gunner's mates around it. One of the gunner's mates was really seriously wounded. He was told by a shipmate that all that could be done was to keep his head out of the water, which we did. Shells continued to burst in the water around us and each time one would hit, it really felt like someone was really trying to force a sea bag up your rectum.

A couple of hours later, the whale boat from the USS *Fitch* (DD-462) arrived and towed this floater net alongside. By this time we were almost incapacitated due to the coldness of the water. Our hands were so numb that they were unable to grasp and hold a line to pull us out of the water. The *Fitch* people reached over the side and some literally came down and dragged us out of the water and brought us aboard. They gave us coffee, heavily laced with alcohol, that they had somehow or other appropriated from, I suppose, the torpedo alcohol or water-testing alcohol, but it was so cold you couldn't hold a cup. The chief gunner's mate aboard the *Fitch* held the cup for me. He said, "Buddy it's great to see you. Everything is going to be all right." The *Fitch* was just unbelievable in their generosity. They opened their lockers to provide us with dry clothes and prepared food and gave us medical help. You name it, they gave it to us.

I started to check on the *Fitch*, (to see) who was there from the *Corry*. I was saddened to find that Charlie Brewer, the chief machinist's mate from the aft engine room, lay in a bunk on the *Fitch*. He was dead. A piece of shrapnel had hit him in the back of the head. It was such a small piece that you could barely see it. Later we were transferred to the USS *Barnett* (APA-5), a troop transport, and this ship was loaded with the bodies of sailors, soldiers, airmen, and the wounded, plus survivors of sunken ships. On board this ship was the body of my good friend, Chief Peterson, the chief who told me where the life jacket was at. Shrapnel from an exploding shell also cost his life. Also on this ship was Chief Felix Rovinski, big chief of the forward fire room. He had steam burns over 99 percent of his body. We tended to him and he could talk a little, but the burns were too much. He passed away the next day. We were offloaded in England and in time were transferred back to the States.

After his transfer to the United States, Gullickson joined the commissioning crew of the USS *John Q. Roberts* (DE-235), a destroyer escort. He finished the war in the Pacific and re-enlisted in November 1945. Gullickson became an officer in 1954.

The *Corry* was hit at 6:33 a.m., just three minutes after H-Hour. The actual cause of the *Corry's* sinking was debated for years. The official US Navy report states the ship hit a mine, but many individuals aboard the ship believed she was sunk by 210-millimeter (8-inch) shells from the German battery known as the Crisbecq Battery, in the village of Saint-Marcouf. German records confirm the battery sank an American destroyer on June 6, conflicting with the US report. Cause aside, the sinking of the *Corry* resulted in the loss of 22 sailors, and reminded American sailors of their vulnerability within range of large German guns. The US Navy needed to silence the German guns before more American ships became casualties.

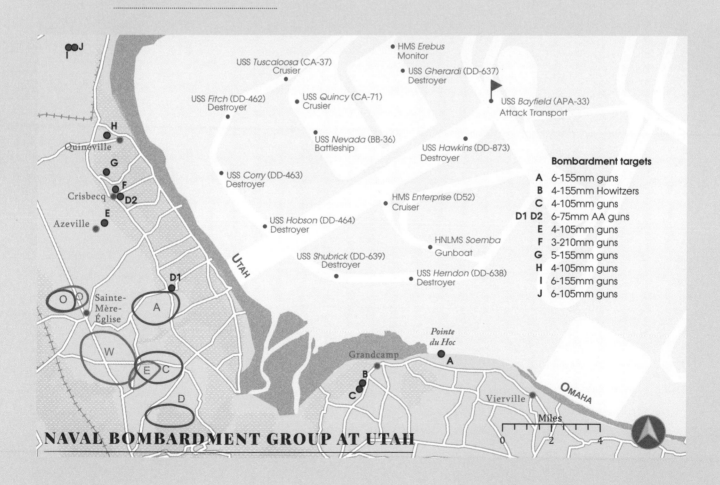

Bombardment targets

A 6-155mm guns
B 4-155mm Howitzers
C 4-105mm guns
D1 D2 6-75mm AA guns
E 4-105mm guns
F 3-210mm guns
G 5-155mm guns
H 4-105mm guns
I 6-155mm guns
J 6-105mm guns

NAVAL BOMBARDMENT GROUP AT UTAH

John Richard Blackburn

Lieutenant Commander, US Navy, Air Defense Officer

USS *Quincy*

West Virginia native John Blackburn graduated from the United States Naval Academy in 1939. After serving on two battleships and two destroyers, Blackburn served as a gunnery officer aboard the cruiser USS *Quincy* (CA-71). As an air defense officer Blackburn was stationed high up in the ship's sky control. As the invasion began, Blackburn worked to coordinate with Shore Fire Control Parties and spotter planes to destroy German guns threatening invasion forces.

USS *Quincy* in 1945. She was named after CA-39, which was sunk by
Japanese gunfire during the Battle of Savo Island in 1942.

After the landing area had been thoroughly worked over
(by bombers), a group of brilliant million-candlepower
parachute flares were dropped north of our beach, in the area
where the heavy gun emplacements were supposed to be. The
flares drifted down slowly in a long, unbroken line. When the
Cap de la Hague and Barfleur had been lightened like day,
the big boys opened up their bomb bays, and again the sear of
yellow flashes tripped across the black beach lands. It was one of
the most awful and shocking things I had ever seen. I tried to
imagine what those pleasant, quiet French natives were doing as
they trembled in their cheese cellars.

Soon the dust filled the skies and reached out to us at anchor.
The dust had the smell of fresh cut grass. For a moment I had
a twinge of homesickness for the fertile valley of my home in
West Virginia—rich green, fragrant fields of alfalfa awaiting the
mower. But the mood was as short-lived as it was out of place.

The first hint of dawn began to fill the sky about 4:00 a.m.
About 4:30 we got underway and started moving towards our
bombardment anchorage, three miles north of the Saint Marcouf
Islands. Low water about 5:40 and sunrise at 6:00 and H-Hour
scheduled for 6:30. That gave the boat waves almost two hours
of light to get organized and run in to the beach. Everything
was worked from an amazing timetable that took, so it seemed,
everything into consideration. The *Quincy's* secondary battery
of 5-inch guns was supposed to open fire on a machine-gun

emplacement in the middle of the northern or Green Beach.
The ship was supposed to fire for about 40 minutes—16 rounds
of 5-inch a minute, plus a number of 8-inch rounds from the
turrets. We would stop if a black smoke rocket was shot up,
indicating that we were to check fire because of the first wave's
contact with the beach.

As we rounded the bend about 5:15, heading down towards
our anchorage, we heard a sharp splat on our starboard bow and
looked over to see three shells fall and explode about 1,000 yards
away. We were being fired upon. We were the target of one of the
shore batteries. Everyone looked at the other man with a mingled
feeling of fear and excitement. I put on my helmet, and the rest of
the lads followed suit. The next salvo of enemy projectiles landed
even closer—only about 500 yards short this time. Instinctively,
we all placed ourselves behind the three-quarter-inch armor
shield around sky control, feeling a little sheepish as we did so.
All of us were doing some rapid mental calculations along the
same lines: will the next one be a hit for the German gunners
and, if so, what is the chance of it getting me?

Our three 8-inch turrets were trained toward the beach targets
with their guns somewhat elevated to provide the necessary

A shell from a German 88mm gun explodes near an LST.

range. The crews of the 20- and 40-millimeter gun mounts in the vicinity of the muzzle blast were directed to move to a more sheltered position, subject to telephone recall. The visibility in morning twilight had improved to the point at which targets could be located on the beach.

Lieutenant Commander Bill Denton, our ship's senior aviator, had been checked out by the Royal Air Force and was flying a Spitfire fighter over the target to provide spotting for our main battery. He was given our selected target coordinates for softening up the Green Beach landing area. Well before sunrise, the first day of many 8-inch salvos erupted from our turrets and sped toward the offending German battery. The belch of nitrous, brown smoke and yellow flames from the *Quincy's* two forward turrets gave us the reassuring feeling that at last we were in the fray and doing something about those pesky gun emplacements that were firing at us.

We all wondered about the next enemy salvo. The *Nevada* and (destroyer) *Tuscaloosa* (CA-37) cut loose with their main batteries at the troublesome shore emplacements. The next incoming salvo landed short and farther to the right of us. Apparently, the point of aim was being shifted to *Tuscaloosa*. We must have been about at the extreme range limit for the shore batteries. A few more salvos of 8-inch and 14-inch high-explosive American ammunition seemed to discourage the German artillery. They closed up shop when the big stuff started going off around them.

At last it was time for us to open fire on the machine-gun emplacement in the middle of Green Beach. A destroyer had already been shelling the beach for some time. Bomb clouds of dust and rubble obscured the beach, but I could see where the salvos from the tin can were landing. Since she was much closer and better able to see what she was shooting at, we would just plunk ours in nearby—one four-gun salvo every fifteen seconds. I watched them landing and called in the spots to our plotting room people. They applied the spots so that the shells would cover a maximum area.

At last it was nearly H-Hour—the moment long-awaited by both the Allies and the Germans. The first waves of tank and infantry lighters approached the beach under heavy fire. One of the lighters stubbed her toe on a mine and was lifted almost bodily out of the water amid a column of spume some 100 feet tall. She settled back down and began sinking stern first. I anxiously watched for the black rockets that would give us the signal to stop shooting. At 6:30, with still no sign of the rockets, the destroyer was blanked out by the smoke. I gave the order to cease fire.

Our next target was another strongpoint in the coastal network, a small white blockhouse. The *Quincy* opened fire with 5-inch, but had trouble bringing the shots on target. I discovered that air plot was trying to combine and evaluate spotting corrections from both Lieutenant Charlie Biltimier in spot two and me. We were apparently looking at different targets without realizing it. We tried to order the corrections in opposite directions to get on target. Lieutenant Paul Anderson in the plotting room was in a dilemma. He tried using my spots on one salvo and Charlie's on the next. The result was the 5-inch battery got nowhere. Our bullets were falling into a swamp on the other side of a neck of land and throwing up columns of spray. Eventually, we realized the problem and got things worked out. Just in time, too, because the shells were walking toward a French farmhouse.

While all this was going on, I was watching the *Corry*, another of the close-in fire-support destroyers. She was having a duel with a shore battery to the northwest of our target. I saw the splashes falling around the little destroyer and saw her blazing back with grim determination. Suddenly, her stern hit a moored enemy mine, opening her smoke-making tanks. Her steering gear was disabled by the mine. The shore battery seemed to sense a victory and kept pouring out more shells at the disabled victim.

As we were watching this drama unfold, the *Quincy* was ordered to use 5-inch projectiles to lay a smoke-screen on the landward side of the *Corry* because she was sinking by the stern. All the while, I wondered why the destroyer didn't get the hell out of the way of that German battery. It took us a while to start blasting out the 5-inch white phosphorous shells that might provide something of a curtain for the stricken destroyer. We had to empty the anti-aircraft shells from our ammo hoists and bring up the white phosphorous from the magazine and lower handling room. Finally after the seeming passage of hours, our smoke began drifting between the *Corry* and the shore battery. But it was too late, because the plucky little tin can was mortally wounded by the mine blast and sinking rapidly. A white mist of steam spouted up from her smokestacks.

We watched as boats and life rafts pulled away from her sides. Several landing craft came alongside to assist in the evacuation. By this time the big guns of the *Quincy* and the other heavy support ships were blazing, aimed at the batteries on the hillside and using spotting corrections called down from a pair of our pilots circling overhead in Spitfires. The shore guns fell quiet at last, and rescue operations proceeded. The *Hobson* (DD-464) steamed up alongside the *Corry* and put her two bits worth of shooting into the cloud of dust arising from the offending guns. The destroyer *Fitch* also aided in picking up survivors.

Finally, hunger prevailed over the excitement that was coming at us in waves, and we sent down for breakfast about ten o'clock. We had hot beans and hot coffee, and they tasted wonderful. By then the gun crews and I were feeling a bit cocky. Our landing craft seemed to be getting ashore, and the fighters overhead were warding off the Luftwaffe. And then, with our stomachs refilled after the long night and morning of waiting, we felt a sense of drowsiness in the morning sun. We could not afford to be complacent for long, however, because in the early afternoon we had a series of "duels" with a persistent and elusive shore battery designated Seven Able.

....

John Blackburn was aboard the *Quincy* in late June as she battled shore batteries at Cherbourg. In January 1945, the *Quincy* transported President Roosevelt to the Malta conference. Blackburn remained aboard the *Quincy* for the duration of the war, supporting carrier strikes in the Pacific.

The remnants of a destroyed building are evidence of the fighting at Utah Beach.

UTAH BEACH

Marvin Perrett

Coxwain, US Coast Guard, USS *Bayfield*

A New Orleans native, Marvin Perrett left high school and joined the US Coast Guard in 1943 after being told navy quotas were filled. He recalls from training in England: "We knew we were going to hit France. We didn't know where, we didn't know when." Assigned to the USS *Bayfield*, flagship for Utah Beach landings, he served as a coxswain aboard an LCVP, delivering troops to the beach. Perrett was eighteen years old.

As the US Navy battled shore batteries, sent high explosive shells onto targets miles away, and ferried soldiers ashore, they were not alone in their work. The US Coast Guard played a vital role in Overlord. Normandy became the largest combat operation of the war for the Coast Guard, as the branch contributed 97 vessels to the invasion, not counting landing craft. Off Utah Beach, Rear Admiral Moon was aboard the Coast Guard attack transport USS *Bayfield,* where Major Generals Barton and Collins had their command posts for D-Day. Loaded down with troops of Barton's 4th Infantry Division, and crewed by Coast Guardsmen, the landing craft headed for the shore.

We left at 9 o'clock on the morning of the 5th, and at 2 o'clock the next morning, June 6th, we would arrive on location, off the Normandy beachhead. At that time a very interesting thing took place. The armada split in two, 12 miles offshore; 2,500 of these ships and craft would lay up off of what was going to be the Utah Beach area. The other 2,500 would go off downrange a ways and set up off what is going to be the Omaha beachhead area. In my case I landed at Utah, which was a lot better than what was experienced by the poor kids that landed down at Omaha. That was a terrible scene down there.

At 2 o'clock in the morning, the armada dropped anchor twelve miles offshore and at 2:30 in the morning it was "away all boats." And it meant exactly what the words said. They sent all of us over the side, in total darkness. We traveled in what would be waves, ten to twelve boats to a wave.

On my first trip to the beach that morning, I had 36 assault troops as my guests, heading into the Utah beachhead. These troops were elements of the 4th Infantry Division. As we went in one of the gentlemen, one of the soldiers, was staring me down

USS Bayfield off Utah Beach on D-Day.

and reminded me that they had landed at Sicily and Salerno a few months ago and he was almost ordering me to make sure I didn't land them as they did there (in Italy) and put them off in three or four feet of water. I didn't want to argue with this young man because I saw that he was caressing a Thompson submachine gun. So I promised him that I'd do the best I could.

Unfortunately, we landed like a city block from dry land (because of) the tide configuration at that time. Had we come in on a high tide, which everyone (the Germans) expected us to do, Rommel had set up tetrahedrons, hedgehogs and different obstacles, with a *Tellermine* positioned on top of them as well, to blow us back into the sea. Seeing this caused us (Allied planners) to change our landing tactic and go in on a low tide. I would go in with these 36 troops and I would have to let them go a good city block from the beach. And if you've ever been swimming and are familiar with sand bars, it is true that when they got out of my boat with nearly knee deep water, they may be walking into four, five feet of water by the time they got to dry land.

On my way in that morning, I had noted that there was an army lieutenant standing in front of me where I was driving the boat, and of course these fellas are packed in there like sardines. They can't move, they can't even squat down in their own spot. This one gentleman, he was a lieutenant; a chaplain, no less. I noticed his face was white as a sheet. He was seasick. And not being able to move, he just stuck his head over the side of the boat and into the wind—he let go of his breakfast, and of course I caught it all. I couldn't see where I was going because I caught it, in my eyes and all. It was a mess. My trusty motor mac saw my dilemma and he promptly reached over the side, got a bucket of seawater and dashed it in my face and said, "You want another one?" I said, "Yeah, that was strong medicine." When I said that,

Reproduction LCVP on display at The National WWII Museum. This LCVP was built by volunteers, and numbered *PA 33-21* in honor of Marvin Perrett's LCVP.

all these troops burst out laughing. And that was what it took to break the tension in the heat of battle. It was almost like these kids were saying in unison, "If the kid can take this, I guess he can get us in safely." Which I did.

Marvin Perrett remained with the *Bayfield* for the duration of the war. Perrett landed Marines on Iwo Jima and Okinawa, losing his landing craft on the first day at Iwo Jima. Perrett returned home to New Orleans and graduated from high school in 1946.

Above: These Coast Guardsmen bound for Normandy paid tribute to Union General William Tecumseh Sherman's feelings on war.

UTAH BEACH

Orval Woodrow Wakefield

US Navy, Naval Combat Demolition Unit 132

Orval Wakefield was born in Toronto, Canada, in 1913. He was almost 30 years old when he joined the US Navy in late 1943. Wakefield went through Seabee training at the Naval Construction Training Center at Camp Peary, Virginia, before attending the Naval Combat Demolition Unit school in Fort Pierce, Florida. There Wakefield became an expert in demolitions, learning how to eliminate underwater obstacles to clear beachheads for amphibious landings, and joined NCDU 132.

Not all Coast Guardsmen were as fortunate as Perrett. The US Coast Guard suffered more losses on D-Day than any other point in the war. Vulnerable coxswains were anxious to unload their boats and get them out of harm's way. While navy and Coast Guard coxswains delivered soldiers ashore, not all sailors remained aboard ships on D-Day. Many were attached to Naval Beach Battalions or Naval Combat Demolition Units (NCDU). Experts in demolitions, NCDU teams, working with army combat engineers, landed in the second wave with the mission of blowing up beach obstacles. Each man carried 60 pounds of explosives; one false move with explosives could be lethal.

On June the 6th at midnight, we were standing around for hours, wondering what it would be like ashore as we watched all of the explosives going off. It seemed everything was lit up. There were shells going in and bombers and it looked like the biggest Fourth of July anyone could make. I told my CPO (chief petty officer) that no one could survive that and he said, "You can bet there will be someone waiting when we get there."

After we got off our amphib ship and into our LCPL, there was just our eight-man team that had been expanded by two young seamen who had volunteered, as well as two army engineers.

The navy was responsible for the obstacle removal and our team had the explosives. Our LCPL went around with other LCPLs in order to line up to make the first wave go ashore. The big guns from the battleships were booming and it felt like it shook the boat, it was so loud. Eventually, we all got seasick. By the time we got to shore I think we were not afraid anymore. We were just glad to get our feet on solid ground. For me it was desperate. I got off the boat and the water was up to my chin. I was only five foot six inches tall. I found that my legs would hardly hold me up and I knew something was wrong. I thought I was a coward. I finally found that I was carrying two sea bags full of water and explosives and it probably weighed about one hundred or more pounds. I used my knife to cut both bags and let the water out. I was able to get up on the beach which was about 250 yards to the seawall.

All the obstacles on our part of the beach were like children's jacks, only they were made out of 6-inch I-beams five feet high. I doubt if anything could have crawled over those. We had all previously been told that we had to get rid of those obstacles by the time the fourth wave came in. While we were working on the obstacles, the incoming GIs were dodging around the obstacles. We were tied to the obstacles by Prima cord which is a quarter-inch cord that is an explosive itself, not a fuse. If one man was hit by a tracer bullet, the Prima cord would all instantly explode. We

This aerial reconnaissance photo shows Germans working on beach obstacles on Utah Beach, May 1944.

looked down the lines of obstacles and started working on them, having to keep chasing the GIs out from hiding behind them. Finally we got everything loaded and we got the GIs out of the obstacles. I don't think anybody stopped to think about being in no-man's-land loaded down with high explosives, knowing that if anything hit you it would be a disaster to the whole unit.

We finally shouted "Fire in the hole!" and then we went up to the seawall where we found a slight trench by the seawall along side of a German 88-gun enclosure. We got in the shallow trench, if you can call it that, and we watched what was happening on the beach. We realized that when we first came in, there was nothing there but obstacles, then men running, turning, and dodging. All of a sudden it was like a beehive. Landing craft were able to come through the water and vehicles also on the land. Caterpillar earth movers had pushed sand up against the seawall and into the interior. It looked like an anthill. By middle afternoon it changed from nothing but obstacles to a small city.

It turned out to be a pretty good day for our team NCDU 132. I understand that our units at Utah beach had 30 percent casualties that day and at Omaha beach they had 70 percent casualties for that day. I guess we were lucky we lost only two of eight men. There was one problem, some of the paratroopers who had been wounded inland had been brought to the beach and they were more or less laying there in a group. Also there was a group of German prisoners that were down a ways from the beach. Those wounded paratroopers were trying to do anything they could to get to those German prisoners. I guess they had been mistreated very badly in the rear or something. Bloody or not, they were still ready to do more fighting if they could have gotten to those Germans.

The US Navy's role in the invasion extended to the beaches. Members of a Naval Beach Battalion work on clearing obstacles on Utah Beach.

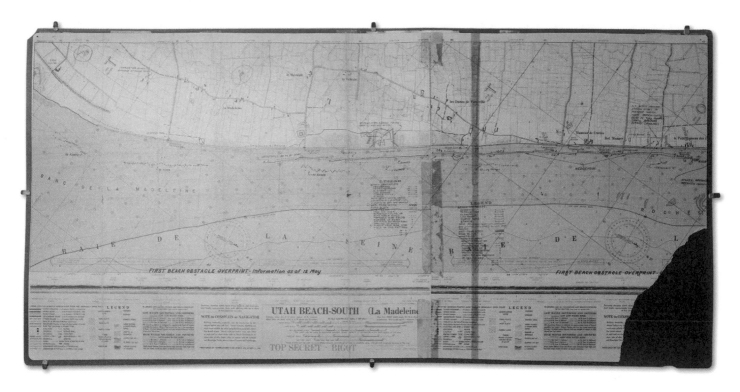

UTAH BEACH-SOUTH (La Madeleine

TOP SECRET BIGOT

By evening it was no longer a rush of men, it was a rush of vehicles. It was as busy as you could possibly believe. It was apparent all of the other NCDU units had done their job well, because as far as I could see to one side of the beach, all the beach was opened, there was nothing holding landing vehicles back. We figured our day was well done, no one ever knew who we were. We were always questioned, "Who are you guys and what do you do?" The captains of the ships didn't like us because we had so many explosives with us. When we were inland the army would ask, "What is the navy doing in here?"

Beach obstacles are marked in red on this map carried by Edward Gilleran, who landed in the second wave with the 116th Anti-aircraft Artillery Battalion.

Orval Wakefield participated in the invasion of Southern France in August 1944, then the Borneo Invasion in early 1945. Just before the war ended, Wakefield dove too deep during an exercise and "broke something in my head." This left him unable to dive deeper than a few feet and ended his service with NCDUs.

Another special unit that landed on Utah beach was an OSS (Office of Strategic Services) counter-espionage unit. OSS Agent Charles Hostler carried this folding-stock M1 Carbine, traditionally used by paratroopers, when he landed on Utah Beach.

John Ahearn

First Lieutenant, Commanding Officer, C Company

70th Tank Battalion

Drafted one month before the Japanese attack on Pearl Harbor, New Yorker John Ahearn joined the US Army in November 1941. Ahearn attended Officer Candidate School (OCS) and graduated in July 1942. He then joined the 70th Tank Battalion. After training French military personnel in the use of armored equipment, Ahearn participated in the invasion of Sicily. Ahearn received a Silver Star for gallantry in action during the Sicilian Campaign. In January 1944, he became the commanding officer of C Company, and prepared to land in the second wave on Utah Beach.

This American flag flew from the mast of *LCT(R)-439*, commanded by Lieutenant Elmer H. Mahlin. *LCT(R)-439* was modified with launching racks that were used to fire a barrage of rockets at German positions on Utah Beach in preparation for landings there.

Demolition teams had to work quickly as waves of troops and tanks continued to pour onto the beach behind them. The 70th Tank Battalion, a veteran unit that had landed and fought in Sicily, was scheduled to land in two waves, both preceding and following the demolition teams. A and B companies were made up of Duplex Drive tanks, Sherman tanks outfitted with canvas skirts and two propeller drives. Ideally, these additions allowed the roughly 40-ton tanks to swim to shore. Tragedy struck quickly for the 70th Tank Battalion as an LCT struck a mine, sending tanks and men flying through the air. Watching the disaster unfold, C Company moved up to land in the first wave.

As the dawn broke, we got a clearer picture of where everybody was, and it became evident that there'd been some problem with the DD tanks, and that we were not going to come in at H-Hour+15, in back of (behind) these tanks, but we were indeed going to be the first tanks on the beach, or alongside some of the company B tanks. As it turned out, we all of course had mounted into the tanks. The tanks did not have this flotation gear, but we had been weatherized, and we were able to get into five or six feet of water, because we had these frontal-like objects (snorkels) over our engines. Everything else was sealed, and eight boats brought us in on the beach just as far as they could. We got off in five or six feet of water, as I recall. Well, as it turned out, Owen Gavigan, because his tank was in front, was the first tank to land on Utah Beach and mine was the second. We then proceeded onto the beach, and it became evident that the beach area was not the same as it had been planned we would land on. It was also evident to me that not all of my tanks had got in. As it developed subsequently, about six of the tanks had to return to England because of boat difficulties. I was faced with a decision as to what to do at this time. I saw General Teddy Roosevelt on the beach and I got out of my tank and reported to him, and told him who I was and what my mission was. He told me to go ahead, via the lateral parts of the beach, both north and south, and to take care and to get inland as fast as we could, and to be generally supportive. I then directed my lieutenant Yeoman who was my second-in-command, and told him to take half of the tanks and proceed up to the north, and I would proceed to the south.

At this time I was leading seven tanks. Of the original 24, as I said, 6 had returned to England. Four of the dozer tanks had reverted to the control of the engineers, so the remaining fourteen had been divided by me between Lieutenant Yeoman

and myself. Anyway, we proceeded southward, trying to find an opening off the beach and subsequently—I don't know how many yards down the beach—did find an opening. However, at this opening, there was a small tank-like object that I had never been informed about, and had never seen in the operations in Africa or Sicily. Although I was concerned, my mission was to get in as rapidly as possible, so we proceeded through. As it happened, nothing happened. Later on, I read about the fact that there were a number of these so-called "Little Goliaths" that had been controlled from one of the strongpoints of the Germans and that during the bombing apparently the controls to these had been severed. Luckily for us, as it turned out.

We then proceeded when we got inside the seawall; we then again proceeded laterally between the seawall and the road, where we saw a number of infantrymen from the 2nd Battalion of the 8th Division who were at this time proceeding northward. As we looked down southward, it became evident to us that there was another strongpoint of the Germans and, although we saw

A *Tellermine* atop a wooden pole on Utah Beach.

no activity there, I had our tanks fire some shells into it. With this a number of Germans—as it turned out, to be impressed soldiers who were not really of German nationality—came out with their hands in the air, and began running towards us. So then I dismounted from the tank so as to take them as prisoners. As I did, the most unusual thing happened. I got out of the tank and, as I began to approach them, they began yelling to me and gesturing me to stay still, because they were yelling: "Achtung Meinen." With this I gestured toward them to move toward the road, and the tanks moved toward the road, and we delivered these 30 or so odd prisoners to the infantry. After doing this we again proceeded southward to where we came across a country road leading to the town of Pouppeville. At this juncture, I told Lieutenant Tighe, who was one of my junior officers and who was commanding the platoon with which I had associated myself, to proceed inward and that I would, along with a couple of other tanks, continue to proceed down this rather narrow road across the dunes and across the hedgerows to see if there was any further strong points that we might assault.

Shortly after this, as my tank proceeded down this small lane, the tank hit a land mine and the front left bogie (external suspension component) of the tank was blown and we, of course, were immobilized. At this time I radioed this information to Lieutenant Tighe, and then I proceeded on foot to cross over to

go down the lane, crossing over several hedgerows, to see if there was anything I could view that we might take a look at.

At this time I heard cries for help and looking toward the beach, I saw three figures who I surmised were paratroopers and had been injured. I immediately returned to the tank and got the rather large first aid kit that we carried in the tanks and I came back. I proceeded in back of the hedgerow that separated them from the hedgerow to the north and, when I saw a break in the hedgerow, I proceeded to cross it. I was going to try to get as close to them as I possibly could. At this time, while I was standing there contemplating my next move, a personnel mine went off under me. The mine explosion threw me into the bank of the hedgerows, and I was unconscious for a while. Subsequently I awakened and began yelling and two of my crew, Technician Anthony Zampiello and Private Felix Beard, came out to take a look. It was hard to find me, because I had rolled up against the embankment, but when they did, I cautioned them not to come over because of the presence of mines. Incidentally, I subsequently learned from our battalion maintenance officer, who wrote me a letter back in the hospital, that they had discovered some 15,000 mines in that vicinity. So the odds were not very good that I was going to be unharmed.

Anyway, they went back to the tank and got a long rope, and threw the rope to me, and then dragged me out from over the

The German minefields featured a deadly combination of different types of mines. This German *Tellermine* 35 is an anti-tank mine. It contained 12 pounds of TNT and required 200 pounds of pressure to activate. Mines like this disabled tanks such as the one commanded by John Ahearn.

The *Schützenmine* 42 is a German anti-personnel mine used extensively in the Normandy defenses. The half-pound charge of TNT was enough to shatter the lower extremities of anyone unfortunate to step on it, and its wooden construction made it difficult for mine detectors to locate.

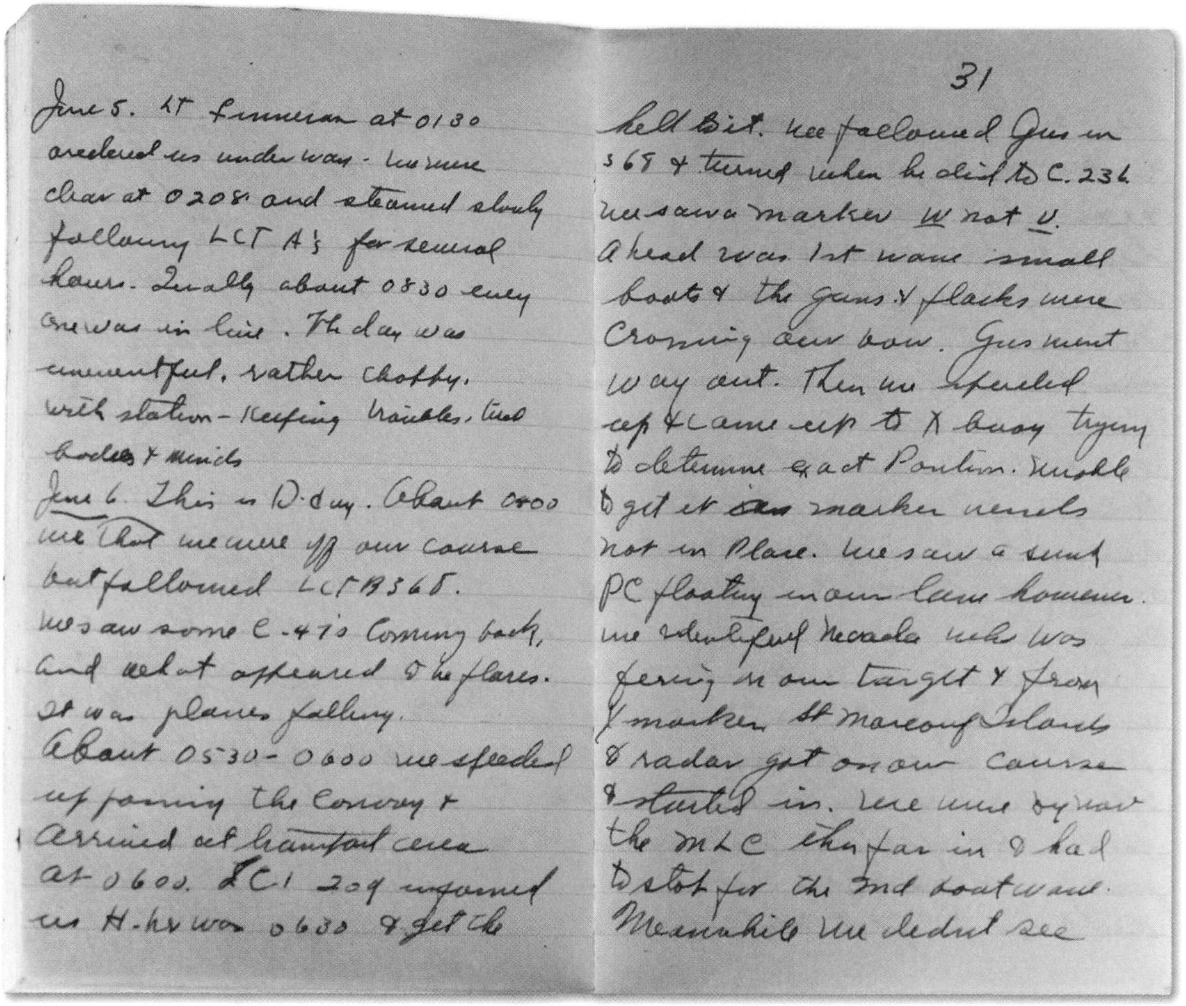

31

[Handwritten diary entry, left page:]

June 5. LT Finneran at 0130
ordered us under way. We were
clear at 0208 and steamed slowly
following LCT A's for several
hours. Finally about 0830 every
one was in line. The day was
uneventful, rather choppy.
with station-keeping troubles, two
bodies & winds
June 6. This is D-day. About 0400
we that we were off our course
but followed LCTB565.
We saw some C-47's coming back,
and what appeared to be flares.
It was planes falling.
About 0530-0600 we speeded
up passing the convoy &
arrived at transport area
at 0600. LC1 209 informed
us H-hr was 0630 & Jet the

[Handwritten diary entry, right page:]

held Bit. We followed Gus in
565 & turned when he did to C-236
We saw a marker W not V.
Ahead was 1st wave small
boats & the guns & flacks were
crossing our bow. Gus went
way out. Then we speeded
up & came up to X buoy trying
to determine exact Position. Unable
to get it our marker vessels
not in Place. We saw a sunk
PC floating in our lane however.
We identified Nevada who was
firing in our target & from
X marker St Marcouf Islands
& radar got on our course
& started in. We were by now
the MLC thus far in & had
to stop for the 1st boat wave.
Meanwhile we didn't see

Lieutenant Elmer H. Mahlin's June 6 diary entry while in command of
LCT(R)-439.

hedgerow. Subsequent to that time my memory is a little bit fuzzy as to how I got back to the field hospital which thankfully, had apparently arrived in four or five hours after the invasion and been set up. I do know that I was on stretchers, and on jeeps, and had been transferred from one group to another and subsequently arrived at the hospital.

During that night, it was decided that I would need surgery. I had heavy paratroop boots on. Both feet, I guess, were still on at this point but were terribly mangled and they decided that they would have to operate on me. I was given about six bottles of plasma and, of course, was visited by the chaplain. Then in the early evening, in this makeshift tent, with white sheets covering the walls of the tent, I was operated on. Subsequently I found from notes that the decision was made that they would just amputate the one foot because they felt that I would not be able to withstand both operations. So during the night, the one foot was amputated, and I was then prepared for a transport the next day to England.

Gravely wounded, John Ahearn ultimately had both legs amputated below the knee. For his actions on June 6 Ahearn was awarded the Distinguished Service Cross. It was given to him by General Raymond O. Barton, commander of the 4th Infantry Division, at Walter Reed Hospital in the United States.

Joseph Louis Camera

Pharmacist's Mate Second Class, US Navy

2nd Naval Beach Battalion

Eighteen-year-old New Yorker Joseph Camera enlisted in the navy in February 1942, in response to the Japanese attack on Pearl Harbor. After basic training he reported aboard the battleship USS *Massachusetts* (BB-59), as a plank owner (member of a ship's first crew) at her commissioning on May 12, 1942. On track to become a hospital corpsman, Camera trained at the Hospital Corps School in Portsmouth, Virginia. As a corpsman Camera landed in Sicily and Salerno in 1943. Assigned to the 2nd Naval Beach Battalion, Camera was an experienced corpsman when he landed on Utah Beach.

US Navy Signalman First Class Herb Davis used these signal flags to communicate with ships offshore while on Utah Beach on D-Day.

Members of a Naval Beach Battalion participate in an exercise prior to D-Day. Dressed like soldiers, naval personnel painted distinctive markings on their helmets to distinguish them from soldiers ashore.

As tank companies cleared the way inland, troops continued to pour ashore. In order to provide specialists to assist in operations such as demolitions, medical care, and traffic control, mixed units were put together under army direction. The 2nd Naval Beach Battalion provided medics, signalmen (to communicate to ships offshore and ships landing on the beach), and demolition experts to clear obstacles. Navy corpsmen, the equivalent of army medics, joined army forces landing on the beaches to provide vital medical care to the wounded.

We boarded an LST (Landing Ship Tank) with part of the 4th Infantry Division, and lay in wait for the operation to begin. The next thing I remember is sailing in the midst of horizon-to-horizon ships, transport, warships, amphibious ships; every kind of assault craft imaginable. It was Tuesday, June 6, 1944. H-Hour was 6:30 a.m. We began to transfer from the LST into smaller landing craft. We boarded an LCVP. I could now see the beach a good distance off. It was about 9:00 a.m. Wave after wave of assault troops were landing on the beach. Artillery from German big guns was now beginning to explode on Utah Beach.

I prayed to God to protect me and, if I didn't make it, to take me into His kingdom. I was 21 years old. I had just learned to smoke. I don't really think I was frightened about it. After all, I was a veteran of other major engagements. They sort of become matter-of-fact. The first one is the toughest. After that you seem to acquire a confidence that overcomes fear. Something like riding a bicycle. When you begin, you wonder how will you ever get used to it, but then it becomes automatic. Then there's that feeling of pride, when you tell yourself: "I did it before and I can do it again. I am a veteran. I wear battle stars I earned in major engagements. I know what to do and how to do it." And one more very important thing: I always told myself, "I'm on the winning team."

We were now moving towards the beach, Utah Beach. It was between 9:00 a.m. and 10:00 a.m. I could see a shell explode intermittently here and there on the beach. I could see the seawall just off the beach, pillboxes spaced along the seawall, GIs moving inland, wave after wave. The ramp dropped on our LCVP. I had to get out and move up the beach as fast as I could. When I reached the seawall, I could hear yells for a medic. I moved towards one yell, and another medic moved towards another.

I reached a wounded GI. I poured some sulfa crystals onto his wound, placed a battle dressing over it, gave him a shot of morphine, hung a bottle of blood plasma and injected it into his veins. I then tagged him to wait for an ambulance pickup to take him to a field hospital. This procedure was repeated time after time throughout the day. Some made it, some didn't. There wasn't much concern for your own safety, but a job had to be done or duty performed, and my main concern was to help whoever I could. The most distressing thing I heard was later in the day, my best friend, Ernie Verdun, another medic, had been killed trying to help a wounded GI. Some GIs were wounded by shellfire and Ernie and another medic ran over to help them. While the two medics were treating the wounded GIs a second shell hit and killed them both.

I took my equipment, used it as much as I could, and I knew I had accomplished what I was supposed to do. There was something else George Patton told us that made a lot of sense: "It's alright to have fear. It's only natural. But if you're afraid to have fear, then you're no damn good."

Towards evening the shellfire began to let up, and the beach was operating successfully. GIs were moving in regularly and advancing inland. German POWs were taken back the other way. We had tremendous air coverage protecting us from enemy aircraft. It was strange: our planes had new markings I had never seen before. Instead of the familiar stars on the wing tips, they were marked with stripes.

I remember when I was in combat, there was always a doubt of whether you would go back home alive. I used to think about the hot dogs I used to get back home in a little restaurant on a side street. How delicious they were and what I would give to have one of them. The spaghetti dinners mom used to cook. You get kind of tired after eating C-rations and K-rations for three years. You'd dream about the wonderful food back home. After sleeping on the ground for three years, I used to think how comfortable my bed was to sleep in at home. Not always, of

Corpsman C. Ed Nelson landed on Utah Beach to assist in evacuating the wounded. His unit could not find red paint for the crosses, painting them with orange paint instead.

Medical pouch carried by C. Ed Nelson on Utah Beach.

course, but quite often. The actual combat was unreal. Before you went into it, you anticipate all sorts of horrifying things. Not that they got to you, but the thought was still there. After it was over—the heavy fire, that is—you thank God that you lived through it. I think the toughest thing about the war was the training for the engagements. The dry runs, the discipline, the timing procedures; they made the actual engagements seem easy, sort of a relief.

After Normandy Joseph Camera remained in Europe, supporting army operations across the continent. Camera was in Bremen, Germany when the war ended in Europe in May 1945. He returned home in November 1945.

Top: The crew of *LCM-73* at Utah Beach.   Above: *LCM-73*, intentionally grounded on Utah Beach.

Clair R. Galdonik

A Company, 359th Infantry Regiment

90th Infantry Division

Minnesota native Clair Galdonik was drafted in early 1942 at the age of 22. Assigned to the army's 90th Infantry Division, Galdonik participated in Louisiana Maneuvers. After two years of training, Galdonik shipped out for England with the 90th Division in March 1944. A devout Catholic, Galdonik spent much time in prayer on June 5, knowing there was nothing more he could do to prepare for the invasion.

Not every man landing on Utah Beach had Joseph Camera's combat experience. For some, it would be their first and last taste of deadly fighting. The 90th Infantry Division had not yet been in combat, though lengthy training in 1943—including village fighting, and attacking fortified positions—prepared the division for battle. Although most men had faith in their training, doubts still arose on the eve of battle and many young men wondered what their fate would be.

About 5 a.m., all heck broke loose. The battleships and cruisers started throwing salvos of shells from their big guns on four to five pillboxes on the beach we would be going in on. What a show. Immediately, it gave me some assurance that no Germans on the beach could survive this bombardment.

We went out on deck and a couple of our squads huddled together to exchange stories of our home life. How we long to be back home, what our plans for the future would be if we survived this horrible war. How will we react in battle? Would it be easy to kill German soldiers? And a lot more discussion revolving around our mission when we are committed in battle. I loved those guys and I believe their feelings toward me were the same. We knew that some of us would not live to see our loved-ones anymore. We talked openly and freely and even shared a few laughs.

Now it was time to crawl into the rest of our battle gear. The Higgins boats were starting to come our way and that meant

GIs unload from LCMs at La Grand Dune, Utah Beach.

Troops unloading on Utah Beach, D-Day.

it was time to move out. The scramble nets were thrown over the side and as my name was called, I started the descent into a Higgins boat. Do I remember my thoughts as I crawled down the rope, and how I felt? Oh, yes. "Please, God, give my parents the necessary strength to carry on if I become a casualty and give me the strength and courage that I need this day to see me through the perils of this long day." For a fleeting second it brought to mind a favorite wartime song of mine, recorded by Sammy Kaye, entitled "Dear Mom." I remember a few of the words to this day. They are:

"Dear Mom, the weather today was cloudy and damp. Your letter arrived but was missing a stamp… That's all for tonight, the bugle just blew. Tomorrow's a big day with plenty to do. I like it here, but I'm kind o' homesick for you. For I love you, Dear Mom."

Seeing and hearing all these strange sights before me almost put me in a state of hypnosis. Was all this for real, or was it merely a dream? I soon found out as I dropped to the bottom of the boat that it was no dream. We were packed in, 30 tight, because of all of our extra equipment and every piece was vital to us. As each boat was loaded, each followed the other in line in a circle around the ship we had debarked from, until all the troops were unloaded and ready to start inland toward Utah Beach.

With the beach in sight, more clearly now, I didn't like what I could see. German artillery on the beach area was heavy, (judging) by the clouds of black smoke rising. Because of many beach obstacles, our boat could not move in close to shore. As it came up on 10:00 hours, the ramp went down. Then something dreadful happened. A boy in my squad started crying and yelling that he could not leave the boat and begged to be left on the craft. I had to make a quick decision, for the beach area was no place to hang around. I inflated my life jacket and grabbed his arm and pulled him into the water with me. I needed help, so another soldier came to my aid and grabbed his other arm. We inflated his life jacket and got him going. But the crying had not stopped. I felt so sorry for him, but it did make me forget my own fear as we headed for the beach. A shell came in close and we had to duck in the murky water with just our heads showing and rifle held high over our head. I moved closer to shore and another whining shell came in. Again I went down, trying to escape the flying shrapnel and trying to watch my buddy who had stopped crying and was facing up and trying to get on shore safely. After the third time of this I was so exhausted, being weighed down, that I lost my fear of becoming a casualty on the beach.

I remember cursing the Germans, then I told someone close, "I'm going for dry land and I won't stop until I get there." This was indeed an unsafe act by me. Fortunately, I got ashore as did my buddy whose emotions got the best of him. It made me feel good that we got him safely onto the beach. Something I feared more than their artillery was the danger of stepping on a landmine. There were so many of them that we had just one little area to work our way through that had been cleared of mines. So far, so good. The beach area had taken its toll from enemy shelling. Tanks and trucks were gutted and burning, but only a few dead Americans were there. It shook me up. Just a short while ago, they were among the living.

Since the 4th Division was the spearhead we encountered no German soldiers yet, but that would soon change. I cannot say how long it took us to get a little elbow room, or what time of day it was getting to be. Now we began to get intermittent artillery fire and we wasted no time hitting the ground. We moved rapidly inland but were limited for space because the areas off the road

The patch of the 90th Infantry Division. The T and O originally stood for Texas and Oklahoma, as the majority of its members were from those states. In World War II, the division adopted a new slogan to fit the patch: "Tough 'Ombres".

were posted with signs in German reading "Mines." We were in a most precarious position. If German artillery spotted us or if the German Luftwaffe got through we would not have made it.

I lost all track of time even though we continued to move inland, still not losing a man. The only Germans we saw thus far were the good ones, all of them dead. I saw the lifeless bodies of some 4th Division men. It was a dreadful feeling seeing this loss of life of our comrades, but later I was able to adjust to it. The invasion was going well, because the 82nd and 101st Airborne had pretty well sealed off the German reinforcements heading for the beach, although I didn't know it at the time.

We moved into position just behind the front lines as it started getting dark. My dear buddy Tom, with the mosquito net, and I dug a foxhole and sat back to back in it. There would be no sleeping tonight, just a long wait for tomorrow, when our company or regiment would get its baptism of fire from mortars, artillery, and small arms fire. We already knew the danger from artillery fire. I could have hugged Tom for bringing his mosquito net. The mosquitoes were vicious as we sat huddled in our foxhole, so we made good use of his net. I shivered the night through but, having someone next to me made it a bit warmer. Tom made the supreme sacrifice to help liberate France. He was gunned down about a week later. It was a terrific loss to me.

Clair Galdonik remained with the 359th Infantry Regiment, as it fought its way across Europe, taking part in the Battle of the Bulge, and ended the war in the Czech Republic.

David Paul Roderick

Staff Sargeant, H Company, 22nd Infantry Regiment

4th Infantry Division

By age sixteen, David Roderick and his five brothers were orphans. Roderick joined the army before the war so there would be "one less mouth to feed." Roderick left his Decatur, Illinois, home and attended basic training at Fort McClellan, Alabama. Assigned to the 22nd Infantry Regiment, 4th Infantry Division, Roderick trained in amphibious landings at Camp Carrabelle, Florida, before shipping out to England for the invasion of France.

The 4th Infantry Division's 8th Infantry Regiment led the assault at H-Hour, followed by the 22nd Infantry Regiment later in the morning. Although small arms and machine-gun fire was less of a threat, Utah Beach was heavily fortified with large artillery. Some enemy guns miles inland were perfectly calibrated and trained on the beach, capable of wiping out men and landing craft with little or no warning. German forces would not easily give up these vital fortifications. The men of the 22nd Infantry Regiment faced a tough battle in order to silence the German artillery.

I never really felt the tension of it. And I don't remember any of the guys feeling it. If you've been together as long as we had you knew each other really well, and you knew you could depend upon them. So your idea was well, "here we go. We've got a job to do. And whatever happens, happens." All I remember is when I transferred from *LCI-229* (Landing Craft, Infantry) into an LCVP down a little rope ladder, I cracked my knee and hurt it. It was cold and damp. So we got in there, got in our circles, and then pushed off. When they pushed off there I'm sure the thought came, "well, here we go." Here we go. But we really had no understanding of what the force was that we were going to meet.

I knew that it was a big beach because I'd seen that in the tent. There was about 200 yards of beach to go to. I knew what the fortifications were like. I knew that they had different obstacles on the beach, and that they were exposed because the tide was out. Matter of fact, that was another good thing because the Germans didn't really think we would land during bad weather and with the tide out. But we did. So the obstacles were exposed which made it easier for the engineers to get in there and blow them out.

Of course, they had the projections up with the mines on top and the wire and so forth. I could see that. Also there was about a four- to eight-foot concrete seawall on Utah Beach. I could see the seawall and the sand behind it and that sort of thing. I couldn't see, but I knew that behind it the Germans had flooded all of that area for two miles inland, with only four causeways in—we called them one, two, three and four causeways or exits. That was the reason, matter of fact, that the airborne was dropped inland because we knew that if we got caught out on those causeways we'd be annihilated.

It was a gray day and a little chilly. Of course, by the time that we got close enough there's a lot of noise because of the firing that was going on by battleships and so forth. But you just kept your head down and out of the spray of the water that was coming in and that would get you wet as you were going in. So you weren't thinking too much about what it was that I needed to do when I got there (laughs).

There was shelling and snipers, particularly when I arrived. I arrived in the third wave. So H-Hour was at 6:30. I got in about eight o'clock. By that time, the fighting in the fortifications had

The ivy on the 4th Division Patch is a nod to the Roman numeral four, IV, or "ivy" as the division became known.

210 mm German gun at Crisbecq. This battery claimed to have sunk an American destroyer, the USS *Corry* on D-Day. The 210mm gun was one of the largest German guns on the French coast.

already taken place. So the only thing I had to worry about was artillery and snipers. Matter of a fact, I only lost one man on the beach. He was shot right between the eyes by a sniper.

Now the next day, I lost eight, which is half of my men, in Azeville and Crisbecq. That's one of the things that concerns me about the media and so forth. When they show D-Day, usually they talk about Omaha and the carnage that was there, which there certainly was. They make it look like we didn't have any difficulty really. And we did. The 4th Division lost 197 men there right on the beach on D-Day. But when we attacked Azeville and Crisbecq, we lost fifty percent of our men within three or four days.

So that was our D-Day, that's what I always say. Our D-Day was really the second day because we had to wade through all that water. The exits weren't all open and we all landed at different places than we were supposed to. The one open exit (exit three), was really crowded. So the 22nd Infantry (Regiment) and the 12th (Infantry Regiment) which came in behind us walked through that. It took about seven hours for us to walk through all that water. And then we hit a road. And then we went up the road to a place called Saint-Martin-de-Varreville. And then we spread out and made our scrimmage line and waited until morning. I was surprised to find that it didn't really get dark over there until about eleven o'clock at night. So at about eleven o'clock, we began to put out our scouts and dig our holes and that sort of thing.

Azeville and Crisbecq were actually a complex of fortifications; about four big fortifications. They were connected underground. Then they had smaller ones out front or to the side where they would put in machine gunners. So they had their protection, fire. Then of course, they had communications back to artillery. They had mortar people. And the German's Screaming Mimi which was a rocket. So they had all these kinds of things. They were all prearranged as far as firing range was concerned and location. All they had to do was wait for you to get there and then open up. That's the way I lost eight men on that second day, matter of a fact. They got Screaming Mimis on us. That's what we called them, Screaming Mimis, because of the screeching noise from the rockets. (The fortifications) were anywhere from three to ten feet wide or thick with reinforced concrete. It was really, really tough to knock those babies out of there.

The hedgerows were really difficult for fighting. Again, the Germans would sit back there. They had all of the avenues of approach to those fortifications zeroed in already. They were

German gun emplacement at Azeville. The 22nd Infantry Regiment suffered high casualty rates in fighting to capture the batteries at Azeville and Crisbecq.

Roderick served as an 81mm mortar section leader. Deployed at the battalion level, the M1 81mm mortar provided indirect fire support to American infantry units. The high angle of fire and range of 3,000 yards enabled the M1 to hit targets behind walls, buildings, and dug into the ground.

mapped, and fire arrangement already been made. So they just sat there and waited for you to come. You had to go over the hedgerow and cling to the sides of them. Our standard way of fighting was that we would have artillery fire for fifteen minutes to an hour on positions over there. But the Germans, again, were dug into the hedgerows, and so it was hard to get to them. Hopefully we would then get the P-47s (Thunderbolt)—which we called the infantry air force—to come in and dive bomb with their 500-pound bombs and with their 50-caliber machine guns. As soon as that lifted, then we would push off. As soon as that lifted, the Germans would come out of the holes and were waiting for you.

When you actually got to the fortifications, they had radios connected with each other; Crisbecq back with Azeville. They also had a back door where they would sling out their troops, come around to your side and hit you from the side without you knowing it. So that was really tough. Matter of a fact, the very first day, we got on top of Azeville and the commander of Azeville, the German command there, he knew what was going to happen. He radioed down to Crisbecq to actually fire their artillery on us while we're on top of it. We thought it was friendly fire. We had to retreat.

The next day we then had to do the job all over again. This time, they did get troops out the doors in the back. They came around and hit us on the side, and we had to withdraw that day. So for two days there, we lost a lot of men. We didn't take it.

The third day we finally got in there. What we did was, we brought the 3rd Battalion off the beach in behind them. Once you get behind these fortifications, then you can do your thing. We discovered that worked really well when we got to the Siegfried Line in Germany because there we'd pin them down, bring a tank destroyer in behind them, stick their big 98-milllimeter gun in through the aperture and shoot about five or six rounds. What was left, they'd come out. We used flamethrowers, of course, too, against Azeville and Crisbecq.

Sergeant Riley eventually ran 75 yards, got behind Azeville and gave some squirts and nothing happened, gave another few squirts and nothing happened. He was about to give up. Then, all of a sudden, he heard this bang and a flash. What had happened was that the gas had gotten inside in their ammunition and blew it up. They came out pretty fast after that one. We used that kind of practice for the rest of the way all through the Quinéville Ridge. The idea, of course, the real goal of our troops on Utah Beach, was to eventually capture Cherbourg on the harbor there in the peninsula. That took us until June 25th.

....

David Roderick stayed on the front lines until he was wounded during the fighting in the Hürtgen Forest in Germany in November 1945. He quickly recovered and was with the 22nd Infantry Regiment's 1st Battalion headquarters during the Battle of the Bulge. Roderick was awarded three Bronze Stars and by March 1945 was shipped back to the United States.

CONCLUSION

Though its forces met less resistance than expected on June 6, the VII Corps faced a long and bloody fight northward to capture the Cotentin Peninsula and the vital port of Cherbourg. The hard-won success of the inland airborne operations was critical to securing the beachhead and demonstrated that an attack by both air and sea was the right strategy. Failure of any element of the Utah Beach assault might have jeopardized the entire invasion.

Results of the Utah Beach operation were decidedly mixed. Despite their inexperience in combat, the highly motivated infantry coming ashore overwhelmed the Germans' first line of defense. But for the US Navy, the attack resulted in significant losses. German mines wreaked havoc on US Navy, US Coast Guard and Royal Navy forces. Along with the loss of the destroyer *Corry*, the minesweeper USS *Osprey* (AM-56) and Patrol Craft *PC-1261* were sunk by mines. A total of nine warships were sunk off Utah during June 5/6, not including a considerable number of smaller landing craft which struck mines or were destroyed by German shore batteries.

The nearly one-mile miss of the designated landing zone posed an obstacle that was overcome through leadership on the beach, most notably that of Brigadier General Theodore Roosevelt, Jr. At 56, Roosevelt was considered much too old by many superiors to go ashore that morning but he was not to be deterred. His presence on the fire-swept beach and his ability to rally the troops would be long remembered. Upon determining the location of the landing, Roosevelt proclaimed, "We'll start the war from here." The VII Corps forged ahead, and by the end of June, Cherbourg was in American hands.

Brigadier General Roosevelt died of a heart attack on July 12 just outside Cherbourg. He would posthumously receive the Medal of Honor for his actions at Utah Beach on D-Day.

OMAHA BEACH

CHAPTER THREE

6.6.44

If America, Great Britain and their allies did indeed commit to "throwing everything we have" into the invasion of German-occupied France, to recall Supreme Commander Dwight Eisenhower's rallying proclamation, the assault at Beach 313—code-named Omaha Beach—would be the ultimate test of resolve. The fiercely contested shore was a linchpin; the fate of the campaign in Europe seemed to rest on the action at Omaha and the other D-Day beaches. Strategy and symbolism, hardware and fears came together there on D-Day.

Eisenhower's message carried life-and-death significance for the riflemen, combat engineers, tankers, coxswains and others targeting Omaha, a five-mile-wide sector offering Germans near-

ideal defensive positions among cliffs reaching more than 100 feet high. At this site, ending Nazi tyranny would come at a deadly cost.

American forces had numbers, if not geography, in their favor as their landing craft thrashed through English Channel waves, headed toward a hazy shore. The infantrymen in the invasion boats were intensely trained and well-equipped. They were backed by a stunning assembly of air and sea power. Plans called for the 1st and 29th Infantry Divisions and the 2nd and 5th Ranger Battalions, together numbering more than 35,000 men, to storm across the shoreline and move inland, with soldiers and firepower

Above: American soldiers hunker down in a Coast Guard-operated LCVP bound for the Normandy coastline.

steadily destroying German strongpoints. The Omaha invasion sectors had been given easy-to-remember names like Charlie, Dog White, Easy Green and Fox Red. Within a few hard-fought hours, it was hoped, the Americans would provide a critical link between American units landing to the west (at Pointe du Hoc and Utah Beach) and the British and Canadian forces to the east (at Gold, Juno and Sword Beaches), and by nightfall, Omaha's victors would establish their own defensive line several miles from the sea. Just a few miles west of Omaha the 2nd Ranger Battalion would carry out a daring assault up the jagged cliffs of Pointe du

Above: Commissioning Pennant flown by the USS *Augusta* on D-Day. It was picked up by Seaman William E. Lamont as it fell from the halyard during the landings. Fearing a courtmartial for leaving his battle station, Lamont kept the pennant tied around his waist and kept its existence a secret until after the war.

Below: USS *Augusta* (CA-31), flagship of the Western Task Force, lies off the invasion coast, ready to provide gunfire support to troops landing on the beach.

Hoc to find and disable heavy artillery threatening both the Omaha and Utah landing beaches as well as offshore support ships.

Everyone expected a fierce struggle. Landing forces faced an elaborate mix of beach obstacles—including poles tipped with explosives to destroy landing craft—and thousands of German defenders peering out from hidden bunkers, trenches and a string of "resistance nests." What they did not expect is that Omaha would become one of the war's more infamous killing zones, a place of almost unfathomable sacrifice.

The Omaha experience stirred bitter memories of amphibious invasions at Anzio in Italy and Tarawa in the Pacific—and of the slaughter of British forces at Gallipoli during the last world war. "Bloody Omaha" confirmed British Prime Minister Winston Churchill's fears that a broad attack on entrenched forces would prove a "heavy and hazardous adventure" carrying a "fearful price."

At Omaha, German defenders came closest to achieving the explicit strategy of "Desert Fox" Field Marshal Erwin Rommel to stop the Allied invaders and annihilate them at the shoreline, where they were most vulnerable. More than elsewhere across a perilous five-part beach invasion front, everything seemed to go wrong for the Americans.

First, a gap in Allied intelligence and communications resulted in a failure to warn invasion forces that the Germans had recently

18th Infantry Regiment officer Lieutenant Leonard Stoddard wore this helmet in three invasions: Operation Torch (North Africa), Operation Husky (Sicily) and Operation Overlord. Soon after landing in Normandy Stoddard was struck with malaria and returned to England.

Known as the "Big Red One," the 1st Infantry Division was formed in 1917. This simple shoulder patch is still worn by the division today.

reinforced their defenses by reassigning the 352nd Infantry Division from reserve to coast duty. Secondly, intensive aerial bomb strikes just before dawn were supposed to significantly impair German defenses and create beach craters for Americans taking cover and dodging bullets. The mission failed, as bombers overshot the beaches by hundreds of meters, even miles. Officers looking over the edges of Higgins landing craft packed with infantry—some battle-hardened, others encountering deadly resistance for the first time—were aghast to see there were no shell holes, no cover, leaving their men utterly exposed. German defenders were dazed but their fortifications and gun nests were mostly intact.

The first waves of incoming troops and coxswains faced hell on earth. Landing craft struggling with rough waves and offshore sand bars veered off course, most dropping their human cargo at the wrong locations. Mortar fire and mined "Belgian Gates" erected at low tide by Rommel's crews destroyed or damaged some craft.

June 8, aboard the USS *Augusta* US officers watch operations ashore. From left to right are: Rear Admiral Alan G. Kirk, Commander Western Naval Task Force; Lieutenant General Omar N. Bradley, Commanding General, US First Army; Rear Admiral Arthur D. Struble (with binoculars), Chief of Staff for Rear Admiral Kirk; and Major General Ralph Royce.

D-DAY AT OMAHA

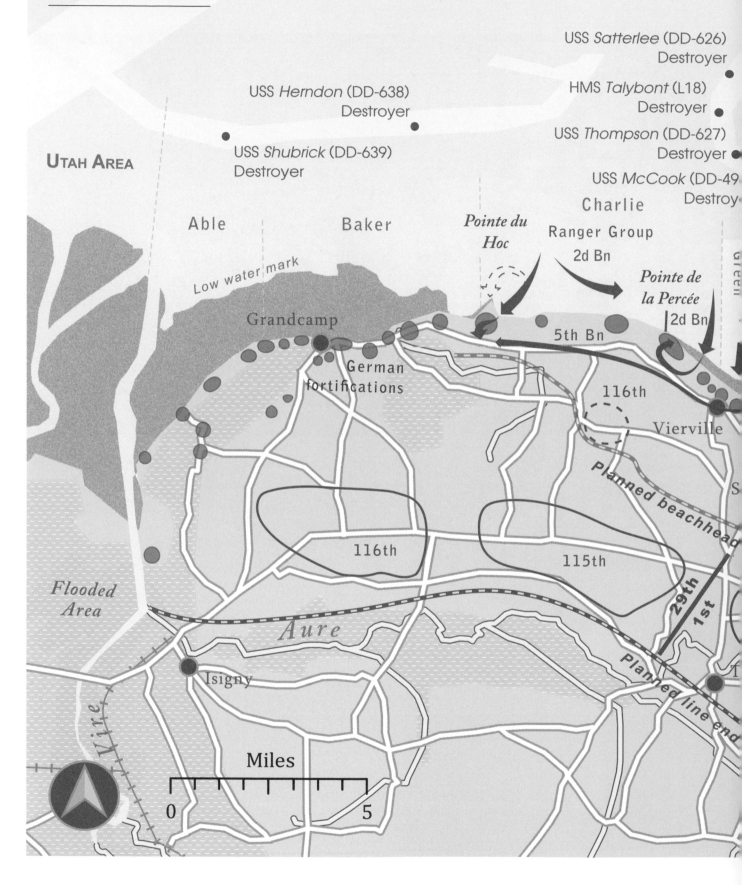

USS *Satterlee* (DD-626)
Destroyer

USS *Herndon* (DD-638)
Destroyer

HMS *Talybont* (L18)
Destroyer

USS *Thompson* (DD-627)
Destroyer

UTAH AREA

USS *Shubrick* (DD-639)
Destroyer

USS *McCook* (DD-49
Destroy

Able

Baker

Charlie

Pointe du
Hoc

Ranger Group
2d Bn

Low water mark

Pointe de
la Percée
2d Bn

Grandcamp

5th Bn

German
fortifications

116th

116th

Vierville

Planned beachhead

Flooded
Area

116th

115th

29th

1st

Aure

Planned line end

Isigny

Miles

0   5

128

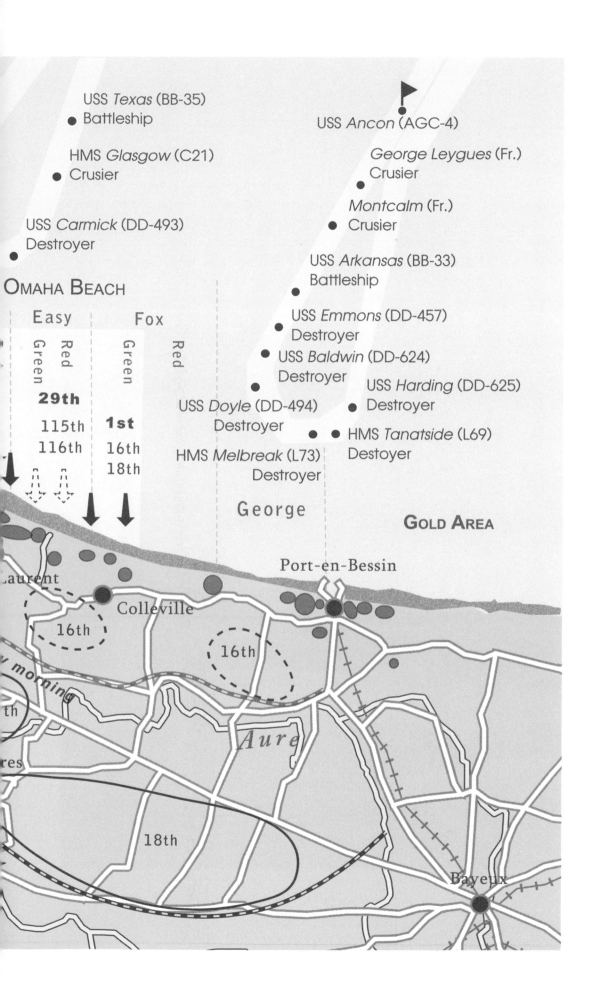

USS *Texas* (BB-35)
● Battleship

HMS *Glasgow* (C21)
● Crusier

USS *Carmick* (DD-493)
Destroyer
●

OMAHA BEACH

Easy			Fox	
Green	Red		Green	Red
	29th		**1st**	
	115th		16th	
	116th		18th	

USS *Doyle* (DD-494)
Destroyer

HMS *Melbreak* (L73)
Destroyer

George

USS *Ancon* (AGC-4)

George Leygues (Fr.)
Crusier
●

Montcalm (Fr.)
● Crusier

USS *Arkansas* (BB-33)
Battleship
●

USS *Emmons* (DD-457)
Destroyer
●

USS *Baldwin* (DD-624)
Destroyer
●

USS *Harding* (DD-625)
● Destroyer

● ● HMS *Tanatside* (L69)
Destoyer

GOLD AREA

Port-en-Bessin

Laurent

Colleville

16th

16th

Aure

morning

18th

Bayeux

129

Death and dismemberment came at the boat exits. Many died before they could exit or, laden with gear, either drowned or came close to doing so after leaping into the surf. Wounds from the dead and dying turned the water to blood red. The beach became an appalling scene of soldiers crawling, huddling behind debris, and falling to shell fragments or machine-gun bursts. Floating tanks designed to move ashore and provide cover for infantry and fire on enemy bunkers instead capsized in the surf, their crews lost. Engineers defused many mines but struggled to blow up beach obstacles because injured or terrified infantry, still hundreds of yards from the base of the cliffs, were using hedgehogs (a collection of steel rails welded together designed to rip out the bottoms of landing craft) planted by the Germans as meager cover.

Amid thundering explosions and screams from the wounded and dying, an invasion traffic jam ensued, bringing fresh complications for still oncoming waves of soldiers. Thousands of American survivors huddled against the sea wall, their advance halted, as the enemy held the high ground.

This German 8.8 cm anti-tank gun, part of *Widerstandsnest* 72, is positioned at the mouth of the Vierville draw, allowing for a deadly line of enfilade fire down Omaha Beach.

With the experience of WWI gas attacks still fresh in the collective memory, gas masks were standard issue for all troops, especially assault troops. This M3 lightweight gasmask was carried by Captain Frank H. Walk, attached to the 6th Engineer Special Brigade Group, on Omaha Beach.

Harold Baumgarten

Private B Company, 116th Infantry Regiment

29th Infantry Division

In an act of defiance toward the Nazis, Harold Baumgarten, a Jew from New York, drew a Star of David on the back of his field jacket. He wore the altered jacket during the opening attack at the infamous Dog Green sector on Omaha Beach. Drafted in June 1943, Baumgarten learned during training that he would be part of the spearhead for an Allied second front in Europe. In his detailed remembrance of D-Day, he methodically called out the names and home towns of fellow soldiers, saying, "I don't want people to forget about them."

D-DAY

Elements of the 116th Infantry Regiment were brought ashore by Coast Guard *LCI(L)-94*. This photograph, taken by crewmember Charles Jarreau, shows soldiers wading ashore. On the beach are three of the DD tanks that made it ashore.

We're in this camp (in England). Got all-new equipment. They issued a special combat jacket. They issued a new first aid kit which had one grain of morphine—injectable, revolutionary. First time in the American army they let soldiers have their own morphine. Saved a lot of lives because it prevented death from shock. They gave us a secret invented seasick pill, a little maroon capsule, which became known as Dramamine. They gave us cellophane bags which we were supposed to put our rifles in, but I put a rubber condom on mine and it worked just as well. They gave us a half-pound block of TNT. TNT is very safe. We used to play touch football with it, a half-pound block. It will only explode if you put a blasting cap in the middle of it and a lighter fuse. So I carried it in my back pocket on D-Day. I carried the fuse and fuse lighter and blasting cap in the netting of my helmet which, if I had gotten shot in the head, would have blown my head off. People asked me, "Why'd you do it?" Because all the other guys did.

May 15 we got driven in a truck to a special camp called a sausage, because it was shaped like a sausage. We were in Camp D1. Companies A, B, C and D were in Camp D1. When I went into the tent of headquarters for Company A, they had a mock-up of the beach we were going to hit, a clay mock-up. We even had airplane pictures taken from P-38s of the Germans working

on the beach with those terrible obstacles they were putting in, four rows.

I looked at the mockup of that beach and I saw the pillboxes elevated over 25 feet above the beach, three pillboxes, WN71, WN72, WN73, three huge pillboxes. Their sides were part of the bluff, so the navy couldn't see them and couldn't knock them out. The airplanes would not be able to knock them out. The one on the left flank had a 75mm gun. The one in the middle had a 50mm gun on a swivel and could fire both east and west. The one on the right flank, which I didn't realize till I got on the beach was camouflaged as a seaside cottage, was firing an MG 42 machine gun sideways, covering the entire beach.

So when I saw these elevated pillboxes and the way we were trained (not calculating for Dog Green's extensive mix of defenses), I wrote a letter home to my sister Ethel in New York, and she lives in the same apartment house with my parents. I said, "Break the news—get the telegram first, because I'm not coming home." There was no way I was going to get off that beach alive, with those guns and those four rows of obstacles that General Rommel was putting in, Erwin Rommel, the Desert Fox. He put in 6.5 million more mines and he put in these diabolical obstacles, starting at 300 yards out from a 25-foot sea wall.

(After pre-invasion reassignments) we were either lucky or

unlucky, but we were in Company B now. Very nice guys. My best buddy there, Robert Garbett Jr., of Newport News, Virginia, made a leather band for me for my watch, the watch that's in the D-Day Museum with his band, because he saw my wrist was getting irritated from the hot weather.

I was in Company B, boat team number one, and I was assistant BAR (Browning Automatic Rifle) man in that outfit. I was number five on the left side of the boat.

On June 3, they loaded us up in trucks and took us ten miles down past Dorchester, England and down to Weymouth, England, which is about twelve or fifteen miles, and we got off and marched down boardwalks to the little boats. And the people were making the V sign for victory, "Good luck Yanks" and so forth, because they knew it was the real thing.

We went on the *Javelin* (British troopship SS *Empire Javelin*) and it started raining every day. On June 5, we were anchored off Dog Green sector, about ten or eleven miles off, and we were getting ready. We had our so-called last meal. I ate some Cadbury chocolate bars—I didn't like the British food. I took my shower with saltwater and lava soap—I had had my head shaved for hand-to-hand combat.

Private Harold Baumgarten wore this watch when he landed in the first assault wave with the 116th Infantry Regiment. Baumgarten watched German fire decimate his unit in the opening moments of the landing and suffered multiple wounds himself before being evacuated.

At 3:30 in the morning (on June 6) we started getting off the ship. It was pitch black, the weather was horrible, wind going at ten miles an hour. The waves were up to twenty feet high, and they had to lower us over the sides already in the (landing) boats. The minute we were lowered over the side and the boats hit the water, we're thrown around like matchsticks. Every man was immediately soaked with the icy cold English Channel water, so we were freezing. The water got up to our knees and First Lieutenant Harold Donaldson, from Texas, said, "What are you waiting for? Start bailing out with your helmets." The bilge pumps weren't working with the LCAs (Landing Craft Assault). Had we landed an LCVP (Landing Craft Vehicle, Personnel) Higgins boat we wouldn't have had that problem. The sides are higher and the water wouldn't have come in.

Elaborate Allied plans for battering and softening German defenses at Dog Green sector through aerial bombing, naval shelling and amphibious tank attacks proved a failure. Soldiers and their landing boats were left badly exposed.

My Company B only landed with four boats. A total of 210 men coming in to face 450 on the bluff, in bunkers, with all that firepower. Almost impossible, isn't it? The first thing I saw, a Company B boat on my left, port side, blew up. Hit a mine. We were showered with wood, metal, body parts and blood. And so we had 180 men now. When our ramp went down (it became) the signal for every machine gun on that beach to open up on the exit to our ship. So Harold Donaldson, the lieutenant, was gunned down in the boat like you see in *Saving Private Ryan*, and several men around him.

The fellow in front of me, Clarius Riggs, was machine-gunned on the ramp. I dove in behind him—the left side of my helmet was creased by a bullet. I was standing in neck-deep, bloody water with my rifle over my head.

They put these combat jackets (assault vests) on these guys. I didn't wear it 'cause my best buddy, who was the radioman of the boat, he said, "Hal, don't wear that jacket, it's liable to drown you." Now I listened to him because he was an old man; he was 25 years old and I was only a kid of 19. So I listened to Robert Garbett. And he went through that water. I (later) met him at the wall. He wasn't in great shape; he was face down, dead.

Anyway, the guys that wore these jackets when they stepped off the ramp—they were (typically) only 5 foot 4—these jackets pulled them down further. They were dark green, canvas jackets. Four pockets in the front, two in the back. They struggled to get

The 29th Infantry Division was nicknamed the Blue and Gray Division, for having been formed by the descedents of Civil War veterans. The division patch combines a yin-yang design of Union blue and Confederate gray.

their jackets off and they couldn't. Some of them bobbed up and down. They got machine-gunned in the water.

The tide was treacherous. It went out fast and it came in fast. So we hit the sand, we were running across sand at 300 yards out (from the sea wall). There were a group of us running across the beach with our rifles at port arms, which is the rifle across your chest. When I got to about 135 yards away from the sea wall, a machine-gun spray came from the trenches, up on the bluff. I heard a loud thud on my right front and my rifle vibrated. I turned it over; there was a clean hole through its receiver, which is a little rectangular plate in front of the trigger guard. My seven bullets in the magazine section had stopped the German bullet. Another thud behind me to the left, and that guy was gone.

I hit the sand behind the hedgehog, which was about 130 yards from the sea wall, and I observed to my right, Private Robert Dittmar, Fairfield, Connecticut. He tripped over the hedgehog, spun completely around, lying on his back, yelling, "I'm hit! I'm hit! Mom! Mother!" And then he was silent. I looked over to my left and Sergeant Clarence Roberson, of Lynchburg, Virginia, was staggering by me without his helmet, gaping hole in the left side of his forehead. His blond hair was streaked with blood. I was yelling "Get down!" This used to be my nightmare. I guess he couldn't hear me anyway. The noise on that beach was horrendous. All those shells coming in, flame-throwers blowing up with the guys getting on fire. He staggered all the way behind me to the left, knelt down on the sand behind me—in about

three inches of water at that time, 'cause the tide was coming in—and he started praying with his rosary beads. And the machine gun on the bluff fired over my head and cut him in half.

Now there are only two of us alive from my boat team, Charles Conner and myself. We had 85 percent casualties, first 15 minutes.

I was wounded five times, three times on June 6, twice on June 7. Now you might say to yourself, "what kind of an idiot would keep fighting, being wounded?" We were left with options: stay there and die, give up the beach to the Germans, or fight wounded. We decided to fight wounded. I started cursing that machine gun that was on the right flank. I never used foul language, but I had to curse him because he was killing all the guys around me. A fellow named Nicholas Kafkalas was next to me when (he was) cut in half—I saw the machine gunner up there by the glare, the shine on his helmet. So I took my rifle, I was a super-expert, and that rifle fired. I shot at him—no more firing from that machine gun. Later on, when I got up on the bluff, he had his head shot off, armor-piercing ammunition.

I was cursing that pillbox on the right flank and a shell went off in front of me, 88mm. It blew off this cheek (gestures to his left cheek), gave me a hole in the roof of my mouth. I had teeth and gums lying on my tongue. This jaw was shot away, left upper jaw, the cheek was flapping over my ear. And I looked to my left front and Bedford Hoback, of Bedford, Virginia, got hit with the same shell, right in the face. He was dead. Next to him was a fellow named Elmer Wright of Bedford, Virginia; he was already dead. I figured I'd better get off the beach.

....

Baumgarten barely survived. He was wounded five times in 32 hours and was evacuated to England in a hospital ship. Later in life his story influenced development of riveting opening scenes in the movie *Saving Private Ryan*—including the soldier who had a Star of David on the back of his jacket.

OMAHA BEACH

Arthur Seltzer

Communications Specialist attached to

the 29th Infantry Division

Depression-era struggle loomed large in the memory of Arthur Seltzer, a native of Norfolk, Virginia. His father had prospered from the sale of a broom factory, but the family suffered major losses during a run on bank deposits. Lacking funds for college, Seltzer responded to an ad promising education dollars in exchange for a commitment to serve in the Signal Corps if drafted. He was indeed drafted in early 1943, at the age of 18, after his freshman year at the University of Pittsburgh. In the spring of 1944 Seltzer's signal company crossed the Atlantic on the RMS *Queen Elizabeth* without convoy escort because the passenger liner could outrun U-boats.

Baumgarten's battle at Omaha was horrific, but could have been worse if the Allies had not confused enemy leaders about the location of the invasion beaches for D-Day. The landing site was among the best kept secrets of the war. Every possible means of deceiving the Germans with misinformation was employed and rigid secrecy was maintained for the actual plans. Top-secret communications teams, based in England, broadcast bogus information into German-occupied territory. They were effective, but American communications officers faced confusion and chaos themselves during the assault.

There is an island off the coast of England, and it is called the Isle of Wight. And from there, we were sending (bogus) messages in hope that the German army would pick up our messages. We were hoping they would (believe) that the invasion was going to come to Calais, France, and they would move all the

Panzer divisions up there. Naturally, the Germans had probably the best tanks that were available.

I was called to the commanding officer and told I was being transferred down to Portsmouth to be attached to the 29th Division, where I was going to be involved in the D-Day invasion. The equipment that I operated was normally put into a trailer, and the trailer was attached to a half-track. When I went down to Portsmouth, naturally the trailer and my half-track went with me, but that was loaded onto another ship. I was loaded into a (different) ship with the 29th Infantry.

We were on this ship for about, I'd say, five days—it was raining for the last three days down there. Finally, on June 5th we got the O.K., the ships pulled out of Portsmouth and started across the English Channel.

At Omaha Beach *LCI(L)-85* hit an obstacle rigged with a German *Tellermine*. The explosion severely damaged the vessel's bow and disembarkation ramps. German shore batteries, taking advantage of the situation, zeroed-in on the floundering vessel. After sustaining over twenty hits by German shell fire, the vessel backed off from the beach and made it back to the relative safety of the armada in the channel. Despite damage control efforts, *LCI(L)-85* capsized and sank.

M-1 Helmet used by Coast Guardsman Elmer Carmichael aboard *LCI(L)-85*. Carmichael survived the explosion and subsequent German gunfire that fatally damaged the landing craft, but fifteen men were killed and over thirty others were wounded.

Above: *LCI(L)-85* sinking off Omaha Beach, likely seen from the USS *Samuel Chase* (APA-26), which rescued the men aboard *LCI(L)-85*.

Left: Elmer Carmichael, kneeling, tends to a line aboard *LCI(L)-85* as she begins to sink.

The sea was pretty rough because of the weather conditions. When we got about three quarters of the way over, the beginning of June 6th, the sergeant in charge of the landing craft that I was attached to asked me if I would like to sign a dollar bill. He asked all of his men to sign a dollar bill. There's thirty-six men to a landing craft. The landing craft, by the way, are the Higgins boats, which were built in New Orleans by Mr. Higgins himself.

I said sure, I'd be happy to sign the dollar bill. That dollar bill I still have at this time. My dollar bill has thirty-six names on it, which include my own plus the other thirty-five (men assigned to the craft).

At 6:30 or 7:00 in the morning, we went over the side of the ships into the landing crafts. We were in the third and fourth wave that hit Omaha Beach. About 80 percent of the first and second waves were casualties immediately.

Before we went off the landing craft, I had a radio which was attached to my back, which was the communications that I was operating from the landing craft back to the ship. Naturally I still did not have my original equipment, which would not come ashore until the beach was secured.

When we landed we were told to go over the side of the ship rather than out the front—we had a better chance. Naturally, over the side we went. And when I went in—I can't swim, and with all the equipment—down I went. I had two choices, either drown, or take my chances above. I figured I'll take my chances above. There were quite a few of us that couldn't swim, and we helped each other between bullets flying all over, and finally we got to the beach.

You could not dig a foxhole in the sand because, as quick as you dug, that's as quick as it filled up with sand. So we hid behind dead bodies, wounded, wherever we could find a place to hide. The machine guns at the bluff and the big guns on top of the bluff were firing down on the beach constantly.

It was probably late in the afternoon of June 6th when we were finally able to make our way off the beach. And when I was walking along the beach, I happened to bump into that sergeant that was in charge of our landing craft. He told me that he and I were the only two that were able to survive.

Seltzer later was attached to the 7th Armored Division during the drive across France and took part in the Battle of the Bulge. His unit drove all the way to Munich near the war's end and participated in the liberation of the Dachau concentration camp.

Captain Frank H. Walk, attached to the 6th Engineer Special Brigade Group, carried this M1911A as he controlled beach traffic on Omaha.

Above: British Battle Dress Jacket given to Elmer Carmichael at the time of his rescue from the waters of the Channel after the sinking of *LCI(L)-85*.

OMAHA BEACH

Bob Miksa

Staff Sergeant, Platoon Leader, B Company

745th Tank Battalion

When the Japanese attacked Pearl Harbor, Chicagoan Bob Miksa joined the rush of young men to enlist. "Naturally we resented (the assault) and we thought, let's get it over with." Seventeen years old, a new high school graduate, Miksa first tried to join the Marines or paratroopers but their quotas were full, so he signed on with a tank battalion. He recalls months of training in the Louisiana Maneuvers before shipping out for Great Britain. On D-Day he left his landing craft as one of the lead tanks headed for Omaha Beach, where he faced tank traps, mines and the chaos of the early landings.

Amphibious tanks were modified for Operation Overlord with flotation attachments and waterproofing to allow them to move through the water under their own power. Once on the beach, they were expected to offer firepower and a measure of protection to foot soldiers facing a fierce German crossfire from hillside bunkers and trenches. Because of waves and choppy waters, many tanks never made it to dry sand, while a few others managed to fight their way across and off the beach and accomplish their mission.

I landed on D-Day as a driver (of an amphibious tank). If you want to get promoted, that's the place to be—in combat, because one after another, your platoon sergeant gets shot, killed, your lieutenant gets hurt, and you just graduate. Before I knew it I was a platoon leader, staff sergeant, and half the time I didn't have any lieutenants so I ran the platoon as a staff sergeant.

We knew (the invasion plan) a few weeks ahead of time (in England). They showed us an exact replica of Omaha Beach, where we were going to land. We were quarantined. We couldn't go out or nothing because they didn't want the news to be leaked out. So we could see where we had a church steeple we were going to guide on, and the whole thing was just laid out. They had it down perfect.

(During training) we used to go out on nice days and tried the Mae West type of flotation on the tank. A 32-ton tank could float. Then we tried (moving through water) like a SCUBA diver, you had a big exhaust valve and intake valve. We tried everything. When we landed (on D-Day), we had two other platoons from two other battalions. They had the Mae West on their tank. My platoon was going to go up the middle and we had only the SCUBA thing on there; and we had everything waterproofed. If

Miksa's tank (similar to the one shown here) was outfitted with "snorkels" over the exhaust and intake to allow for travel through shallow water.

Charles Bulkley, of the 301st Counter Intelligence Command, collected this fragment of the canvas flotation skirt of a Duplex-Drive Sherman tank knocked out on Omaha Beach.

they dropped us in the water we could go right under it and keep going. After (the air snorkel) was in place it was a good five, six feet tall. The other two battalions with the Mae West, as they got off the LCM (Landing Craft Mechanized), and with the weather being so windy and cold and the waves so high, every one of them turned over. And the guys were all in there, all buttoned up—we lost them all. We lost all ten tanks. Our battalion was the only one that came in because we had a snorkel.

The coxswain that drove this (LCM), he was a young fellow, and as you get to shore there's two sandbars. Hit the first sandbar, you've got to go over that one, and when you hit the second sandbar he's supposed to open up the door, the gate, and you pull out with your tank. Well, coming in, this guy was getting so much fire, he hit the first bar and he stopped, he didn't want to go any further. He opened up the door and there I am, I had my tank going, I had no choice but to pull out. I must have gone into twelve to fifteen feet of water, covered the whole tank practically except the snorkel. I buttoned up and all I could see was out my periscope, straight ahead. I must have gone about 30, 40 yards then I hit dry land, and we finally pulled out of the water. We pulled right in front of the big cliff that you see on Omaha.

It was cold and damp and dark. H-Hour was about 6:30 and we were supposed to land about an hour and a half after H-Hour. The beach master had called back that the beach was so littered with bodies and everything, he said, "Hold up, you guys can't do

A Duplex-Drive Sherman (on the left) ashore in Southern France. Capable of "swimming" in deep water, few Duplex-Drive tanks made it ashore at Omaha Beach. Of the 32 launched by the 741st Tank Battalion, only 5 made it ashore.

nothing here because you would just be running over your own guys." There were half-tracks there and all kinds of equipment was scattered over the beach. So we held back about twenty minutes before we could land.

It was kind of misty, you could just hear the boats, the battleships firing away and a little Air Corps—very few Air Corps were out because of the weather. It was a cloudy day, visibility was bad.

I was the first tank. I was driving for the platoon leader, Lieutenant Davis. I was the first tank out; the other fellows were right behind us. I couldn't see anything because the water was splashing, the periscope was clouded over with water. Finally when I got up on the shore I could see the big cliff in front.

The beach was getting smaller because the tide was coming in already at that time. All along the shore, the guys that were wounded, they were (bunched) all up against the hill so that the Germans wouldn't be able to fire on them. And we couldn't get too close because we were exposed. We were getting a lot of small-arms fire, nothing big, we were lucky—we didn't get hit with an 88 or anything, but a lot of small-arms fire. (It sounded) just like raindrops on the roof, you know—pink, pink.

We eventually moved up until we found a place where we could crawl up, drive up and get out on the road that goes on top of the cliff. The guy from the 1st Division had a bulldozer and he worked back and forth, back and forth, built up enough dirt so we could get up on this road and get on top of the cliff, and we took our first objective. We got there about 4:30 in the afternoon.

(On Omaha Beach) there wasn't much you could do, just wait and pray. See what's going to happen, waiting for orders. We had one tank commander, he stuck his head out and a sniper got him. He was the first guy in our outfit that got killed, Charlie Donoghue. There were a lot of snipers.

When I was sitting on the beach, I could unbutton (open the tank hatch) as long as I wasn't getting any fire. I unbuttoned and

I was looking. You could see guys laying there—I mean bodies, heads blown off, arms off. I thought to myself: "Boy these mothers are going to get a card, a letter, from the government saying that your son got killed on Omaha Beach, but if you would see what he looks like now, you wouldn't be too happy." We had a lot like that.

In the race across France, Bob Miksa was wounded at Mortain. After a quick recovery he fought in the Battle of the Bulge and took part in the liberation of a Nazi concentration camp at Nordhausen. Miksa encountered a Russian army unit near the end of the war in Czechoslovakia and was unimpressed, recalling they "looked like bums … no discipline and a kind of cocky attitude."

Above: Nearly an hour before H-Hour, Companies B and C of the 741st Tank Battalion launched 32 Sherman tanks equipped with Duplex Drive (DD) to enable movement in the water. However, rough seas sank 27 tanks after launch from the LCTs; three were unable to launch at all. Those were the first weather-related casualties suffered in the assault. As a result, the 743rd and 745th Tank Battalions decided to land their tanks directly on the beach. Lieutenant John M. Bruck, a member of Headquarters in the 741st Tank Battalion, received this Top Secret *Bigot Neptune Field Order No. 1* booklet. Dated May 21, 1944, it held maps and documented intelligence for the Normandy invasion.

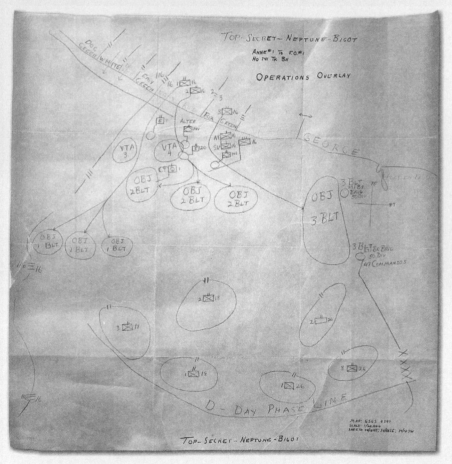

Above: The Top Secret Neptune map of Omaha Beach. Marked "Bigot," the British designation for Top Secret. This map was used by members of the 741st Tank Battalion.

OMAHA BEACH

Lucien Laborde

Captain, Regimental Adjutant, 115th Infantry Regiment

29th Infantry Division

Lucien Laborde was the son of a small-town school principal in Louisiana. He learned military leadership in the Louisiana State University ROTC program but was far removed from war preparations immediately after college. Laborde was preparing flood control surveys for the federal government in Missouri and Arkansas when he was drafted in early 1942 and sent to Army Intelligence School. Before long, he was crossing the icy Atlantic en route to Great Britain. The young intelligence officer was in an ill-fated large convoy that was attacked by German U-boats. Laborde's troopship survived, but the submarines sank the Army transport USAT *Dorchester*, which became famous when four Army chaplains aboard gave up their life preservers to save other frightened soldiers as the ship went down.

Staff officers in the Allied invasion units had the heavy responsibility of analyzing the decrypts of secret intelligence reports. On a daily basis, they received reports on advances made by General Rommel in building up the defenses in Normandy. They studied German troop movements, changes of command and effects of battle stress. They understood that their decisions and performance helped determine the outcome of the war, impacting whether foot soldiers would live or perish.

I was regimental adjutant when we found out that we would be a part of the invasion. The division set up a war room, completely patrolled (and surrounded by) concertina wire. You had to have double codenames to get in, and inside was the whole layout of what we were going to do. We had mark-ups of Omaha Beach, the hill above it, all the little ravines and all the known enemy emplacements. Some of us had the opportunity to fly the beach—I don't know if you remember a twin-fuselage plane, a

fighter plane called "The Mosquito." (Note: the British-made Mosquito, a fast, versatile aircraft, served well in a wide range of reconnaissance and combat missions.) Most of the officers of rank of captain or better had an opportunity to fly that area, make a swipe, get a feel for what we were going to have to do.

Within two hours after that decision (by General Eisenhower to go) we heard the planes going over with the paratroopers. And all through the night we heard planes that were supposed to drop 500-pound bombs on the beach for the infantry, because we knew the (enemy) machine-gun fire was solid, and we were going to have these holes to work through. But they dropped the bombs about two miles inland, so we didn't have a single hole on that beach.

Above: Laborde (standing left) aboard an LCI with fellow 115th Infantry Regiment soldiers. This photo was taken by a crewmember aboard the LCI and sent to Laborde's brother

Left: Carried by his great-great-grandfather in the Civil War and then his great-grandfather in World War I, this Confederate bill was carried by Laborde throughout his service in Europe.

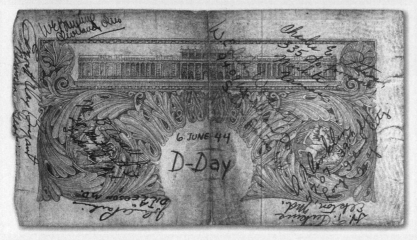

Left: This British one pound note was signed by the men on Laborde's landing craft on June 6.

My boat hit an underwater obstacle, one of those shark-looking things, about 50 yards offshore, so we had to disembark there. We went over the front and worked in. For the first time, we saw these little things popping up in the water—we didn't know what they were, but learned later they were mortar shells, some artillery shells. And just as I got to the beach, I looked back and our boat was hit, badly hit, and I thought that was it for these navy boys.

One of them (landing craft crew members) had taken pictures of a bunch of us as we were crossing in the daylight—had taken pictures of some, had taken some addresses of home people and so forth. Six months later, my brother—one of my older brothers who was an attorney in Marksville, Louisiana, and who had polio as a child and was badly crippled, he always regretted that he wasn't with us—he received a set of pictures from a navy man in a hospital in North Carolina. I have those pictures.

We were supposed to land on Easy Green. I think it was right at a little place called Les Moulins if you're familiar with it. But the naval man in charge signaled us to move further toward the

1st Division, which was further east. So we landed right next to the 1st Division and there was a little ravine in front of us, and some engineers who'd landed ahead of us. We didn't land until 9:30 in the morning, and some of the engineers who'd gone in at 7:30 were working their way, taking the mines out of the ravine.

Most of us were up on top of that ridge, about a 90-foot cliff, by about two o'clock that afternoon. Everybody had spent some time on their belly, crawling in the beach, and it was a marshy area too. I had to stay alongside of Colonel Slappey (Eugene N.), who was a regimental commander—I was his adjutant. I went with him to find General Huebner (Clarence R.), who was 1st Division commander. On the beach, under fire, they had a little conference and decided what they had to do. The 116th was the first to land on Omaha Beach and they were decimated. Their objectives were well known by all units, but they just couldn't accomplish that. It was decided between Huebner and Slappey that the 115th Regiment would take on the mission of the 116th, so we had to turn back toward Vierville and try to clean that area out, starting at Saint-Laurent.

One battalion was given an assignment near the beach, near the top of the cliff, that was the 2nd Battalion, and the 3rd Battalion was right there at Saint-Laurent, south of the 1st. By nightfall, the commander of the 1st Battalion was killed. By the second day, the commander of the 3rd Battalion was removed for what was termed "combat exhaustion" in those days. On the night of D+2, the 2nd Battalion moved into a field surrounded by hedgerows after making

quite a gain for that day—moved into a field, exhausted, three nights with no sleep, three nights with no food, just flopped. The Germans were up ahead and just waited for them to come, eliminated over half of that battalion right there, killing the battalion commander.

The commanding general of the division found out about it. He came down—I had been sent down to help the 3rd Battalion, because the commander had been removed. So I was sent from regimental staff to battalion, to assist the executive officer who had been made commander. The next morning early, General Gerhardt (Charles H.), the commander of the (29th) division, drove up in a jeep, right there to the front line, and he knew me. He said, "Where's Slappey?" I said, "I don't know sir, I haven't seen him since 9 o'clock this morning," or something like that. He said, "Does anybody know where the regimental headquarters is?" Nobody did. He relieved Slappey just like that, so by the end of the second day, we had lost three battalion commanders and our regimental commander. It was a new ballgame from then on.

Things worked the way they normally do in combat. When one drops out, one just below takes over, and it would just keep moving up. So if you stay alive, you can get to be division commander after a while, if the war lasts long enough.

⋯⋯⋯⋯⋯⋯⋯⋯⋯⋯⋯⋯⋯⋯⋯⋯

Laborde's service after D-Day included fighting in the Normandy hedgerows, the taking of Saint-Lô, the Battle of the Bulge and the crossing of the Rhine.

Elements of the 116th Infantry Regiment were brought ashore by Coast Guard *LCI(L)-94*. This photograph, taken by crewmember Charles Jarreau, shows one of the numerous beach obstacles Allied forces faced: a *Tellermine* fixed to a wooden pole.

In another shot taken by Charles Jarreau from the landing craft, one can see the lethal and varied beach obstacles placed by German forces along the Normandy beaches.

OMAHA BEACH

George Morgan

US Navy, Naval Combat Demolition Unit

Baseball commanded the attention of many young Americans during the 1930s and George Morgan, a native of Lyndhurst, New Jersey, was no exception. After Morgan's father lost his job on Wall Street, Morgan delivered newspapers and groceries to help support his family—and picked up change retrieving foul balls for a semi-pro baseball team. "The team could only afford to buy a couple of baseballs at a time," he recalled. Morgan gained skills as a pitcher and could have played professional ball if the war had not intervened. His enlistment in the US Navy was activated before he could sign on with a Brooklyn Dodgers farm team. Morgan was among sailors selected for training to handle explosives and become a member of a demolition team assigned to blow up beach obstacles.

Above: George Morgan, at home after the war.

Rommel's array of underwater obstacles off the beaches became a nightmare for Allied planners in the weeks and months before D-Day. Many hundreds of these obstacles—hedgehogs and poles—were tipped with mines and would be submerged at high tide, or even half-tide, and could impale or blow up landing craft coming ashore, wiping out the soldiers inside. Rommel thought his beach obstacles were equal to a battalion of German troops in defensive impact. The Allies knew they had to clear a path through so that landing craft could make it to shore. To do this, numerous teams of engineers and sailors would follow the first waves onto Omaha Beach and, while waters were still at low tide, blow up the mines and other obstacles. On D-Day, these teams were stymied by bad weather, timing and German sharpshooters who targeted them specifically. Nonetheless these demolition teams were critical to the invasion. Many lost their lives as new waves of landing craft faced bottlenecks amid the fierce German crossfire.

Examples of obstacles along the beach at Arromanches-les-Bains (Gold Beach) laid by German forces to deter Allied landings along the Normandy coast. Mixed engineering units like Morgan's were responsible for clearing these obstacles.

When the Normandy invasion went off, the fellows (assigned to beach demolition tasks) were the NCDU, Naval Combat Demolition Units. They were five-man teams with an officer, usually an ensign, in charge. And these teams were to take care of the obstacles that were on the beach.

Well, what happened at Omaha was that because of the water coming across the Channel and when they got to Normandy—it was so bad, so rough—they lost practically all their explosives. They had nothing to work with. Plus one big mistake they made as far as the invasion was concerned is that these NCDUs should have gone in before the invasion rather than with the invasion—because a lot of the GIs were hiding behind the stuff that we're supposed to blow up.

So even if we had our explosives, we couldn't blow it up because these guys were hiding there, and they didn't want to go any further because of what was happening. So they couldn't get those obstacles out of the way to make the opening that the mechanized units needed to get up to and beyond the dune line. That's what screwed up Omaha real bad, the mechanized stuff couldn't get through because the obstacles hadn't been blown up. That was the real snafu, and there probably were others too.

I saw the Rangers go up the cliff (at Pointe du Hoc). I could see them trying to get up there and I said, "My God, I'm glad I'm not trying to do that."

I didn't know if I was going to see the sunset that day. I was so scared, I pissed my pants, and I was: "What in the world am I doing here?" It was awful. The noise—the noise was terrible. I equated it to a thunderstorm, and lightning cracks right above your house. The crack and then the thunder, that's what it was like continuously, hour after hour after hour. You can't get away from it; it's just terrible, awful.

Two things I remember very clearly. One is (a man), I think he was a Canadian—I'm not sure, but I think it was a Canadian uniform—he had a hole blown through him. You could put a bowling ball through it. And there was another fellow, I saw his arm get shot off.

Evidently he didn't realize what had happened because when his arm was shot off and his rifle was laying there, he saw his rifle and he tried to pick it up with his right arm—but he didn't have a right arm.

George Morgan was pulled out of Europe following the Normandy invasion. He returned to the States for more training and later took part in underwater demolition missions during the Pacific island-hopping campaign.

Army and navy personnel await orders during maneuvers in England prior to D-Day. Navy demolitions experts aided army personnel in clearing obstacles on the beaches.

Above: American GIs aboard a US Coast Guard
assault transport wait for the landing craft which
will ferry them to the landing beaches.

Left: Kenneth Kassel, part of the 299th Engineer
Combat Battalion, working with an NCDU,
lost his helmet while moving to another landing
craft. A soldier remaining aboard noticed Kassel's
loss, gave him his own helmet, and said, "You
might need this." After placing demolition
charges and taking cover, a buddy asked Kassel if
he was alright. Kassel was unknowingly bloody
from a bullet that hit his helmet and deflected,
throwing shrapnel into Kassel's head. After a
doctor removed the shrapnel, Kassel's company
commander told him: "Don't let anybody ever
take that [helmet] away from you."

OMAHA BEACH

Bernard Friedenberg

Staff Sergeant, Medic, 16th Infantry Regiment

1st Infantry Division

The son of a floor-covering merchant, Bernard Friedenberg was born in Philadelphia and grew up in Atlantic City. He couldn't wait to get into the fight after Pearl Harbor but enlistment didn't come easily. "They turned me down several times; I kept going back," he said. "They told me I was a pain in the ass. I fought harder to get into the army than most men who wanted to stay out." He took part in landings in North Africa and Sicily before the Normandy invasion, always driven to be the first off the landing ramp.

When wounded men fell on D-Day, other men ran to aid them. On Omaha Beach, as in all wars, the medic played a heroic and sacrificial role. The swirl of violence and chorus of pleas for help from the wounded and dying tested the physical and psychic limits of one medic who was determined to get into the fight.

I was good with the first aid. I saved a lot of lives. I know that. I wanted to lead my men in, and I did.

They were supposed to let us off the landing craft in waist-deep water. But when I stepped off the ramp—I guess I was the first one off the ramp—(it was) over my head. And I was carrying a load because the only equipment we could have was what we could carry, for an indefinite period of time. It was imperative that we got it all in, and I was loaded up heavily.

It was hairy. You had to go in. But I didn't get far because as soon as I stepped off there was guys who were wounded. And

I went from one to another to another and all around me men were hollering. There were a lot of casualties, a lot of mortalities.

I had to ignore the fact that I was in a minefield. You couldn't tell where—just luck that I didn't step on any mines. And they were plentiful.

I just saw a casualty and I went to them. I did my thing and dressed their wounds and went to the next one. All the time, I didn't know where I was. I was just going from one wounded man to another. No direction. God only knows (how many men he treated on D-Day), and God's not talking (laughs.) I was there to patch up the wounded, and that's what I did. And then my main job was after that to move to cover; and then my job was

116th Infantry Regiment medical base hospital in England before D-Day. Friedenberg's fellow medic, Winston Morris, is far left, back row.

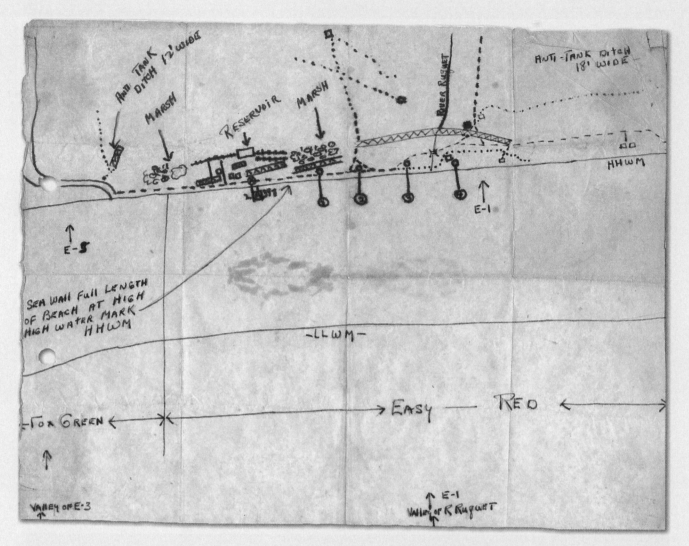

Above: Hand-drawn map of Easy Red sector of Omaha Beach, the landing
zone for the 16th Infantry Regiment.

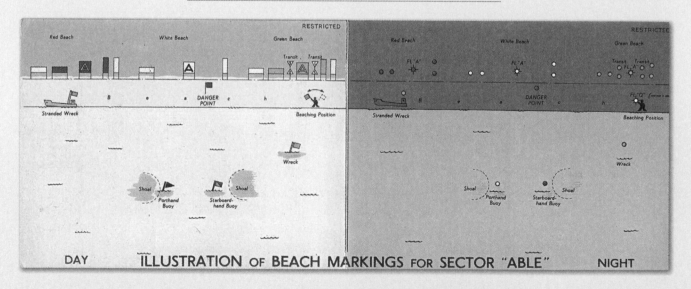

Above: This map illustrates beach markings for Omaha Beach sector "Able" during both
daylight and nighttime. Markings were established quickly in order to facilitate further landings.

Winston Morris at the Red Cross facilities in Cornwall, England, wearing his M1938 Parsons jacket, pictured right. He wore this jacket when he landed, alongside Bernard Friedenberg, with the early assault waves on Omaha Beach. The jacket bears stains, believed to be blood stains from wounded men on the beach.

evacuation. I was in charge of the litter bearers. I would take the wounded men back to where they could get more attention.

You're thrown into someplace where men are getting killed and crippled at one time, and your job was to help them. I did my job, I was really a dedicated soldier, but I wanted to fight. I was an angry Jew. After I saw the concentration camps (later), I got mad all over again. Not that I was a religious man; I was average, I guess, as far as religious faith goes. But I knew what I was, and I knew what I wanted to do. I wanted to fight back. I wanted to fight.

Friedenberg continued to tend the wounded in combat zones as Allied forces pushed into Germany, including the Battle of the Bulge and street fighting in Aachen. Wounded twice by shell fragments, he became adept at playing dead when the enemy was near. He pulled occupation duty after Germany's defeat.

William Dabney

Corporal, Barrage Balloon Crew Chief

320th Very Low Altitude Barrage Balloon Battalion

William Dabney never enjoyed school – "my sisters would have to grab me under each arm and sort of take me" – so he dropped out of high school in 1942 to enlist in the army, following his brothers into wartime service. As an African-American he faced rigid racial segregation during training, seldom seeing a white officer. In England, he remembers kind treatment by civilians. Dabney learned how to operate barrage balloons that would rise into the sky carrying explosives that could ensnare or destroy strafing enemy planes. He landed on Omaha Beach on the night of D-Day, following waves of infantry and hauling balloons that would protect artillery units.

In addition to bombarding shore installations and providing anti-aircraft defense of the invasion fleet, the USS *Augusta* acted as General Omar Bradley's headquarters ship until June 10.

Many critical roles in the Allied invasion are mostly invisible in D-Day narratives. Minorities and women contributed in medical wards, aboard ships and on loading docks and in combat settings. Among notable groups serving was the barrage balloon battalion that went ashore at Omaha Beach, a segregated unit of African-American soldiers.

We came over from England on a ship called an LST (Landing Ship, Tank); it was a large ship that carried a lot of troops. From the LST you would climb down the rope and get on the landing barge. The landing barge carried us to the beach with about 55, 65 soldiers. Had a 50-caliber machine gun on the back. You had to get off, there wasn't any turning back. The landing barge ran as far as it could on the water and the door would fall. You'd come out of the water with your rifle over your head and your pack—sometimes the water would be up to your waist—and hit the beach, hit the sand. Once it unloaded that load of soldiers, it would turn around and go right back and bring in another group just as fast.

The tide came in on us while we came in; it must have been low tide, because while we were on the beach the tide came in and we had to raise our heads up out of the water just to get air because we couldn't move for a little while. We were pinned down on the beach. We couldn't move on account of the strafing

and whatnot, and the guns were firing both ways. The ships were firing from the Channel and the German guns were firing from up in the hill—the night was just like day with the firing. We were right up under all the firing.

There was quite a lot of debris, including bodies and body parts, on the beach. The truck—what we call a six-by-six truck—would go around and throw the dead up into the truck. They would pull off the dog tag and throw them up in the truck. I imagine with so many they had to have been burying them in a mound, a big grave. The dog tag would tell who they were, you see.

I saw someone get blown up by mines. They had minesweepers in front of you. That's why you couldn't just rush in.

I had my (barrage balloon) inflated on the LST. It was strapped to me and I brought it off the LST hooked to me, down to the landing barge. I missed (lost) it when I got to the beach—a plane had to hit it, or gunfire, the planes were strafing over and over. The Germans had a plane that would shoot coming down and when it went up. The main purpose of the balloon was to stop the strafing and protect the (American) anti-aircraft, the big guns.

Soldiers of the 320th Very Low Altitude Barrage Balloon Battalion prepare to deploy a balloon on Omaha Beach.

The balloon was inflated—I would say it had a 75-pound pull—and I was a little bit heavier than that. I weighed about 175 pounds and I had a pack on that took care of some of the weight, so it didn't have enough pull to jack me up in the air. It couldn't carry me off.

When we got to shore the first thing we did was dig in. Dig in, in the sand so we would be protected from the strafing. The big guns wouldn't hit us, that was over the top of us, but the strafing would. We had to dig in and wait until the minesweepers took care of the mines, so we could move on. We were pinned down on the beach for a while. At one point we thought we might get pushed back into the Channel because the fire was so heavy up in the mountains from the German side. There was a lot of firing going on.

....

Dabney was asked what went through his mind onboard the LST, on D-Day, as he prepared to climb down into the landing barge.

You were nervous, I guess, in a way. You were scared, but also you were brave. You're going to make it or you're not going to make it. What you had on your mind is: "I'm going to have to try to make it. I'm going to try to save myself. I'm going to have to try (to lead) these guys I've got with me, my crew." I was younger than most of my crew, so that was on my mind. I had to look out for these guys.

....

Dabney moved inland with invasion forces, continuing his work in support of artillery units. He recalled combat at Saint-Lô and in other small communities and interactions with terrified French civilians as they came out of hiding.

Above: The German anti-personnel S-Mine 35 was one of the most feared weapons in the German arsenal. When triggered, a canister filled with 6½ ounces of TNT and 350 steel balls, was projected out of the ground and exploded at crotch height. Inflicting unspeakable wounds, GIs referred to this terror as the "Bouncing Betty."

Left: The German *Glasmine* 43 was made with a minimum of metal parts in order to fool Allied mine detectors. Upon detonation, the glass shards imbedded in its victims were impossible to detect by X-ray.

John Raaen

Captain, Commanding Officer, Headquarters Company

5th Ranger Battalion,

later to support 2nd Rangers at Pointe du Hoc

As Headquarters Company Commander with the 5th Ranger Battalion on D-Day, John Raaen played a key role at Omaha Beach and beyond. His after-action report from Normandy became important to the American D-Day narrative. Born at Fort Benning in Georgia and raised on military bases, Raaen is the son of an Army infantry officer. He began reading Infantry School texts as a grade school student, and graduated from the United States Military Academy. Raaen trained as a combat engineer and secured a place with the Rangers on that basis— his knowledge of explosives was highly valued—but his first love was the infantry. On D-Day Raaen and many fellow rangers launched from the British LSI (Landing Ship Infantry) HMS *Prince Baudouin*.

Above: Raaen in Toul, France, after the invasion.

Long before support units like barrage balloon crews dug in, the 5th Rangers joined other infantry units in the tumultuous assault at Omaha and recorded a memorable encounter with a brigadier general. In following days they fought their way inland in support of 2nd Rangers who had scaled nearby cliffs at Pointe du Hoc to disable German big guns threatening Allied forces at both Omaha and Utah beaches.

We were quite lucky in the Ranger battalions. We were to go to the coast in LCAs, Landing Craft Assault, a great deal like an LCPR (Landing Craft Personnel Ramp) but a hair smaller. It was armored a little bit more, had a lower free-board, and it had muffled Rolls-Royce engines. It was the assault boat of choice for the commandos.

We were lowered away into a sea that was running perhaps three to five feet. It was rough. Of course, as you touched the water, the boats were thrown right and left, up and down, and it was more than a short time before we were able to finally get clear of the *Baudouin*. As we formed in our column to move toward the beach, we heard the captain of the *Baudouin* on his bullhorn saying, "God bless you, Rangers, and good luck."

We formed up and moved toward the coast. By then we probably could see the coast, though it might have been as much as ten miles away. Suddenly we heard a tremendous explosion. We jumped up and looked over the side. At that point the British petty officer said, "Sirs, that is the Battleship *Texas* (BB-35), opening the barrage on the Normandy coast." Sure enough, they opened and every warship out there began firing and the din was tremendous.

Above: Raaen (in front of the small signal mast) and fellow Rangers aboard a British LCA (Landing Craft Assault) en route to their British transport to France, the HMS *Prince Baudouin*.

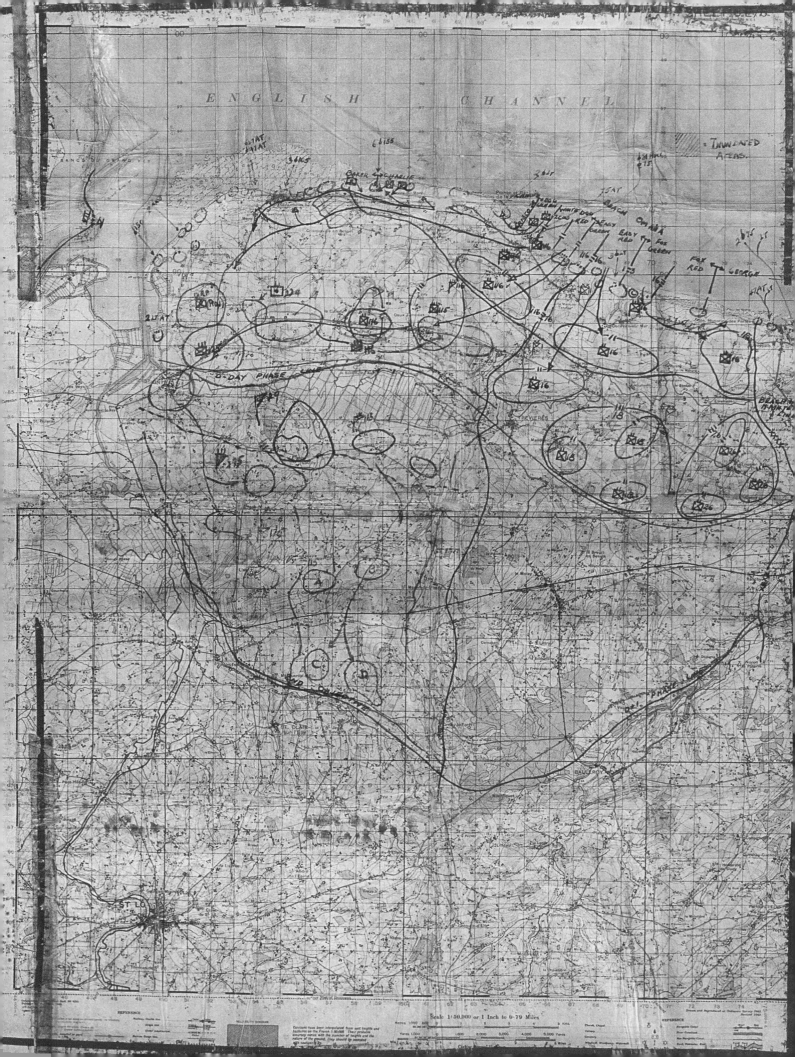

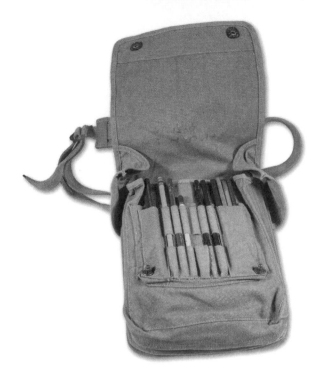

Above: Maps enable individuals to have a better picture of the surrounding terrain and a place to record real time information on units and fortifications. Captain Frank H. Walk carried this map case on Omaha Beach while he worked to get men and materiel moving inland.

You could hear the shells rushing through the air, and a short time later you could begin to see flashes on what until this point had been a not-very-well-defined series of hills. The seas were running heavy; it was all bouncy. A lot of the men were seasick.

(Recalling the landing at Omaha), the first thing is, there's a lot of smoke, there's a lot of noise. There is artillery bursting around. I was never conscious of mortars coming in. I was conscious of a tremendous amount of small-arms fire coming from our right—nothing from straight ahead, and nothing from the left. All of it was just pouring in from the right-hand side, and most of that turned out to be WN70, one of their small redoubts specifically designed to provide enfilade fire on the beach. It also provided enfilade fire on the Omaha Dog Green exit at D1. So there's lots of smoke, lots of smells, lots of blood around. Any water you were near usually had puddles or pools of blood in it. The sound was deafening—artillery when it's detonating is almost as deafening as anything you can have.

We were getting the fragmenting shells as the (German) artillery engaged the boats. The artillery was not shooting at people on the beach because the big prizes were the boats coming in. With one shell you could kill, or at least disable, 250 men on an LCI (Landing Craft Infantry). With just a plain little ol' landing craft, personnel landing craft, you got 35 people with one shot, so they were concentrating on targets that were worthwhile. So once you got onto the beach, you had only that small arms torrent to worry about.

Left: Second Lieutenant Charles Arnett, I Company, 116th Infantry Regiment, landed on June 6, using this map for guidance as his company fought inland.

As we came in, there was an LCI to our right flank that I saw hit by an artillery shell. It apparently hit the flame-thrower tanks of a flame-thrower man at the top of the gangway on the starboard side. The jellied gasoline was spread from one end of the LCI to the other and became a raging inferno in a fraction of a second. It was one of the most awful things that I have ever seen. Very few men were able to survive that. Those that did jumped off into the water and killed the burning gasoline, of course, by nearly drowning. Most men coming in our LCIs were too heavily laden to swim. It was a true holocaust.

Raaen turns to discussing his own landing.
We were lucky because Colonel Schneider (Lieutenant Colonel Max, commanding Ranger Force C) had convinced the British to bring us in on Dog Red beach, and on Dog Red we had fourteen breakwaters, and those breakwaters were about four and a half feet high, made of stone piled up on wooden frames. They performed the duty of, you might say, fort walls for us.

We would (also) have the sea wall on one side and the retards on the other two sides. So once you got up to the retards—they extended about 25 yards from the sea wall, and were about 25 yards apart—you found yourself in a little 25 by 25 fort, and you could stay there all day if they didn't attack, or didn't bring in mortars to reach you. Most inland artillery could not hit the beach because the bluffs were quite high, fairly steep, fairly close to the water, and if shells cleared the bluff they probably would be out in the water.

(As Raaen took cover on the beach) far too many were screaming, "Medic! Medic!" A number were trying to crawl to keep ahead of the tide. The tide was coming up one yard on the beach every minute, so you might fall ten yards beyond the water, and in ten minutes you'd be drowned because that's how fast the water was coming in. The fools were taking shelter behind boat debris because the boat debris was getting shelled and would soon disappear. And they were hiding behind (other) obstacles, those big telephone poles—Rommel's asparagus—they would hide behind that. They would hide behind tetrahedrons, but those only covered fifteen or twenty percent of their bodies, so that was ridiculous. A lot of people were just crawling to get to the safety of breakwaters or the sea wall.

I lost one man, my runner, who was directly behind me. He paused when he saw the bullets hitting the water, and resumed just in time for the next burst. He got a flesh wound in his thighs.

I couldn't get to the sea wall because the 29th Division men, mostly dead, were piled up like cordwood—two, three, four deep. These looked like football pileups at the base of the sea wall. I checked on my men and the noncoms were very good. I said, "Anybody hit?" and I got a report immediately. I had them form their teams, because they came in as teams. As soon as that was done, I went around the base of the sea wall into the next bay where Sullivan was, and we discussed the situation. I said, "I'll go report to (Colonel) Schneider." He says, "No, you stay here and worry about any counter-attack that comes down that bluff,

and I will go and check with Schneider." So we put up a call for Schneider, and within a minute the word came back and he turned out to be three bays from us, and Sullivan went over, checked in. Sullivan came back probably no more than three minutes later, gave me the order that I was to follow—move over three bays, there would be a hole blown in the wire. I was to follow the C Company machine-gun section that was in front of me.

As I was moving out, that was when a couple of guys said, "Hey, captain, look at that crazy guy down the beach there." I looked down beyond the sea wall and there was this man waving his cigar, walking up and down the beach right behind the dunes and yelling at people. We had quite a little discussion, probably 30, 40 seconds worth of it, and decided it was either, one, a stupid reporter who had a concussion and didn't know what he was doing, or he was a very high-ranking officer who was acting stupidly.

So when he came around—he walked his way around to my end of the sea wall/retard, I said, "I better go find out what he is, who he is." And as I approached him I could see the star. (The man was Brigadier General Norman Cota, second in command of the 29th Division.) Don't remember if it was on his collar or on his shoulder. I saluted him and reported to him, and that was when he asked me if I was Jack Raaen's son, and I said, "Yes sir."

"What's the situation here?" "Sir, the 5th Ranger Battalion has landed intact over a 200-yard front." And he said, "Where's your battalion commander?" I said, "Right over there, three bays, I'll take you to him." He said, "You will not. You will stay with your men." And I said, "Yes sir." (Laughs.)

At that point, he started off, but he came back. He turned

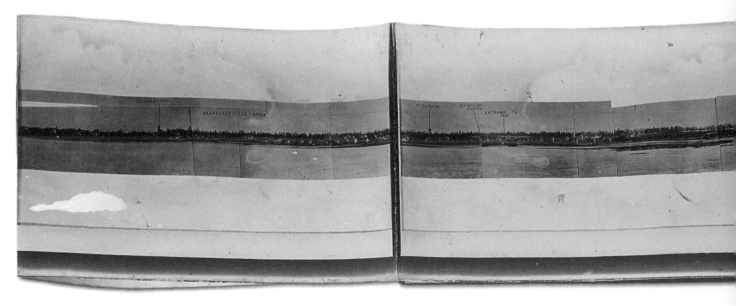

around, and of course every eye was still on him, and he said, "You men are Rangers, I know you won't let me down," and then he was off to see Schneider. And at least three or four times, he stopped with different groups of Rangers and gave them something that gradually evolved into, "Rangers, lead the way." "You men are Rangers, you got to lead the way." "Colonel Schneider, we got to get off this goddammed beach, and you Rangers are going to lead the way." That type of thing. So it (Cota's directive) has many, many versions, all of which are probably correct.

Well, I just follow the orders, "Move to the left, three bays, watch C Company go by, and when their machine-gun section is there, follow him up the hill." That's exactly what we did. The attitude (of Rangers) was, "Let's get on with the job. We trained for it, we're fed up with being shot at, let's do some shooting." We just went up the straight side, and when the path switched back, there was a little hollow there and a dead German, and we just continued on up the hill, sidestepping. The switchback was about halfway up the bluff itself. We didn't take any fire at all going up the bluff.

By the time we got through the (defense) wire we really didn't have to worry, although I admit that I didn't like the men being on this pathway, which was fairly well raised, so I said, "Move over here into a hollow." I knew the hollow could be booby-trapped but I thought it was safer to go into there being careful. It made sure we didn't get hit by small arms for just standing up there. I remember getting up to six stone steps. The column stopped ahead of me, and I sat down at the top step and looked back at the beach.

The boats were coming in, the men were running across the beach to get to the sea wall. There were a lot of troops behind us

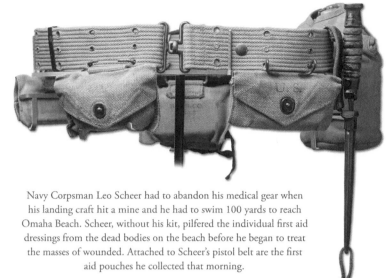

Navy Corpsman Leo Scheer had to abandon his medical gear when his landing craft hit a mine and he had to swim 100 yards to reach Omaha Beach. Scheer, without his kit, pilfered the individual first aid dressings from the dead bodies on the beach before he began to treat the masses of wounded. Attached to Scheer's pistol belt are the first aid pouches he collected that morning.

that were using the four holes that we had blown in the wire—a lot of people coming through those, because nobody wanted to stay on that beach and die. I mean, you had navy people who were just grabbing the weapons of casualties and following right behind us.

Over the next two days, the 5th Rangers fought in a series of hedgerow and roadside skirmishes as they made their way toward a rendezvous with 2nd Rangers at Pointe du Hoc on June 8.

Beyond the invasion, Raaen helped direct reconnaissance patrols and other troop movements during the campaign across Europe. He suffered a broken leg and lacerated face when his jeep came under German artillery fire during the Battle of the Bulge. After recovering from his wounds, he served in ordnance instruction and command positions.

As 5th Rangers topped the bluffs at Omaha Beach and began their drive toward Pointe du Hoc, artillery units were moving ashore at Omaha, providing desperately needed firepower for the battered 29th Infantry Division. The artillerymen were stunned at the scene of destruction at the shore. In the coming hours and days, they had to adjust to fast-changing battlefield conditions and to vexing challenges posed by Normandy's ancient hedgerows.

On the trip across the English Channel, Motor Machinist's Mate Charles E. Jarreau, USCG, aboard LCI-94, saw men of the 116th Infantry Regiment studying these panoramic photos of Omaha Beach. Jarreau picked up the photos after the assaulting troops left them behind.

Frank Denius

C Battery, 230th Field Artillery Battalion,

30th Infantry Division

As talk of the United States entering World War II escalated in the 1930s, Frank Denius lived with his mother and other relatives in the east Texas town of Athens, where his grandfather operated a general store. He was sent off to a military institute at the age of 13 and briefly attended the Citadel, the Military College of South Carolina. He was called to active duty in 1943. Trained as a forward observer for artillery, he shipped out to Great Britain on a converted luxury liner carrying 11,000 troops. Denius received additional Ranger training in England, learning about infantry tactics and the Normandy terrain, as well as "a lot about stamina" during countless marches. His account of landing in the days after the invasion provides insights into the importance of artillery in the Battle for Normandy.

They lost a lot of (soldiers) landing at Omaha Beach, and they lost their artillery. At the time this was occurring, we were on reserve and our battalion was notified that we were to immediately prepare for embarkation to France. We were rushed to the ships in the Channel on the day of June 6, although time and days didn't mean much at that time, quite frankly—we landed as soon as we could.

Those of you who have seen the (American) cemetery at Omaha Beach, if you would go about 50 to 100 yards west of the cemetery, you would see—looking down that cliff—a big draw, and that's the area that I came up along with my radio sergeant and the other members of the 30th Infantry Division. That's our first entry onto the beach. What we saw was a tremendous number of casualties on the beach, and medics attending to those. There were a lot of ships that were

sunk, and you could see what was still left of those that were still above the water level.

We actually came in on a Landing Craft Infantry (LCI); that's the boat where the ramp goes down and you come down the front and you wade through the water onto the beach. You could hear all kinds of artillery fire. There were bombers going over, and there was a lot of noise, and your primary objective was to get up that cliff, crawl up that cliff, and then as soon as you got up the cliff, to organize. And then we were directed by our officers to move into the area to start supporting the 29th Division.

Now remember that the artillery is being landed after we were

Above: The M2A1 105mm Howitzer was one of the most destructive weapons of the war. Capable of firing high-explosive shells at targets miles away, it was used to soften defenses or break up enemy attacks.

because they had to bring it in on different types of ships, the actual field artillery—105mm Howitzers, and all the trucks of ammunition. So it wasn't like you landed and it all started happening. There was a lot of logistics and support. Effort had to be made by everyone to land your artillery, then get it onto the top of the cliffs, and then to begin to take positions where you could start helping the 29th Infantry Division. Everything was somewhat hectic, but at the same time you have to give credit to the discipline of all of the guys, all the soldiers. While it was chaotic to some, it was the best organization we could manage at the time under direct artillery fire and machine-gun fire—and not knowing exactly where the Germans were.

In a forward observer party, there's usually an officer and a sergeant—I wasn't that rank at the time—and a radio operator. There was A, B and C batteries (of the 230th) and we were C Battery. We were all directed to report as quickly as we could to the appropriate units of the 29th Division. There were several hours before the actual artillery was landed, and before we could start directing artillery fire, but in the meantime we became acquainted as quickly as possible with the location and the terrain

that was in front of us, and also the commanders of the 29th units that we were beginning to support. They were extremely glad to see us. All of the infantry was so supportive of the artillery observers—throughout the war. We became loyal friends.

My radio sergeant, and officer, and myself, this was our first time in combat, and you never know how you're going to respond in combat. You have to learn the terrain, you have to learn to protect yourself, and you have to learn how you can position yourself with the infantry units to become the most effective you can—either in defending them, or in preparing them for attacking. We learned very quickly to hug the ground, to get behind any object that could protect you from enemy gunfire. And I might add that with the bombardment of the area above Omaha Beach, with large shells from our battleships and bombs, there were a lot of craters, and these craters and holes afforded you some real protection as you advanced inland from the beach

USS *Arkansas* (BB-33) lays down a barrage of 12-inch gunfire on enemy positions on Omaha Beach.

American GIs rush from a hedgerow near Mortain, France. Dense hedgerows made fighting in Normandy even more challenging.

area. You could get down in one of these craters, and you're pretty well protected, but you didn't have much time to stay there. You had to advance from area to area.

It didn't take long for us to reach the hedgerow country that everyone has heard about, in the early part of June after the invasion, until we broke out at Saint-Lô.

To describe the hedgerows would be like describing a farm that had barbed-wire fences. Only instead of barbed-wire fences in Normandy they were mountains of dirt and trees, and they were anywhere from 75 to maybe 110 or 115 yards apart. They were almost in squares, so you learned that when you were behind, say, the first hedgerow, the Germans might be behind the next hedgerow over. You learned that the Germans had machine guns set up in each corner of their hedgerow as defense. It was the perfect type of position to defend hedgerow by hedgerow, and they could use their machine-gun fire as crossfire.

The other big obstacle from the German defensive standpoint were the German mortars, because they could lay down mortar fire on our side of the hedgerows. And so all the time you were trying to get into position to attack you had to deal with the mortar fire. Further, the Germans dug in their tanks and camouflaged those tanks behind the hedgerows.

Our objective as an artillery observer was protecting our infantry, and preparing for the attack. At night, when you weren't attacking, we directed artillery fire into locations where we thought the Germans might counter-attack. It could be a draw, it could be a trail, it could be an asphalt-paved road—anywhere we thought the Germans might counter-attack at night or the next day, we pre-set artillery. They were called "emergency barrages." And then there was a normal barrage. If the Germans were attacking, it was usually necessary to fire the emergency barrages, whereas the normal barrages were more in preparation for advancement. When you're being attacked it's hard to adjust the fire, because it takes time, it takes position, and it takes exposure of the observer to combat himself, and to being killed or wounded.

Denius earned a reputation as a courageous and skilled artillery observer during an Allied push near Saint-Lô and, later, during a fierce defense of a hilltop at Mortain. There he and a handful of forward artillery officers remained on Hill 314 for six days, directing fire that held off a massive German infantry and tank offensive designed to split American forces. He also played a key role as a forward observer during the Battle of the Bulge. Denius suffered wounds in Normandy and during the Battle of the Bulge.

Walter David Ehlers

Sergeant, Squad Leader, 18th Infantry Regiment

1st Infantry Division,

Walter Ehlers, raised in a devoutly religious family in Kansas, would receive a Medal of Honor for his bravery and leadership in Normandy, but his transition to military life didn't come easily. Eager to enlist in the army with older brother Roland, Ehlers needed his parents' signatures because of his young age. "My mother looked me square in the eye and she says, 'I'll only sign on one condition: you promise to be a Christian soldier.' Well, I was a little bit taken aback, but I said, 'I'll do my very best,'" he recalled. During his service Ehlers avoided cigarettes and strong drink, and privately grappled with the notion of violence toward other human beings.

Above: Ehlers after his battlefield promotion to Lieutenant in December 1944.

For many veterans of the invasion at Omaha Beach, the extraordinary violence, the raw struggle for survival, would continue far beyond the bloodied shoreline. One Army sergeant stared down the enemy day after day and protected his men, in the process achieving iconic status.

To justify being able to kill the enemy (I reasoned) that was my duty. I was fighting for freedom. That's all we've fought for in the United States Army, from the Revolutionary War up to the current wars. World War I and then World War II, that was for freedom. We fought Nazism, fascism and imperialism, and all three (enemy) nations became democracies after the war was over.

When we got ready to go (invade Normandy), in March, the company commander called my brother and I in and told us, "You guys have only $5,000 in insurance apiece when you can have the maximum of $10,000. We'd like for you to increase your insurance because we're going to have a lot of casualties on our next landing." So we said, "Okay, we'll do that." And he said, "The next thing is I have to make a transfer here. One of you has to be transferred to another company." Well, my brother got to stay because he's the oldest; I was outranking, but still got transferred (laughs). I got transferred to L Company, which was a sister company, and we were still close enough to visit in the evenings and things like that. We hardly ever saw one another.

That's the way it went until we got down to Weymouth. We said goodbye to one another at Weymouth, when he went on his ship, an LCI. Each LCI had a company of men on it. Our company had over 200 men, and because we had too many men, my squad got put on the Headquarters Company ship. And so I wasn't with the company when they went in, Company L. My brother was with Company K and I was with Headquarters Company.

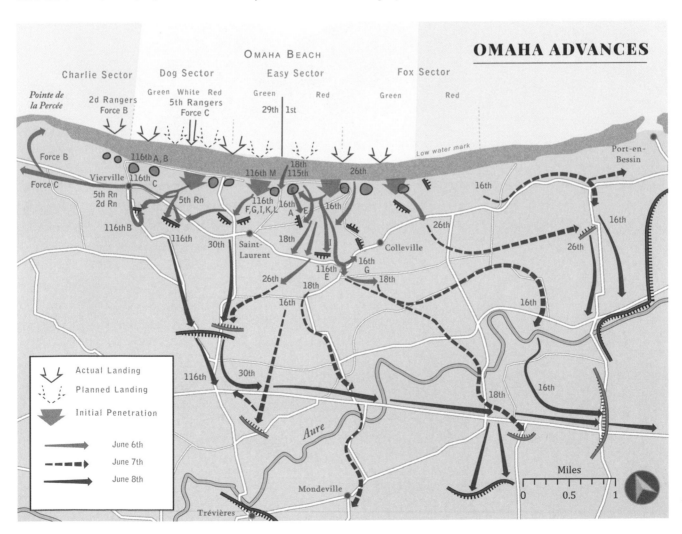

When we go out in the (English Channel), we all go out at the same time, and this is at night. All these planes started going over, and we're out there, moving towards Normandy. We never saw so many planes in the air at one time in our lives. There were planes like the C-47s pulling gliders, and there were bombers going over. There were fighter planes going over. English planes, French planes and everything else was going over at that time. They had about 800 planes overhead at one time. I just couldn't imagine seeing all that, the air was covered all the way across the Channel, practically.

We see all this happening, and then we get close to the beach. They said the first wave got pinned down on the beach. They wanted more people on the beach immediately. The first Higgins boat that came back came to my ship and my squad, because we were excess baggage on the ship, got put on the Higgins boat. There were only twelve of us.

My orders were to go in, take a reconnaissance patrol into the city of Trévières. Well, that was about six miles inland, and I thought, what do I do now? I get on this ship and I don't have a company with me—and I don't know where the company's going to land or anything, because they were coming in later.

As we got close to the beach, we saw Higgins boats that people were bailing out of. We saw two big two-and-a-half-ton DUKWs (amphibious vehicles) that were carrying supplies sink out there in the water. In towards the beach, we could see the smoke and stuff like that. We heard bombing and we saw the ships firing inland. And we thought we were not going to have any problems at all on the beach when we got there.

Lo and behold, we hit a sandbar. We asked the boatswain, "Is this as far as we're going?" because we had another hundred yards of water out there in front of us. He said, "As far as we can go, we're on a sandbar." Then he let the ramp down. So we run out. What do we do? We go down into the water, clear up to my neck. The sergeant who came in with me, it was over his head. We had to pull him through it.

And we got up on the beach. First thing they all wanted was to lie down on the beach. Now we were being fired upon, but we weren't getting hit for some reason. They were still firing artillery

Left: A soldier of the 16th Infantry Regiment looks out over the English Channel from the relative safety of a chalk cliff along Omaha Beach.

shells, but we're not a big enough target. I saw a beach master up there and I asked him what direction we go from here, and he said, "Follow that path there. If you go to the right or left, you'll step on land mines." Well, we headed up the path, and it was true, there were guys on both sides of the path that had been killed by stepping on land mines.

We got up there and there wasn't anybody ahead of us but these two Bangalore torpedo men who were supposed to be blowing a wire, but they were pinned down by a sniper and couldn't move. We fired in the general direction where the sniper was firing from and laid down a field of fire. You couldn't see the Germans and so we were firing at the top of the trenches, you know, the pillboxes and so forth, and apparently kept them down. He finally got the Bangalore torpedo under the wire and he set it off, and it blew the wire. I rushed my squad through the opening and from that on up the hill.

There weren't any mines on the other side, apparently, because we went clear up and got into the trenches, and we were fighting the Germans from there. We captured four Germans and sent them back down for interrogation. The ones we didn't capture were either killed or they ran from us. And we captured the pillbox from the rear. Then we kept going, because that wasn't the end of our fighting. We got up into the hedgerows, then got stopped again. We were kind of holding ground for a while until our company's second wave started coming in.

We were kind of pinned down there, waiting for more troops and so forth, for people to catch up on the right and left, and the Germans decided to strafe the beach. I guess they had a couple of planes that came down and made a straight run on the beach. The navy, of course, lowered their guns to shoot at the airplanes, and when they were shooting at them, the shells were coming over our heads. We were lying in like a hedgerow here and over in the next field the (American) shells were landing. We thought they were going to get us before it was over with—fortunately they didn't come back for a second run (laughs).

The next day, we were in firefights with the Germans off and on, here and there, and we went way further. We had a tank unit that was finally being landed on the beach, and they were a lot of help. They couldn't go on the roads, so they had to get something on the front of them (tanks) so they could go bulldoze through the hedgerows, because every time they go down one of those roads, they'd find *Tellermines* at all the crossings. They didn't have that many minesweepers yet.

Medal of Honor
awarded to Walt
Ehlers.

Medal of Honor Citation for Ehlers:

"For conspicuous gallantry and intrepidity at the risk of his life above and beyond the call of duty on 9-10 June 1944, near Goville, France. S/Sgt. Ehlers, always acting as the spearhead of the attack, repeatedly led his men against heavily defended enemy strong points exposing himself to deadly hostile fire whenever the situation required heroic and courageous leadership. Without waiting for an order, S/Sgt. Ehlers, far ahead of his men, led his squad against a strongly defended enemy strong point, personally killing 4 of an enemy patrol who attacked him en route. Then crawling forward under withering machinegun fire, he pounced upon the guncrew and put it out of action. Turning his attention to 2 mortars protected by the crossfire of 2 machineguns, S/Sgt. Ehlers led his men through this hail of bullets to kill or put to flight the enemy of the mortar section, killing 3 men himself. After mopping up the mortar positions, he again advanced on a machinegun, his progress effectively covered by his squad. When he was almost on top of the gun he leaped to his feet and, although greatly outnumbered, he knocked out the position single-handed. The next day, having advanced deep into enemy territory, the platoon of which S/Sgt. Ehlers was a member, finding itself in an untenable position as the enemy brought increased mortar, machinegun, and small arms fire to bear on it, was ordered to withdraw. S/Sgt. Ehlers, after his squad had covered the withdrawal of the remainder of the platoon, stood up and by continuous fire at the semicircle of enemy placements, diverted the bulk of the heavy hostile fire on himself, thus permitting the members of his own squad to withdraw. At this point, though wounded himself, he carried his wounded automatic rifleman to safety and then returned fearlessly over the shell-swept field to retrieve the automatic rifle which he was unable to carry previously. After having his wound treated, he refused to be evacuated, and returned to lead his squad. The intrepid leadership, indomitable courage, and fearless aggressiveness displayed by S/Sgt. Ehlers in the face of overwhelming enemy forces serve as an inspiration to others."

On the 8th we started fighting and getting up to where those second and third lines of defense were. And then on the 9th of June, we were sending out a platoon in this field over here. I didn't want to get caught out in the middle of a field, so I rushed my men up to the hedgerow in front of me, with me. And then, because I was the experienced one in combat, I could smell the Germans before I could see them. I started going up this hedgerow because the sound of machine guns was down in a corner there. I went up the bank and I heard some rattling, and I came face-to-face with four Germans on patrol. All of them had their guns pointed at me, and they were pretty close together. I didn't have any choice, I had to make a real fast decision—either I shot them or they're going to shoot me. So I pulled my trigger four times and got all four of them. It was with my M1 rifle. I had my men fix bayonets because these guys (Germans) were right there in front of me, and I had to reload. They followed me up the hedgerow.

I came upon a machine gun next out there, and I ran out there and knocked the guy out. I think the guy was still alive. The guys (platoon members) said, "Stab him." I said, "Stab him? I've still got bullets in my gun." I shot him. I wasn't going to stab anybody with my bayonet if I didn't have to.

Then we came to a mound back there, and I went up on the mound. In the back of that mound was two mortar positions, 80mm type mortars, the big heavy ones. They had to be placed there by weapons carriers or something. The weapons carriers weren't there, but the men were there and they had the guns in position all ready to shoot. When they saw me coming, their eyes got big. I asked them to halt and they wouldn't, they started to turn. Well we had to shoot them in order to stop them, I told them (fellow soldiers) they had to shoot them or else they were going to have to fight them again. There was another machine gun later on, up in the hedgerow, further up. We got it that day.

The next day, next morning, we had this similar situation come up, because you know hedgerows, there are square fields all the way around you. So we're going up to this next hedgerow that we were attacking and we started getting fire (from multiple directions). The company commander said to withdraw, because we had to go at this from a different situation. I knew that if we turned around, they'd probably shoot us all in the back. So I went up on the hedge, on a kind of a mound, and I started firing on the left. An automatic rifleman came up and he fired around to the right to keep the Germans pinned down. We kept

Ehlers was struck by a German bullet on June 10, which broke his rib, then passed through his pack, hitting a bar of soap and this photograph of his mother, Marie.

them pinned down, and our squad got back to the hedgerow behind us. Then we turned around to come back, and I saw them (Germans) putting a machine gun in a corner down there.

So I'm busy shooting at these three guys who are putting in the machine gun down there when I get hit in the back. It went through my rib area, glanced off the rib, went out—made two holes, one where it went in, one where it came back—and went into my pack. It hit a bar of soap and went through my mother's picture there, and it came out my trench shovel in the back.

I got up and went over and picked up the AR man. I saw him lying in the field when I got up. So I carried him back, even though I was wounded myself. My arms and legs were fine; he had a right leg wounded, he couldn't walk, and his right arm was wounded. He couldn't carry his rifle. So I carried him back, and after I got him back behind the hedgerow and turned over to the medics—I went back and got his rifle under fire.

After I got back, when we started loading the automatic rifleman on the ambulance, I told the company commander, "You better have the medics look at that wound in my back." He said, "You've been wounded?" I said, "Yeah." So he turned me around and he saw that bullet hole through my trench shovel. He says, "My God, you should be dead, you've been shot clear through." I said, "Oh no" (laughs). It was kind of a miracle. It

looked like I should have been dead, but I wasn't. The word went around that Sergeant Ehlers had been shot. Sometime later in the day, I met some other people that said, "We thought you were dead" (laughs). They passed the word around real quick. Rumors in the army go by word-of-mouth—you always get rumors about the next hill and things like that.

And that's the day for which I received the Medal of Honor. I didn't know I was getting the Medal of Honor that day. I didn't have the least idea of what was happening. I went on, refused to be medevaced. I didn't have to carry my pack because I had a dressing put on my back; it would have rubbed a good couple of wounds there (laughs). And so I carried bandoliers over my shoulder, so it didn't bother my back at all, and I carried my rifle, went on to lead my squad.

Walt Ehlers' brother Roland was killed on D-Day when a mortar shell hit his landing craft; it would be weeks before Ehlers learned of his brother's death. Before the Normandy invasion, the brothers had fought together in North Africa and Sicily. In addition to his back wound, Ehlers suffered wounds in fighting at Saint-Lô and in the Hürtgen Forest, and before returning home was injured in a shooting accident and a jeep wreck.

Gordon R. Osland

Second Lieutenant, US Army Coast Artillery Corps

Artillery officer Gordon R. Osland, from Detroit, entered the service in the spring of 1942, and, according to news accounts, shipped out for Europe in early 1944. He faced the long-anticipated invasion with determination and loyalty to fellow soldiers, but his time in combat was short. Second Lieutenant Osland was struck down by German shelling and never made it past the beach on D-Day. He died of "a penetrating wound of the chest," a War Department official later reported. Osland's letter to his wife Martha days before the combat expressed confidence but was also laced with foreboding. Communications surrounding Osland's death recall a time of sacrifice and mourning for American families.

The hard-earned American victory at Omaha Beach was laced with anguish as word of the deaths of soldiers reverberated among loved ones and wartime buddies. Among the many D-Day artifacts that survive today, and few are more powerful than letters left behind by the deceased and their loved ones.

June 3, 1944

To My Beautiful Wife Chickie:

Good Evening Darling and along with that Salutation, I send my apologies for not writing before this but it was impossible. I think you understand what I mean. Really Darling I don't know exactly how or what to put in this letter but I'm going to violate some of the rules of censorship because when you receive this it will not matter too much. It is almost midnight of June 3rd. I want you to remember that date. I'm going to get my first real test as an officer very shortly Sweet and I don't know just exactly how I'll react to it but at the present I am very calm and not the least bit nervous. As I said before Chickie when you get this letter it will be old news and you will know what the score is. I've been in several air raids and they were not bad compared to some of the things to come.

Honey I'm with a wonderful bunch of men and they are all in the best spirits and morale is high. I sincerely hope every one of them get back home safe and very soon. All of the officers tell me to say hello to you and they say don't forget the wonderful times we used to have when we were at Sheridan and Riverhead. I know sometimes I made you very angry at me but I think it's all forgiven now.

Honey if the first page of this letter was cut up pretty badly (note: letter was intact) it was my own fault but I didn't let out any military secrets. I had to express my feelings somehow to one I love very dearly. Sometimes we had our little squabbles but it was really wonderful to make up again. Guess that's what makes life interesting. I carry that picture of you in the little leather folder with me all the time. It's getting a little soiled now but I'll never let it leave me. I look at it quite often Honey and wish with all my heart I could be with you and could put my hands on you and my arms around you. If everything goes along ok it will not be many weeks before we'll be together again and at the thought I get what you might call little chills of pleasure and excitement. I could ramble on for hours on how much I miss and love you Honey but that doesn't help the present situation any appreciable amount.

I've had a few spare hours the last few days Precious and I read a book titled "Citadel." Remember the picture? If you haven't read it do so for me and you will see the names of towns in that book which I have visited. Every one but a few minor ones I've seen pretty thoroughly. It was real interesting to me on that account.

I haven't received any letters from you for over two weeks Darling but I don't think it's your fault. I know our mail has been held up and I'm hoping very much to receive it in the near future. It gets awful lonesome when I don't receive any from you.

I've just about run out of news Sweet. Just don't forget that I love you and no one else will ever take your place. I'm glad I married you before I came into the service and have since kicked myself for not doing so earlier. Darling say hello to all my friends for me and also a special greeting to a wonderful mother and father in-law. They're grand people. Say hello to the kids also. I'm going to write my Mother and Dad tonight, they should get a letter about the same time as you.

Darling are you still modeling? If so do you still like it? Please don't give up your place at the telephone company at least not while the war is on. Promise me?

Honey it's getting late and I'm a little sleepy but not too tired. Just remember two things Precious. One, I love you and always will. Two, the date this letter was written. I'll say Bye Bye for a little while precious and will be back as soon as possible.

Yours forever

Your Husband

Gordon

P.S. If anything should happen to me Honey please pay H.J. the $25.00 I owe him. It's impossible for me to do so at the present. Don't do it though unless something prevents me from doing it. Goodnight Sweetheart.

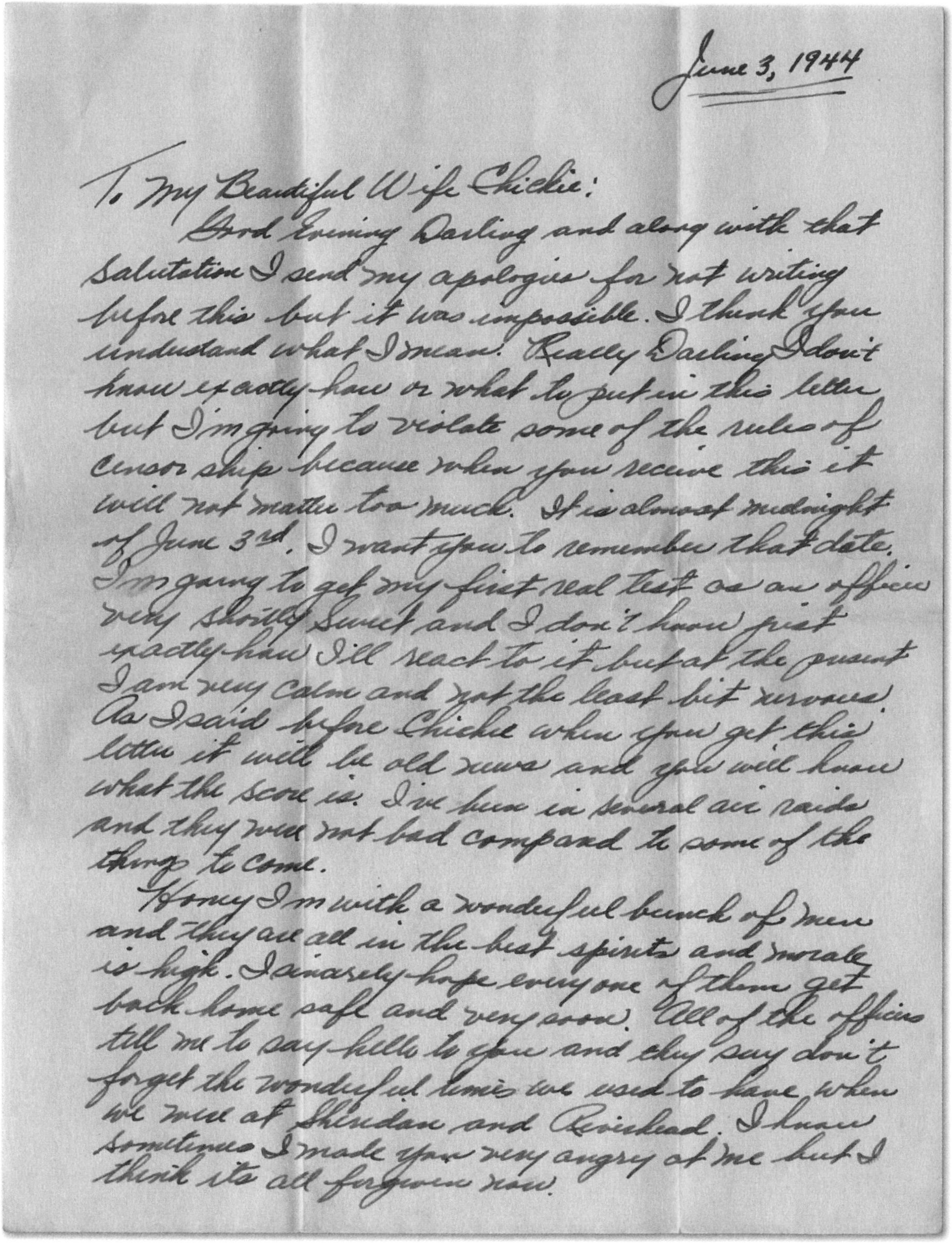

June 3, 1944

To My Beautiful Wife Chickie:

Good Evening Darling and along with that salutation I send my apologies for not writing before this but it was impossible. I think you understand what I mean! Really Darling I don't know exactly how or what to put in this letter but I'm going to violate some of the rules of censorship because when you receive this it will not matter too much. It is almost midnight of June 3rd. I want you to remember that date. I'm going to get my first real test as an officer very shortly Sweet and I don't know just exactly how I'll react to it but at the present I am very calm and not the least bit nervous. As I said before Chickie when you get this letter it will be old news and you will know what the score is. I've been in several air raids and they were not bad compared to some of the things to come.

Honey I'm with a wonderful bunch of men and they are all in the best spirits and morale is high. I sincerely hope every one of them get back home safe and very soon. All of the officers tell me to say hello to you and they say don't forget the wonderful times we used to have when we met at Sheridan and Reinhead. I know sometimes I made you very angry at me but I think its all forgiven now.

Osland's last letter to his wife, Martha, nicknamed Chickie (continues to page 180).

Honey if the first page of this letter was cut up pretty badly it was my own fault but I didn't let out any military secrets. I had to express my feelings somehow to one I love very dearly. I mean that with all my heart Darling. Sometimes we had our little squabbles but it was really wonderful to make up again. Guess that's what makes life interesting. I carry that picture of you in the little leather folder with me all the time. Its getting a little soiled now but I'll never let it leave me. I look at it quite often Honey and wish with all my heart I could be with you and could put my hands on you and my arms around you. If everything goes along ok it will not be many weeks before we'll be together again and at the thought I get what you might call little chills of pleasure and excitement. I could ramble on for hours on how much I miss and love you Honey but that doesn't help the present situation any appreciable amount.

I've had a few spare hours the last two days Precious and I read a book titled "Citadel." Remember the picture? If you haven't read it do so for me and you will see the names of towns in that book which I have visited. Every one but a few minor ones I've seen pretty thoroughly. It was real interesting to me on that account.

I haven't received any letters from you for over two weeks Darling but I don't think its your fault. I know our mail has been held up and I'm hoping very much to receive it in the near future. It gets awful lonesome when I don't receive any from you

I've just about run out of news Sweet. Just don't forget that I love you and no one else will ever take your place. I'm glad I married you before I came into the service and have since kicked myself for not doing so earlier. Darling say hello to all my friends for me and also a special greeting to a wonderful mother & father in-law. They're grand people. Say hello to the kids also. I'm going to write my mother & Dad tonight, they should get a letter about the same time as you.

Darling are you still modeling? If so do you still like it? Please don't give up your place at the telephone company at least not while the war is on. Promise me?

Honey its getting late and I'm a little sleepy but not too tired. Just remember two things Precious. One, I love you and always will. Two - the date this letter was written. I will say Bye bye for a little while Precious and will be back as soon as possible. Yours forever

Your Husband
Andre.

P.S. If anything should happen to me Honey please pay H. J. the $25.00 I owe him. Its impossible for me to do so at the present. Don't do it though unless something prevents me from doing it.

Goodnight Sweetheart.

Western Union telegram from the military, June 19, 1944 to widow Martha L. Osland, 13 days after Osland's death:

> Mrs. Martha L. Osland:
>
> The Secretary of War desires me to express his deep regrets that your husband Second Lieutenant Gordon R. Osland was killed in action on 6th June in France. Letter follows.
>
> Ulio Adjutant General

CLASS OF SERVICE

This is a full-rate Telegram or Cablegram unless its deferred character is indicated by a suitable symbol above or preceding the address.

WESTERN UNION

A. N. WILLIAMS
PRESIDENT

1204

SYMBOLS

DL=Day Letter
NL=Night Letter
LC=Deferred Cable
NLT=Cable Night Letter
Ship Radiogram

The filing time shown in the date line on telegrams and day letters is STANDARD TIME at point of origin. Time of receipt is STANDARD TIME at point of destination

XM14 30 Government Washington DC June 19 1944 536p

Mrs Martha L. Osland.

18365 Dale.

The Secretary of War desires me to express his deep regrets that your husband Second Lieutenant Gordon R Osland was killed in action on 6th June in France. Letter follows.

Ulio Adjutant General

712p

THE COMPANY WILL APPRECIATE SUGGESTIONS FROM ITS PATRONS CONCERNING ITS SERVICE

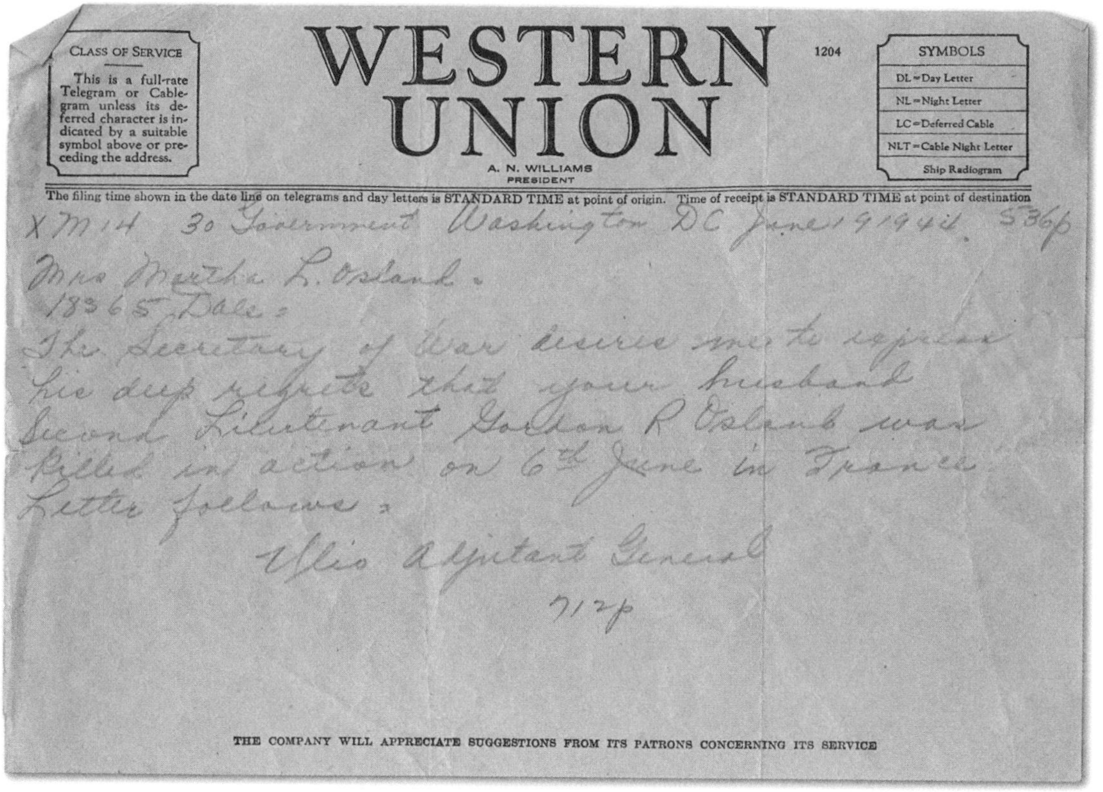

Telegram delivered to Osland's wife informing her of his death on June 6.

War Department letter to Martha Osland, June 21, 1944

Dear Mrs. Osland,

It is regret that I am writing to confirm the recent telegram informing you of the death of your husband, Second Lieutenant Gordon R. Osland … Coast Artillery Corps, who was killed in action on 6 June 1944 in France.

I fully understand your desire to learn as much as possible regarding the circumstances leading to his death, and I wish that there were more information available to give you. Unfortunately, reports of this nature contain only the briefest details as they are prepared under battle conditions and the means of transmission are limited.

I know the sorrow this message has brought you and it is my hope that in time the knowledge of his heroic service to his country, even unto death, may be of sustaining comfort to you.

I extend to you my deepest sympathy.

Sincerely yours,
J.A. Ulio
Major General
The Adjutant General

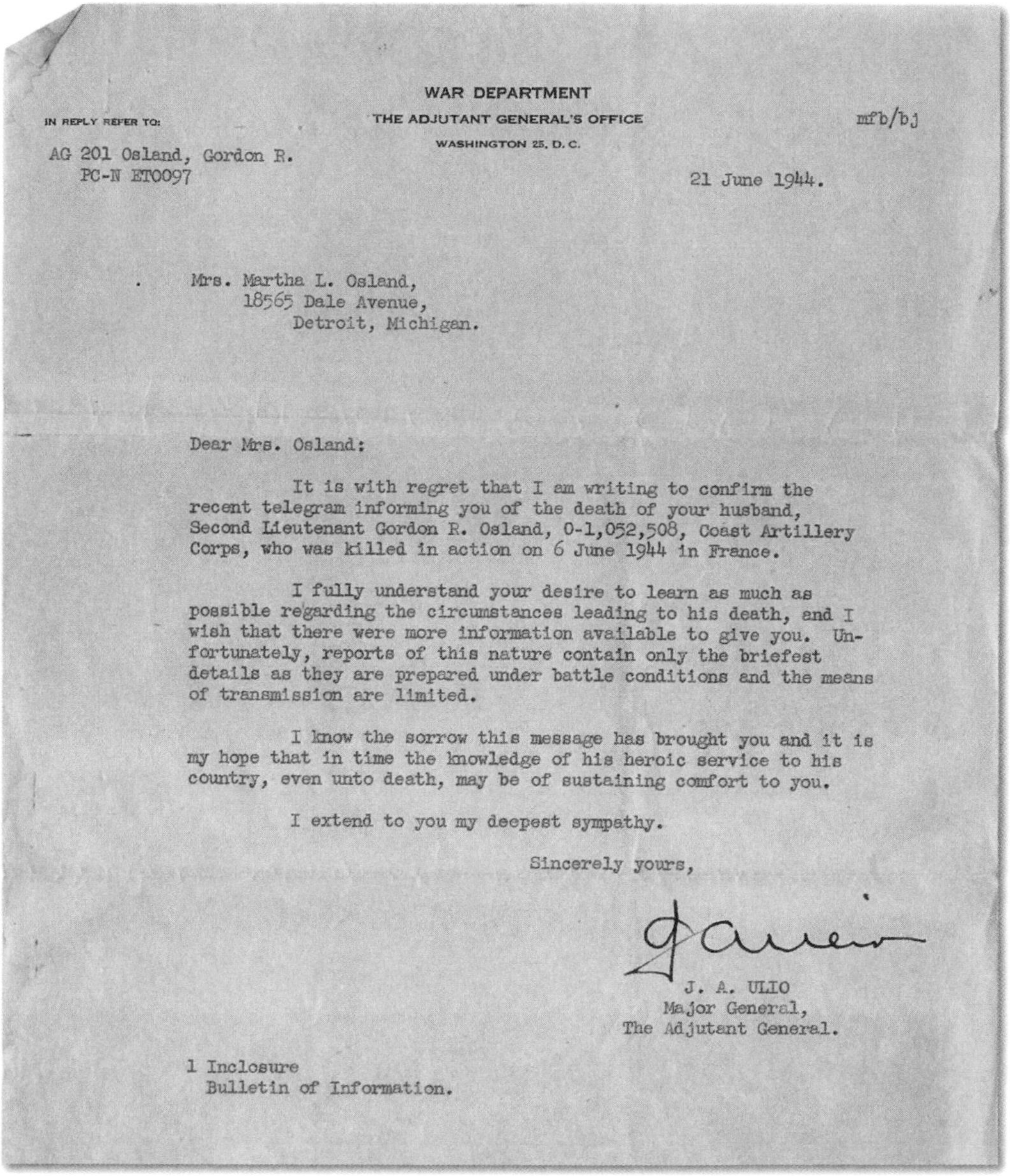

WAR DEPARTMENT
THE ADJUTANT GENERAL'S OFFICE
WASHINGTON 25, D. C.

IN REPLY REFER TO:
AG 201 Osland, Gordon R.
PC-N ET0097

mfb/bj

21 June 1944.

Mrs. Martha L. Osland,
18565 Dale Avenue,
Detroit, Michigan.

Dear Mrs. Osland:

It is with regret that I am writing to confirm the recent telegram informing you of the death of your husband, Second Lieutenant Gordon R. Osland, O-1,052,508, Coast Artillery Corps, who was killed in action on 6 June 1944 in France.

I fully understand your desire to learn as much as possible regarding the circumstances leading to his death, and I wish that there were more information available to give you. Unfortunately, reports of this nature contain only the briefest details as they are prepared under battle conditions and the means of transmission are limited.

I know the sorrow this message has brought you and it is my hope that in time the knowledge of his heroic service to his country, even unto death, may be of sustaining comfort to you.

I extend to you my deepest sympathy.

Sincerely yours,

J. A. ULIO
Major General,
The Adjutant General.

1 Inclosure
Bulletin of Information.

War Department letter to Martha Osland, June 21, 1944.

Letter to widow Martha Osland, nicknamed "Chick," from a soldier in her husband's unit, July 28, 1944:

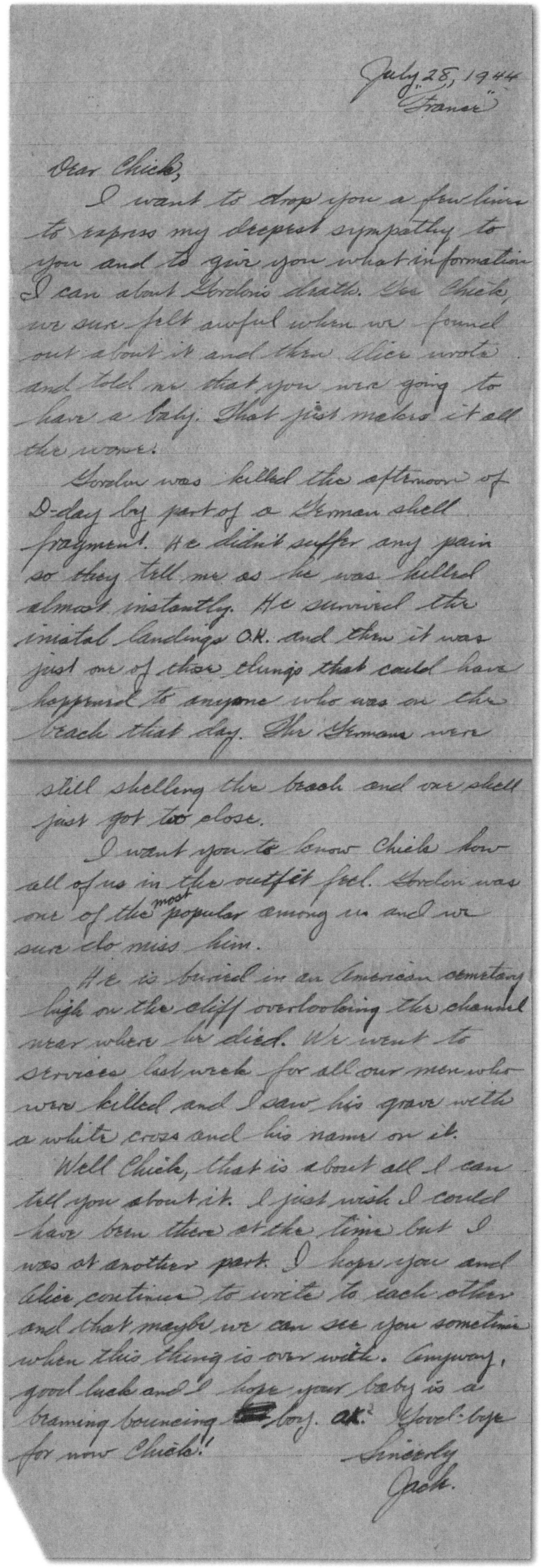

July 28, 1944

"France"

Dear Chick,

I want to drop you a few lines to express my deepest sympathy to you and to give you what information I can about Gordon's death. Gosh Chick, we sure felt awful when we found out about it and then Alice wrote and told me that you were going to have a baby. That just makes it all the worse.

Gordon was killed the afternoon of D-Day by part of a German shell fragment. He didn't suffer any pain so they tell me as he was killed almost instantly. He survived the initial landings O.K. and then it was just one of those things that could have happened to anyone who was on the beach that day. The Germans were still shelling the beach and one shell just got too close.

I want you to know Chick how all of us in the outfit feel. Gordon was one of the most popular among us and we sure do miss him.

He is buried in an American cemetery high on a cliff overlooking the channel near where he died. We went to services last week for all our men who were killed and saw his grave with a white cross and his name on it.

Well Chick, that is about all I can tell you about it. I just wish I could have been there at the time but I was at another part. I hope you and Alice continue to write to each other and that maybe we can see you sometime when this thing is over with. Good luck and I hope your baby is a beaming bouncing boy. OK? Good-bye for now Chick!

Sincerely,

Jack

Letter to Osland's wife from Jack, a soldier in Olsand's unit.

Note to Martha Osland from another soldier, undated:

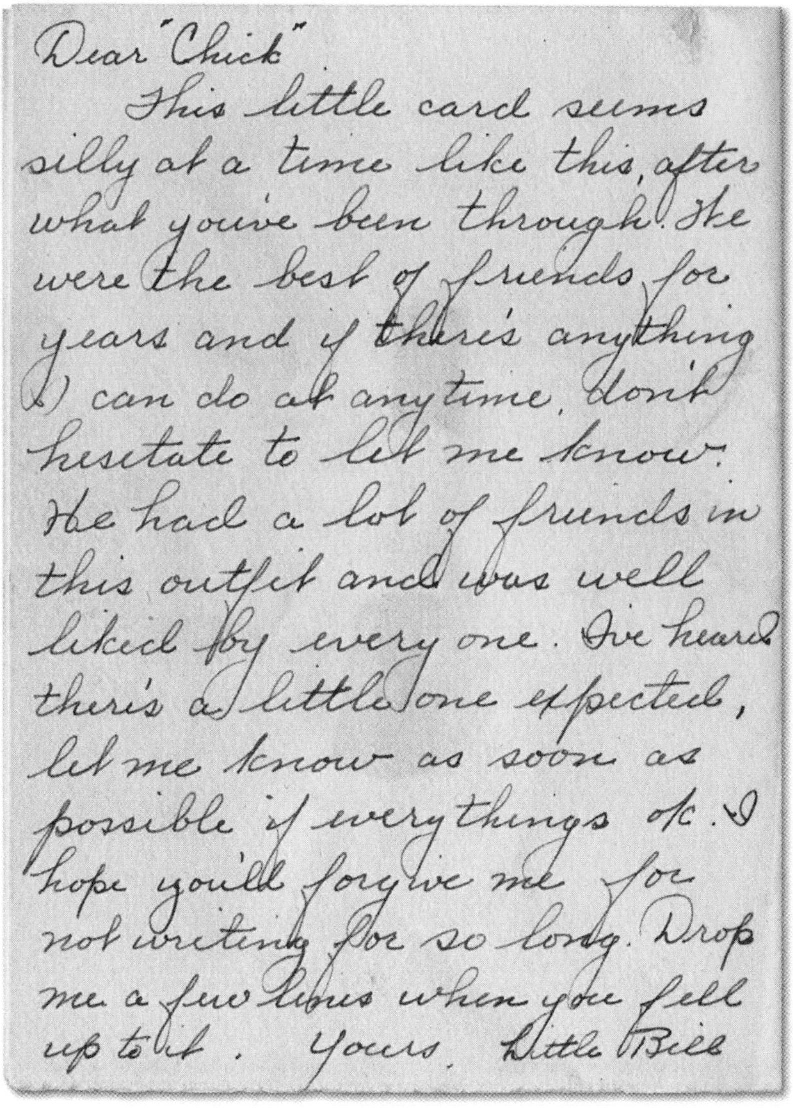

Dear "Chick"

This little card seems silly at a time like this, after what you've been through. We were the best of friends for years and if there's anything I can do at any time, don't hesitate to let me know. He had a lot of friends in this outfit and was well liked by everyone. I've heard there's a little one expected, let me know as soon as possible if everything's ok. I hope you'll forgive me for not writing for so long. Drop me a few lines when you feel up to it.

Yours,

Little Bill

Letter to Osland's wife from Bill, a soldier in Olsand's unit.

CONCLUSION

The assault at Omaha Beach made history as one of the most chaotic and devastating episodes of the war. Historians calculate that about 4,700 Americans were dead, wounded or missing by day's end—more than triple the German losses in that sector of the D-Day struggle.

Individual heroics notwithstanding, Omaha Beach's fundamental story was one of epic tragedy and anguish. Many years later, historian Stephen Ambrose quoted Private John MacPhee of the 1st Division, who said he was "so seasick I thought I would die" before reaching shore——and then, hit three times on the beach, almost did perish. Of Omaha Beach, Ambrose noted, "No tactician could have devised a better defensive situation. A narrow, enclosed battlefield with no possibility of outflanking it; many natural obstacles for the attacker to overcome … high ground looking down on a wide, open killing field for any infantry trying to cross no-man's land." Rick Atkinson, in his account of the invasion, dubbed Omaha "Hell's Beach," and wrote that survivors would long remember "the shapeless dead, sprawled on the strand like smears of divine clay, or as flotsam on the making tide, weltering, with their life belts still cinched."

In the moments after the first wave of boats hit Omaha Beach at 6:30 a.m., the invasion forces faced chaos, confusion and death. Most of the 116th Infantry Regiment of the 29th Division was annihilated. In other sectors, troops that survived the carnage in the water or on the beach huddled behind the sea wall at the base of the cliffs. The main draws for exiting the beaches were still held by the Germans—and other waves of landing troops were stalemated in the face of withering fire from defensive positions. Many senior American officers were dead and the foot soldiers and junior officers still able to fight were stacking up, paralyzed. Colonel George Taylor, the 16th Infantry Regiment Commanding Officer, rallied the terrorized troops with the words, "There are two kinds of people who are staying on this beach—those who are dead and those who are going to die. Now let's get the hell out of here!"

Small bands of soldiers began making their way up the cliffs, attacking German strongpoints and trenches even as enemy snipers continued to pick off the attackers. As the day wore on, improvised tactics and sheer determination began to extinguish the German threats. American tanks and ground forces finally pushed beyond the beaches, cleaning up scattered resistance and then bracing for counter-attacks.

In the early afternoon, Lieutenant General Omar Bradley and other commanders on the bridge of the *Augusta* (CA-31) were relieved to hear that troops who had been pinned down on the sand were now advancing. Operation Overlord had managed to pass its great test at Omaha Beach. The desperate hours and sacrifices there would live on in public memory.

POINTE DU HOC

CHAPTER FOUR

6 . 6 . 44

Douglas A-20 Havocs bomb Pointe du Hoc in May 1944.

As Allied strategists prepared for the D-Day invasion, they were especially wary of a battery of 155mm guns looming over the English Channel at Pointe du Hoc. This rocky promontory thrust out into the sea like a jagged knife, a seemingly impregnable position with 100-foot cliffs, one of the finest vantage points anywhere in the German coastal defense system. From there, the German guns posed a major threat to American forces invading Omaha Beach to the east and Utah Beach to the west, as well as to warships and troop transports more than eleven miles out to sea. Repeated Allied bombing of the Pointe had produced mounds of rubble, but the threat remained with no clear indication of the status of the battery of big guns.

A top priority mission for D-Day was to take out the guns on Pointe du Hoc. US Army Rangers—troops with special training and equipment—had to neutralize the gun battery in the opening minutes of the beach invasion. Since German commanders had

planned their defense of the Pointe against a land-based attack, American strategists opted for a bold frontal assault from the sea.

General Omar Bradley gave this critical mission to the 2nd and 5th Ranger Battalions weeks prior to the invasion. According to the plan, the 8th and 9th Air Forces and warships of the Western Task Force would pound the Pointe for an hour before the assault and stop just moments before the Rangers landed at 6:30 a.m., hoping to catch the enemy dazed in their bunkers. The Rangers were to scale the daunting cliffs with the help of grappling hooks, ropes and fire ladders. Their initial goal was to overwhelm the defenders quickly, destroy the big-gun battery and then brace for a fierce German counter-attack. Once they had neutralized the guns, the Rangers' second mission was to seize the coastal road behind Pointe du Hoc to prevent reinforcement of German troops defending Omaha or other beaches to the east.

It came as little surprise that the task of taking Pointe du Hoc fell to the US Army Rangers. This elite force was created in 1942 under the leadership of Major William Darby and modeled after British commando units skilled in irregular warfare and special operations. The Rangers drew inspiration (and their name) from English settlers in the seventeenth century who "ranged the wilderness" as armed scouts, using mobility and stealth in their struggle against Native American war parties.

The 2nd Ranger Battalion called upon for the Pointe du Hoc mission was trained in the same mold—aggressive, innovative and deadly. The man assigned to shape and lead them into battle on D-Day was Lieutenant Colonel James Earl Rudder. "Big Jim" was six-foot and heavy-set, a former Texas A&M University football player, a leader on the gridiron and a tough task-master to his Rangers. Rudder hammered his 2nd Ranger Battalion into shape during more than a year of rigorous exercises in Tennessee, Florida and New Jersey before arriving in Great Britain in early December 1943. The training included relentless drilling, 24-hour endurance hikes, boxing matches, demolition training and cliff-climbing. Their training stressed innovation and taking the initiative to complete their mission even if the cost was high. "Rudder's Rangers" took pride in being among the army's best. Other Ranger battalions had already collected accolades in previous campaigns in North Africa and Sicily, and their brash confidence carried over to these new fighters who would face an extreme test on the Normandy shore.

"These units accepted only volunteers, and men were selected for their mental and physical stamina, their motivation to get the job done," recalled James Eikner, a 2nd Ranger Battalion communications officer. "Sometimes we were called suicide groups, but (we were) not at all—we were simply spirited young people who took the view that if you were going to be a combat soldier you might as well be the very best." Eikner called the Rangers' training "exceedingly tough, and we were made experts in all of the infantry weapons and tactics. I can assure you that when we went into battle it wasn't all shaking of the knees and weeping and praying and so forth. We knew what we were getting into. We were volunteering for extra hazardous duty."

General Eisenhower, General Bradley, and Overlord strategists pushed forward with the daring plan to take Pointe du Hoc (designated Pointe du Hoe on many maps), despite grave reservations in some quarters. The Germans had deployed infantry and artillerymen to defend the gun battery and the steep cliffs gave defenders a clear advantage; one American intelligence officer would warn that "three old women with brooms" should be able to keep the Rangers from reaching the cliff tops. But such observers did not fully appreciate Lieutenant Colonel Rudder's leadership and the determination of his men.

On May 6 Rudder took over a new Provisional Ranger Group, consisting of the 2nd and 5th Battalions, attached to the 116th Infantry Regiment of the 29th Infantry Division. Rudder briefed his men on every detail of the Pointe du Hoc plan, including the precise locations of the beach landings, German pillboxes, barbed wire, obstacles and the casemates for the big guns.

Rudder divided his Rangers into three groups, Forces A, B and C. He would personally lead 225 Rangers ashore in Force A (D, E and F Companies, 2nd Ranger Battalion) aboard British LCAs (Landing Craft, Assault) in the frontal assault on Pointe du Hoc. Their primary task was to climb the cliffs and neutralize the big

This 1943 reconnaissance photo of Pointe du Hoc shows the gun positions targeted by the Rangers.

A-20 Havoc pilot Richard Gates wore this A-2 flight jacket
during missions over Europe, including a mission on June 6.

guns. Force C, commanded by Lieutenant Colonel Max Schneider (with A and B companies of the 2nd Ranger Battalion and the entire 5th Ranger Battalion) would circle offshore for 30 minutes beyond the 6:30 a.m. H-Hour. Force C would await a signal from Rudder's team that Force A had taken its objective and then scale the cliffs as reinforcements. If no signal came, Schneider would divert to Omaha and go in on Dog Green beach to support the 116th Infantry Regiment before looping back west overland to relieve the Rangers at Pointe du Hoc.

Force B (C Company, 2nd Rangers) led by Captain Ralph Goranson, would land on Omaha beach and head to Pointe de la Percée, three miles east of Pointe du Hoc to attack machine gun and mortar positions above Omaha Beach.

Rudder was confident in his Rangers and his plan of attack as the British transport ships came to anchor off the Normandy coast in the early morning hours of June 6. The order "Rangers, man your craft" came over the intercom at 4:00 a.m. and the 225 men destined for Pointe du Hoc began loading into their LCAs and from the ships into brisk weather with rough seas and a stiff breeze.

While the men were ready, leadership and courage would soon be required in large measure. One LCA capsized at the outset,

drowning some Rangers and hospitalizing the survivors. A supply boat sank, killing most of those on board. Rangers in other boats witnessed the boat mishaps and the deaths of their comrades, depressing their morale. In just moments 225 men of Force A were down to 180—20 percent casualties before a shot had been fired. Undaunted, Rudder's reduced flotilla of LCAs pounded through the choppy seas toward the coast as the battle began to heat up. Deafening explosions from 14-inch guns of the battleship USS *Texas* began firing just over the Ranger boats against the Pointe du Hoc fortifications. As Rudder's LCAs drew closer to the coast around 6 a.m., Captain Goranson's Force B was in trouble, taking heavy fire as it tried to take the Pointe de la Percée strongpoint to the east.

When Rudder began to make out landmarks on the Normandy coast at first light, he discovered that a serious navigation error had sent Force A miles off course—well east of Pointe du Hoc. He ordered his boats to correct with a hard right turn back to the Pointe, but the mistake delayed their landing by 40 minutes to 7:10 a.m. By that time the German defenders were over their shock of the bombardment and had come crawling out of their bunkers.

With the element of surprise lost, Rudder's men faced withering fire from German troops at the Pointe as the LCA ramps went down and Companies D, E and F ran onto the narrow beach beneath the cliffs, on the Pointe's east side. A hellish scene unfolded. The Germans tossed grenades or cut the ropes attached to grapnels that were fired to the top of the cliffs with rockets. Rudder set up his temporary headquarters in a cave under the cliff and rallied the men and medics to their mission.

Sergeant Leonard Lomell, though wounded in the side while getting off his boat, was among the first to start up the cliff. Rangers began climbing with any rope they could grab. When one fell, another would take his place. Helped by covering fire from fellow soldiers, Lomell led the way as Rangers clawed their way up the cliff, using piles of rubble created by earlier Allied bombing or shelling from warships to gain elevation. By 7:20 a.m. Lomell and most of the 22 men from his boat were over the top. The German defenders began to fall back. The Rangers rushed from one bomb crater to another, attacking pillboxes and bunkers to get to the casemates where they thought the big guns were located.

Meanwhile, Lieutenant Colonel Max Schneider and Force C circled offshore in their landing craft, waiting for a radio signal from Colonel Rudder that the attack on the Pointe was successful. However, Rudder's E Company radio equipment had been

Above: The USS *Texas* (BB-35) provided fire support for Rangers at the Pointe. Here a shell from a German shore battery near Cherbourg falls short of hitting the ship in late June.

Below: Obstacles on the beach are visible below Pointe du Hoc in this aerial reconnaissance photo from May 1944.

compromised by exposure to seawater on the way to the beach, and what signals Schneider did get were garbled. After a frustrating wait with no clear signal of success coming from Rudder at the Pointe, Schneider executed the contingency plan and headed to the Omaha beachhead. His new mission was to fight his way inland to the coastal road and circle back to the Pointe to rescue any Rangers still alive.

Going in with Schneider's Force C and playing a key leadership role was Captain John Raaen (See "Omaha Beach" pages 160-165) with the Headquarters Company of the 5th Rangers. It fell to Raaen to command the bulk of the Ranger force in two tumultuous days of combat with German troops in the fields and villages just inland from Omaha Beach.

Dramatic episodes unfolded rapidly at the Pointe from June 6 to June 8. After seizing the cliffs, the Rangers were shocked to find that the 155mm guns were missing from their casemates. This discovery set into motion a secondary mission for Lomell and other Rangers. The soldiers first scrambled to seize control of a coastal road a mile inland. Once that was accomplished, Lomell and Sergeant Jack Kuhn did a reconnaissance run down a nearby country lane and found five of the missing 155mm guns. Unseen by German troops a short distance away, Lomell seized the opportunity to spike the guns with thermite grenades.

While the Rangers' primary mission was accomplished by roughly 8:30 a.m. on D-Day, difficulties were just beginning. Lightly armed by design, the Rangers now found themselves in a stand-up firefight with well-armed German forces. Undaunted, the Rangers resorted to using German weapons and ammunition as they fought off fierce counter-attacks during the next two days at the Pointe and along the coastal road. Rudder was the key man, rallying his men even though he was wounded. "Under the leadership of Colonel Rudder," one Ranger said, "miracles almost seemed possible."

Many men would be lost on the coastal road as the isolated Rangers of Company D and parts of E and F defended a shrinking perimeter against determined German night attacks on June 6 and 7. These Rangers held on even as food and ammunition ran short, waiting desperately for the relief that finally came with the 116th Infantry Regiment and the 5th Rangers on the morning of June 8.

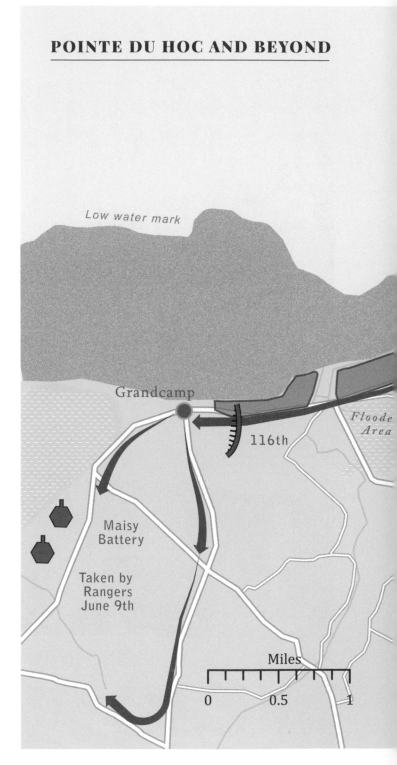

POINTE DU HOC AND BEYOND

Low water mark

Grandcamp

116th

Flooded Area

Maisy Battery

Taken by Rangers June 9th

Miles

0   0.5   1

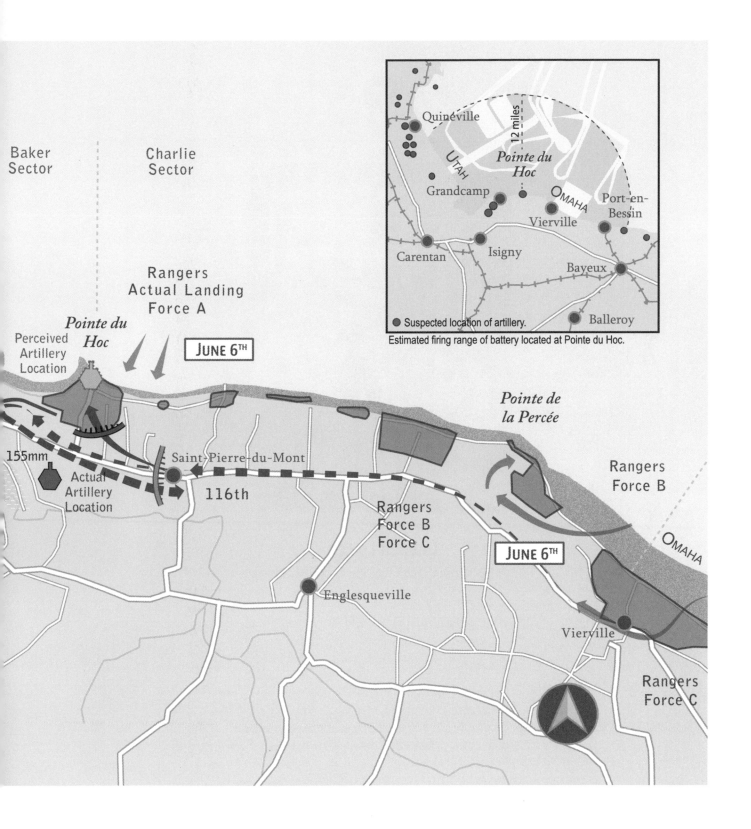

Baker Sector

Charlie Sector

Rangers Actual Landing Force A

Pointe du Hoc

Perceived Artillery Location

JUNE 6TH

155mm

Actual Artillery Location

Saint-Pierre-du-Mont

116th

Rangers Force B Force C

Englesqueville

Pointe de la Percée

Rangers Force B

JUNE 6TH

OMAHA

Vierville

Rangers Force C

Quinéville

UTAH

Pointe du Hoc

12 miles

Grandcamp

OMAHA

Port-en-Bessin

Vierville

Carentan

Isigny

Bayeux

Balleroy

● Suspected location of artillery.

Estimated firing range of battery located at Pointe du Hoc.

POINTE DU HOC

Leonard Lomell

First Sergeant, D Company, 2nd Ranger Battalion

Born in Brooklyn, New York, Leonard "Len" Lomell grew up in Point Pleasant Beach, New Jersey. He dreamed of entering a military service academy after graduating from Tennessee Wesleyan College in June 1941, but the plan was jeopardized by his inability to produce a birth certificate, a consequence of having been adopted as a baby. Drafted into the army months after the attack on Pearl Harbor, Lomell trained with the 76th Infantry Division before accepting an invitation to join the Rangers. Gaining specialized training in commando tactics, including the scaling of high cliffs, Lomell became First Sergeant of Dog Company in the 2nd Ranger Battalion. He would become a central figure in the assault on the German gun battery at Pointe du Hoc.

We got loaded upon the LCAs at four o'clock in the morning—these LCAs were manned by the British navy. It took a few hours to get from that point to the beaches, wherever you were going to land. In our case, we were about 40 minutes late because our British coxswain lost the cliff he was to land at, but that was corrected. We did land, and we did climb the cliffs of Pointe du Hoc.

As our LCAs landed and the ramps went down, we pushed buttons on our switchboard that we had in the gunnel, and that set off these rockets (carrying grapnels and rope lines) that had launchers along the gunnels. And those rockets would sail up there, a hundred and fifty feet—these are all hundred-foot cliffs—grab into the earth, and we would pull on them down on the beach. That would secure them so we could, hand over hand, climb a hundred feet straight up.

Had everything gone right, the Germans would have been in bed when we did this—it was so early. But because we were late,

it gave them enough time to get out there, to welcome us, such as it was. They cut our ropes as we were trying to come up, dropped grenades on top of us, or shot us off the ropes—it became almost impossible to climb those ropes and get up there, and find the guns. We got up there, and fought our way through the Germans to the gun positions. D Company, my company, was assigned gun positions four, five and six on the west flank of Pointe du Hoc.

When we got to the positions where our three (German) guns were supposed to be—these big coastal howitzers—they weren't there. There were nothing but telephone poles sticking out of these immense placements and, of course, we trained for this mission only from aerial photographs, and information that had been given to us. We did not know what we later found out that those guns had been removed before D-Day to another position. We checked quickly, and we could not find any guns on Pointe du Hoc at that point.

By 8:30 am, Sergeant (Jack) Kuhn, my acting platoon

Left: Staff Sergeant Leonard Lomell before joining the 2nd Ranger Battalion.

Above: In the center of the cliff is a ladder used by Rangers to climb the Pointe. Taken after June 6, the photo shows supplies being brought up the cliff.

sergeant, Second Platoon of D Company, and I—after we had been through the landing and climbing the cliffs, and fighting the Germans, and going into position, and finding the guns missing—had our section sergeants set up a roadblock on a shore road from Pointe du Hoc to Grandcamp. They manned that roadblock to keep the Germans from getting up the road to help each other, fend us off, or whatever they would do.

As they were assigned, Sergeant Kuhn and I went looking for the (missing) guns, and we just happened upon this little road that ran from the coast road along the English Channel. It ran inland, and it looked like wagon marks, or something on the dirt road between these mammoth hedgerows. The hedgerows

Below General Dwight Eisenhower, seen here with (L-R) General Omar Bradley, General Henry "Hap" Arnold, Admiral Ernest King and General George C. Marshall, examine what is believed to be the hidden 155mm German artillery site near Pointe du Hoc. The inspection came about a week after D-Day and the successful Rangers assault.

The *Stielhandgranate* 24 was the standard high explosive hand grenade of the German Army. It consists of a sheet-metal-wrapped bursting charge on the end of a wooden handle. The long handle gives the thrower mechanical advantage and enables a longer throw. A fragmentation sleeve has been added to this grenade to increase its anti-personnel effect.

in Normandy are not like here in America where they're three or four feet tall, maybe five-foot from time to time. These were giant; the tanks couldn't get through them, with fifty-foot trees out of the top of them. Sergeant Kuhn and I leapfrogged—that is to say, I'd run up fifty feet and look over the hedgerows and see where I could find any evidence of any guns. I'd hold that position, whilst he'd run up and get (a look), and take over the position while I ran another fifty feet, and we kept doing this—protecting each other, never knowing if we're going to run into a machine-gun nest or something.

As luck would have it, within the first couple of hundred feet, we came to this hedgerow—it was my turn to peer over it and examine what lay on the other side. And there were the guns.

We were lucky. We were at the right place at the right time, and we watched over each other. Jack got up on top of the hedgerow while I went into position (to neutralize the guns). We just immobilized them; never touched the barrels. As a matter of fact, you couldn't touch the barrels. Most of them were too damn high. There wasn't any discussion about it, we knew that the only weapon we had to handle the destruction was a thermite grenade to melt the gears of the traversing mechanism and the elevation mechanism. My gun butt destroyed the sights. The thermite grenades were brought along for this very purpose. Whatever we could do to render it inoperable, we did that with the limited things we had to work with, you know, we were traveling awful light.

Jack and I were scared to death that we couldn't get this mission accomplished fast enough. We've got to get in and out of here because we're so badly outnumbered.

We destroyed those guns so they could not be used, and got back to our roadblock men. We fought there for two days and then were relieved. We had heavy casualties. I think out of sixty-five men, I had fifteen men left. Those of us that did survive of course were just plain lucky.

We knew what we were doing, and we accomplished the

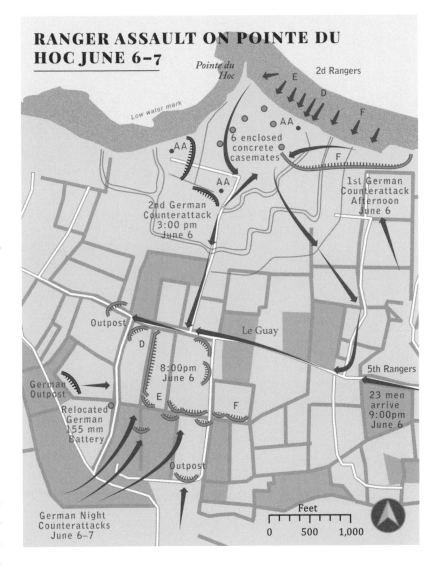

RANGER ASSAULT ON POINTE DU HOC JUNE 6–7

mission by about 8:30 in the morning of D-Day which, as they said, was so important because it (the gun battery) was the heaviest firepower along the Atlantic Wall that could have killed tens of thousands of service members, (threatening) our whole invasion fleet of thousands of ships off the coast. They were all visible when the sun rose. They were visible targets for those guns.

Lomell was sent to England to recover from wounds suffered in the Normandy assault. He later took part in the Allied drive across France, into Belgium—where he fought in the Battle of the Bulge—and ultimately into Germany. Wounded repeatedly, Lomell earned a Silver Star for his bold leadership in the capture and defense of "Hill 400" during the Battle of Hürtgen Forest.

Frank E. South

Medic, Technician, Fourth Grade, 2nd Ranger Battalion

Frank South, a native of Norfolk, Nebraska, left college as a freshman in March 1943 to join the 106th Infantry Division as a medic. He became "extraordinarily bored" with training at Fort Jackson, South Carolina, and jumped at the chance to volunteer for the Rangers. After specialized training in Tennessee and Florida for both infantry and medic roles in combat, he was among Rangers enjoying nice accommodations—arranged by Colonel Rudder—on the *Queen Elizabeth* during the voyage to England. Cliff-scaling and other assault training followed in the run-up to D-Day, and he became fond of the young boys from a nearby village on the Cornish coast who wanted to "help" the American soldiers with menial tasks.

Ranger patch, as worn on uniforms.

Following the capture of Pointe du Hoc, Lieutenant Colonel Rudder, top right, directed the movement of German POWs. The American flag on the ground signaled "friendly" to Allied aircraft.

On the first of June, we went aboard our mother ships and lay at anchor until very, very early on the sixth. We weighed anchor while or after having breakfast at about 2:00. As a medic, I was on the (British transport) SS *Ben My Chree* and spent the night in the ship's surgery along with a British commando medic. I had read in one of the army medical journals about problems with hair, etc. entering head wounds and I figured that this would be a good time for me to shave my head. If I took a head wound, I might keep it as clean as possible. Youth! I was all prepared for D-Day with a shaved head and a newly grown mustache.

I spent much of the night talking with the commando, and since we were allowed to carry arms if we wanted to, or at this time, side-arms, as long as we didn't have our medic brassards on, I compulsively worked on my .45 automatic, cleaning it, re-cleaning it, checking it, working the slide, and making sure that the clips and rounds were in order. Next I turned to sharpening my fighting knife, and again inspected my large medical pack. All our personal packs were, of course, on the supply boat, but I had also a huge specially prepared pack which was a pack board with a large mountain pack attached. It had everything from bandages to morphine to plasma and anything else I, or anyone else, could think of in it.

About 2:00 a.m., we were served breakfast, which consisted of flapjacks and lots of coffee. Following that, we made a final check of our arms, and equipment. We were all issued one D ration bar and started lining up on deck. About 4:00 a.m., they called out "Rangers, man your crafts," and we started boarding the LCAs. Mine was number 884, one of the two F Company crafts. My huge pack and I were, of course, placed in the stern of the vessel. I was to be one of the last off.

The boats were lowered away without incident, got into formation and started on the way in to the cliffs. The seas were fairly heavy for the small British LCAs. One of them carrying part of D Company started taking on water, foundered and sank;

Rangers climb a ladder used to scale the Pointe on D-Day.

boat that was to pilot us in had wandered off course. Apparently he had not properly adjusted for set and drift and we were, instead of going towards Pointe du Hoc, headed in towards Omaha Beach. The situation was picked up by Colonel "Big Jim" Rudder and by 1st Sergeant Len Lomell, and the proper course change was made. But this meant that we had to come in more or less parallel to the cliffs and started picking up fire from the German positions along the top of the cliffs. On our boat, one of the British sailors returned fire with a Lewis machine gun, to little or no effect. As we began to close with the shore the battleship *Texas* and the British destroyer *Talybont* could see the action on top of the cliffs and started laying down some very effective shell fire.

As we got in, close to the cliffs, we were not in the planned positions, so that our boats were crowded too closely together. The rockets with the grapnels attached were fired, bringing up the climbing lines and ropes. Many fell short because they were fired too soon, or because the ropes were wet and heavy. The grapnels were designed to go to the top of the cliffs, dig in there, and then we would be able to scale the cliffs, using either rope ladders, which some of them had, or simply straight ropes, which most of us preferred.

Some of the ropes that made it were cut by the Germans. In any case, we were getting constant machine-gun fire from our left flank, alongside the cliff, and could not, for the life of us, locate the source immediately.

As soon as my LCA landed, the ramp dropped and the Rangers waded ashore the best they could and I followed. But instead of finding knee or hip deep water, my pack and I found a bomb crater and the world turned completely to water, green water. Somehow, I clawed my way out, my pack still on my back, and got up onto the beach. Then, instantly, I was being shot at. I found and ducked into a dry crater, but before I could take a good breath, the first cry of "Medic!" went out and I shrugged off the pack, grabbed my aid kit, and ran to the wounded man.

While I was working on him—he had been shot in the chest, as I remember—we came under fire again and I was able to drag him in closer to the cliff where we could get out of the line of fire.

At the same time that this was happening, I felt a blast over to my left. The other F Company boat was unable to get its rockets into position to fire them properly. So, Technical Sergeant (John) Cripps had taken the rockets off, two of them as I remember, put them on the beach itself, and hand-fired them while standing only three feet off. In the process of firing the first one, he was

most of the men were saved later. Also lost was one of our supply vessels with much of our spare ammunition—and personal packs.

Dawn broke with leaden overcast skies. The seas were gray and white-capped and it was cold. Planes were overhead giving us air cover and the big guns from the warships were firing, to what effect we couldn't tell. I remember it as being extraordinarily spectacular. The huge armada on our left and behind was made up of the warships as far as our eyes could see. The noise of the ships' fire and aircraft bombings was persistent and impressive.

A problem did arise in that the British Combined Operations

partially blinded, with carbon particles embedded deeply in his face. Nevertheless, he went on, and again, in almost direct line of fire from the machine gun, was able to get the second one in position, fired it, again taking a terrible blast. It took extraordinary courage, determination and self-control. I still feel this act of bravery was never properly recognized or rewarded.

I'd no sooner taken care of the first wounded man, than I had to go to another and another and another. Most of the time I was either trying to drag our men to cover or patch them up the best I could. The one somewhat amusing incident which I still remember concerned Bill "L-Rod" Petty, one of our more assertive combat types. He was standing and cursing at the bottom of the rope. The rope was slippery, muddy and wet. Captain (Walter) Block, our medical officer and also an assertive type, said "Soldier, stop fooling around and get up that rope to the top of the cliff." Petty, with his usual short temper turned

to Captain Block—Petty a buck sergeant at the time—stared at him and said in his Georgia drawl, "I've been trying to get up the goddamned rope for five minutes and if you (Block) think you can do any better, you can f——g well do it yourself." Block, furious and red-faced returned the stare, looked at me, shook his head and turned away.

First one, and then another, and then a few more, made it to the top, all within a period of maybe five minutes, ten minutes, fifteen minutes. Time was fluid and passed in erratic leaps. The battle for Pointe du Hoc began in earnest.

After a half or three quarters of an hour or so, Block got the other medics together to go up to the top of the cliff and set up an aid station. I was given the job of staying below, taking care of

A wounded Ranger is brought aboard USS *Texas* for treatment.

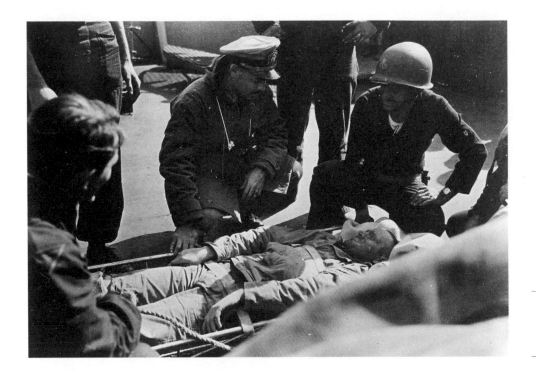

Left: A wounded Ranger talks to Chaplain Moody aboard USS *Texas*.

Right: GIs inspect damage to a fortification at Pointe du Hoc.

any newly wounded individuals, and those already wounded. As I recall I spent most of this time moving them the best I could into a more secure part of the cliff structure where they couldn't be fired upon and I would continue with (medical) patch work.

In about an hour or two, I went up to the top of the cliff where I was now more needed. Since we were taking heavy casualties, Rudder had set up his CP (Command Post) just seaward of an anti-aircraft bunker and shelter, a concrete emplacement with two rooms. We turned the structure into our aid station and, since it was pitch-black in there, at first we worked using only flashlights. Later, someone was able to get some gasoline lanterns off the remaining supply boat before the British sailor left with the rest of our supplies.

The wounded were coming in at a rapid rate, and we could only keep them in rows a few on a few litters we had or on the floor in blankets. The dead we took into the adjoining room.

I don't recall how many we treated. It was just an endless, endless process. Periodically I would go out and bring in a wounded man from the field, carrying or leading one back, and ducking through the various shell craters.

At one time, I went out to get someone, and was semi-carrying him back, more or less on my shoulders, when he was hit by several bullets and was killed. Remembering that is still bothersome; depressing and a burden of some weight. I didn't realize he was

dead until I was almost all the way back to the aid station.

Later on in the day it turned much warmer and, though we had first begun fighting in what seemed very cold weather, in the afternoon men were opening their shirts to cool off a bit. The day wore on. The casualty rate dropped off towards evening. The medics kept working that night and I don't recall how, when, or if we slept.

On day two–that is, D+1–the fighting again became more intense. The sailor who backed off with our other supply boat also left us without additional backup ammunition, so we were running very low. Rudder ordered Block to ration out the ammunition, and Block had assigned me to carry it out. There were a few people who kept coming back for all the ammunition they could get. We were starting to experience some counter-attacks, and Rudder was worried about being able to maintain a solid perimeter defense.

After taking care of a few men in the morning, I took off my Red Cross armband and, arming myself with a captured German Schmeisser machine pistol, volunteered to go out on perimeter defense. After about four hours it was apparent I was no longer needed and I returned to the aid station with a wounded man.

On the 8th, I went out of the aid station and over the field. The firing had died down, and coming across towards us were the rest of the battalion. Near the front of them, I recognized the

tall figure and the peculiar loping gait of my closest friend, Bill "Willy" Clark, also a medic and also, at this time, not wearing a brassard (armband) but carrying an M-1. It was a great sight, and a relief. But then we started counting heads. Of the 225 men who had landed on the Pointe, there were less than 95 who could still bear arms.

Put together, the three Ranger companies that had landed on Omaha Beach could now form no more than a single company having lost over two-thirds of their men, killed or too severely wounded to carry on.

After being relieved, we did get some C rations. We made sure that the wounded were fed first, and then we started taking them down to the beach for evacuation. Later that day, we were able to leave the Pointe and move on to a swampy area outside of Cricqueville and Grandcamp, where we were able to wash in the creek, rest and wonder about what would come next.

South and other Rangers regrouped as they received reinforcements after their defense of the Pointe. He was part of the campaign to take Cherbourg and later joined the fight in northern France, Germany and Czechoslovakia.

POINTE DU HOC

Elmer H. Vermeer

First Lieutenant, Engineer/Demolition Specialist

2nd Ranger Battalion

Farm chores and two-mile walks to school were central to the youth of Elmer "Dutch" Vermeer in rural Iowa. At an early age, Vermeer learned how to hunt and use explosives, as he and an older brother took black powder used by their father to reload shotgun shells and applied it to splitting logs. After a few years of college, Vermeer enlisted in the army in the summer of 1941. He attended Officer Candidate School and, after commission as a second lieutenant, was assigned to the Second Engineer Battalion of the 2nd Infantry Division, which trained in amphibious landings and rapid bridge-building. The battalion shipped out for Ireland in mid-1943 and faced more training there before Vermeer was recruited to handle demolitions for the 2nd Rangers as they prepared for D-Day.

Several of the other boats hit the beach before we did, and by the time we landed there were men already on top of the cliff. One of the big problems on the little, short beach was that the (German) machine gun which had fired on us in the boats was now firing on everybody as they crossed the beach on their way up the cliff. When we got to the cliff, we could get out of his sight, but there must have been about 15 men hit right on that short 30 yards of beach between the boats and the cliff.

Our boat landed high and dry, and I didn't even get my feet wet before crossing that beach. About the time we came in, the only DUKWs (amphibious trucks equipped with ladders for the assault) that did make it into the Pointe put up the fire ladder out in the water—they could not get on the beach because of the shell holes made by the bombardment which had preceded our landing. The fire ladder was swaying at about a 45 degree angle, both ways. The Ranger with the machine gun at the top of the ladder did fire short bursts as he passed over the edge of the cliff. However, the DUKW floundered so badly that they had to put the fire ladder back down.

Two of our grapnel hooks carried to the top of the cliff, so our boat had at least two ropes that we could climb. When I got to the top of the cliff, I found that we were in Captain (Otto) Masny's F Company sector. He had already moved his troops in a short distance, so we got to the top of the cliff safely. There was still an awful lot of machine-gun fire and, I think, the Germans were also shelling the area from the Maisy batteries near Grandcamp. Colonel Rudder was already topside, and he set up a CP in a bomb crater.

There were a number of men attached to the Rangers for this mission. One of the groups was a Shore Fire Control Party, headed by Captain Jonathan H. Harwood from the artillery and a navy lieutenant, Kenneth S. Norton. They were talking to Colonel Rudder when I came into the CP. They had found out that not one of the radios that were brought in to direct fire from the navy ships was working. They had all become water-soaked in the trip across the channel, and we didn't have any communication with the ships out at sea.

One of the major problems was the machine gun over to our left, just a little over a quarter of a mile from the CP. This gun could cover the beach area, and it was almost impossible for men to cross that beach and get ammunition and supplies up the cliff. The first thing Colonel Rudder asked me to do was to go after the machine gun. (Vermeer and two other soldiers) moved through the shell craters and had just reached the open ground where the machine gun could cover us also, when we ran into a patrol from F Company who were on the same mission. Captain Masny had also seen that the machine gun was a real obstacle. The six of us no sooner got together when a Ranger came running up from the CP saying to back off and wait until they could try and shoot the machine gun off the edge of that cliff with guns from a destroyer.

Although we were really facing some major problems, such as coming in late, being hit by the machine gun along the coast, losing a number of our supply boats and men at sea—some of them were actually picked up and again came to join us at a later date—one thing seemed to work in our favor. Lieutenant James Eikner, the signal officer, bought a small lamp with shutters in England from his own personal collection. It proved to be the only communication we had with the navy for quite a period of time. He was able, with his signal lamp, to relay our problem to the navy, and one of the destroyers was able to see the machine gun and did blow it off of the cliff with its guns. I think it would have been virtually impossible for us to knock out that machine gun since the gunner had about 300 yards of completely open field to fire on us, and he was in a fortified position, almost impossible to hit with mortars or any other kind of artillery except the guns on the destroyer. We were short of mortar ammunition anyway that, fortunately, we didn't have to use.

We came back with the F Company patrol and stopped at Captain Masny's CP, which was under siege by the Germans from over on the left front and from straight south of where we had landed. The Germans were mounting a very heavy attack with riflemen, machine guns and mortars. Masny and his men stayed cool and killed a great number of German soldiers, truly displaying the Ranger spirit and training. Captain Masny was an excellent leader. One of his men was operating a mortar by placing it against his knee. He could see where the Germans were, and without using a bipod or any instruments, he was firing the mortar just by sight. He almost dropped every shell right where he wanted it. Later reconnaissance let us know how effective he had been. An orchard, just beyond where the Germans had attacked, was literally covered with dead Germans who had been killed during that raid.

After the fight, (fellow Ranger) Gerald Eberle and I returned to Colonel Rudder's CP. When we got to within about 25 yards of the CP, we found a Ranger who had captured a German soldier from an underground pillbox or sleeping quarters. We had just

An underground storage vault at Pointe du Hoc, damaged by a bomb.

started to question him, since I do speak some German, when the German was shot right between the eyes by someone farther inland. I don't know if it was a German or an American who shot him. He was facing inland, we were facing the channel, and they nailed him between the eyes while he was standing between us.

Upon getting back to the CP we found out that, since the only communication we had was Eikner's signal lamp, it proved to be impossible to get a message through to higher headquarters telling them that we had landed and were established on the Pointe. For this reason headquarters had ordered the remainder of the Second Battalion and the 5th Ranger Battalion to come in on Omaha Beach, which was the alternate plan. Had we been able to report within 45 minutes of our landing that we had been successful, they would have come in to Pointe du Hoc. So we lost all of the reinforcements and supplies when they went to Omaha Beach.

Also on returning to the CP, we found out that Jake Hill had been killed. Lieutenant Hill was an F Company officer who was one of the first men on top of the cliff. The story goes that on reaching the top he called back to those below, "Those crazy SOBs are using live ammunition." This even brought a smile to some of their faces while they were being shot at. Hill was killed after throwing a grenade—turned out to be a dud— into an enemy position.

I remember shortly after returning that Colonel Rudder came back into the CP having been shot through the leg. It was a flesh wound and Doc Block, I think, ran a swab through it and put a little iodine on it. Colonel Rudder refused to stay in the CP and soon went out again with Captain Harwood and Lieutenant Norton. We understood that one of the men who were working on the radio in one of the gun emplacements had gotten it operational and the three of them went out to do some fire directing.

(A stray naval shell) hit the gun emplacement the three were in while trying to use the repaired radio. Of course, it was a serious mishap. Evidently the Germans had reoccupied another gun emplacement, which was just farther in from the one where the Colonel and the shore fire control party were working. The target number that was given may have been in error since the area was so thoroughly shelled and bombed.

The direct hit turned the men completely yellow. It was as though they had been stricken with jaundice. It wasn't only their faces and hands, but the skin beneath their clothes and the

Captain Jonathan Hartwell Harwood

clothes which were yellow from the smoke of that shell. It was probably a colored marker shell.

Captain Harwood died, and his body was left on a stretcher placed just outside the CP. We could see his body until the third day, when we were relieved. Lieutenant Norton was taken into Doc Block's hospital. The quarters were just behind the CP, down concrete steps and into a concrete bunker which had been the sleeping quarters for the personnel who operated the German ack-ack (88-millimeter) guns.

I must digress to say something about one of the biggest things that saved our day on Pointe du Hoc. That was seeing Colonel Rudder controlling the operation. It still makes me cringe to recall the pain he must have endured trying to operate with a wound through the leg and the concussive force he must have felt from the close hit by the yellow-colored shell. As far as I know,

it was the concussion which probably killed Captain Harwood, and Colonel Rudder, I understand, was right next to him when the shell exploded. He was the strength of the whole operation through the next day-and-a-half in spite of his wounds, and he was in command all of the time.

In order to secure the CP during the night, Colonel Rudder appointed me officer of the day and asked me to post guards. They were not very far out from the CP since we probably did not have much more than 35 acres under our control. We didn't have any "changing of the guard" since there were so few men left able to fight. We even used some of the lesser-wounded men as part of the guard for the CP.

One incident happened to me in the middle of the night. I had gone out and checked the guard and also visited with Captain Masny of F Company whose CP was not far from the battalion headquarters. As I came back into our CP, whether I failed to hear the password call or what, I don't know, but one of the men fired at me. I could hear the bullet snap as it went right by my head. Fortunately, it missed.

Though hard to recall specific times, I still distinctly remember when it got to be 12 o'clock that night (of D-Day), because the 7th of June was my birthday. I felt that if I made it until midnight, I would survive the rest of the ordeal.

During the early morning hours of D+1, the Rangers from F Company and E Company, who were across the perimeter road, came back, a few at a time, into the area where we were. They had taken an awful beating, and there were many casualties. The walking wounded and even some of the wounded that had to be carried were brought back in to the Pointe. Their return gave the perimeter more strength with the additional men and weapons. However, the area now being held against the Germans was getting very small.

On June 7 we dug in and held on to everything we could in the hope that the 29th Division and the 5th Rangers and the remainder of the 2nd Rangers would get to Pointe du Hoc. The day wore on and our defenses probably covered 35, no more than 40, acres. About noon Colonel Rudder, in making sure that he had done everything he could to secure the area, asked me to take

a patrol and see if we could blow the observation post which was right at the tip of the Pointe. This was an area where a number of E Company men had been killed on D-Day trying to cross, and they had left the post in the hands of the Germans. One man, however, had been left in front and one behind to guard the area. Our problem was getting to the observation post across the open area which was subject to German fire from a position west of the Pointe.

When the colonel asked me to blow the Pointe, I again called on my friend, Eberle, who had gone with me earlier on D-Day toward the machine-gun nest. We found a 20-pound sack of C2 explosives and took about five other men from other companies who were at the CP with us to blow the Pointe. We stayed together and went from shell hole to shell hole until we came to the open ground. Then we moved as rapidly as possible and into position right behind the observation post. Eberle and I set the charge at the back door of the concrete bunker, and I hardly remember getting around the corner. We used a very short fuse, and I think the explosion probably lifted us right off the ground.

It wasn't long until we heard the Germans calling, "Comrade," as they were coming out. We captured eight prisoners from the bunker. One of them carried a gun pointing at us as he came out, and he was hit by three or four rounds of rifle fire from the men who were watching.

Toward evening Otto Masny's men had seen Germans going in and out of an ammunition dump, which was along the road leading down from the perimeter road straight to the Pointe. It was well behind the German lines at this time, but Otto felt that we should try to destroy the dump. Colonel Rudder asked him to pick a crew to do this. He asked me to go with him and he also took G. K. Hodenfield, a writer for the *Stars and Stripes* (newspaper), and a man by the name of William F. Anderson from F Company.

We moved out very rapidly and Lieutenant (Richard) Wintz, who was holding the area that we went through, gave us a lot of fire cover so we could get to the ammo dump. When we got there, we all passed our Bangalore torpedoes, pipes about 41-inches long which are filled with high explosives, to Anderson. He crawled through the entrance of the ammo dump, which was nothing more than a shed of tin with some wooden planks. Anderson placed the charge and ignited the fuse. We all crawled back a few feet, got into one of the shell holes and let it blow. The rain that we received included pieces of steel, tin, wood and shells that came falling down after the explosion. We went back to the CP and reported that we had accomplished our mission.

Shortly before dark, a boat from one of the ships came in and brought us a few additional men, including a Ranger from the 1st Battalion who had fought down in the Mediterranean. They also brought some bread, and Doc Block issued out jam sandwiches. This was really the only food that most of us had for the two days we had already been up on the Pointe.

In the early morning hours of June 8, I went back out to the gun emplacement where we had the radio working earlier, crawled in a corner and fell asleep. I woke up—it must have been close to noon—when the gun emplacement was being shelled accidentally by American tanks attached to the 29th Division, when the 5th Rangers and 29th Division men were coming into the Pointe. I think that two of Lieutenant (Charles) Parker's 5th Rangers were killed during this episode. Again Colonel Rudder displayed his great courage and leadership as he helped the men in his CP hold up an American flag as high as they could, so the troops advancing would know that we were Americans and not Germans. They had mistaken some of the firing of the weapons which we had used. Since our ammunition supply was low, many of the Rangers on the Pointe were using German weapons.

The sounds and smells of the battlefield still remain vivid in my mind. You can see the battlefield and hear the battlefield, but it's the smell of death on the battlefield that really penetrates everything. You smell it as soon as the shells explode and the bullets fly, long before the dead bodies of your comrades start to decompose. It is a smell you'll never forget.

Vermeer received a Silver Star for destroying the German ammunition dump. He fought with the 2nd Rangers in Europe until the end of the war.

Originally designed as a heavy anti-aircraft gun, the 88mm proved to be one of the most versatile and feared weapons in the German arsenal. This 8.8 cm Flak 37 could hit an aircraft at 32,500 feet, put indirect fire (firing without a line of sight) on infantry out to 16,000 yards, or penetrate the armor of most Allied tanks with direct fire.

John Raaen

Captain, Commanding Officer, Headquarters Company,

5th Ranger Battalion

As a ranking officer in the Force C Ranger force, John Raaen became part of the Omaha Beach invasion when the force did not receive a clear signal from Rudder's team to follow them up the cliffs at Pointe du Hoc. He led a drive by Rangers to protect the Omaha beachhead en route to reinforcing the 2nd Battalion Rangers holding out against German counter-attacks at the Pointe. (Note: Biographical details on Raaen are found in the Omaha Beach chapter—see pages 160–165.)

This destroyed German pillbox at the Pointe illustrates the capabilities of Allied firepower.

I got up to the top of the bluff. Our mission was to go to our west, so we turned west along the wall and ran into C Company. They already had their mortars in position. I talked with Captain (Wilmer) Wise, asked where Major (Richard) Sullivan was. He told me where Sullivan was and warned me not to go into that particular field because the Germans have it under fire, but to go in this field and you'd be alright, and we did. I moved forward, finally found Sullivan. He asked me to reconnoiter a path along a fence line. It was not a hedgerow, it was a fence line right in the middle of the field. I did. It was perhaps 200 yards, 300 yards. And these are big fields.

I went across the fence line, got to the other side where there was a hedgerow; lying there nicely was a dead German. I'd been shot at a few times on the way over, but it was probably mostly friendly fire. I went back, told Sullivan it would be a proper route for the battalion to go. And so that's the way we did it and the battalion moved across, followed the little pathway into an irregular field. In this irregular field we received quite a bit of artillery fire. It was the first artillery fire that we had received— our baptism. Of course, the first time we heard a shell, we all hit the dirt. But by the time we got out of that field we listened to the sound of the shell coming and we could tell where they were going to hit. If it wasn't very close, we'd pay no attention to it.

We moved through that field and up toward the road and finally ran into Sullivan again. He gave me another mission, and it was to find the left flank of the battalion. What had happened was that B Company was our lead company and had tried to go around Vierville to the south, and machine guns in

the hedgerows beyond that road prevented them from doing it. So the battalion commanders sent a platoon to envelope the problem, which also ran into machine guns, and another platoon run and so on, and we had the whole battalion strung out in the wrong direction—five companies. He said, "Find me the left flank," so I proceeded down the road alone—which was stupid. I should have had somebody with me. I found the last platoon and ran into a patrol from the 1st Division, and this was the linkup between the 29th Division and the 1st Division. I took the patrol with me—there were about three paratroopers who'd been dropped in the water ten miles from where they should have been dropped, and they joined us and we took the whole bunch back to the headquarters. We then proceeded down the road directly to Vierville principally because the B Company commander said, "I can't get through here, there are too many machine guns." We were fired at by snipers and a few things like that, maybe some long-range machine-gun fire, but we got through Vierville.

At that point, we were to continue on to Pointe du Hoc to relieve the 2nd Battalion. That was our mission. But the 29th Division, particularly the commander, the 116th (Regiment) and General Cota, thought that the beachhead was too fragile. He made us stay to defend the beach that night. We went into a night position in two farmhouses that were a couple of hundred yards from the main Vierville intersection—my company in one of the farm houses and headquarters in the other.

We didn't receive any counter-attacks during the night, but I found out I'd forgotten my entrenching shovel, or I'd lost it. So I couldn't dig a foxhole or sleep trench and though the men offered to do it for me, I said, "No, no, I'll wait until you are through and then I'll take one of your shovels and a pick and dig my own." And I said, "Meanwhile, I'll go over in that haystack—it probably is nice and warm—and I'll be comfortable there watching what you do." I went over to the haystack and parted it and climbed in. And being a city boy, I didn't know the difference between a manure pile and a haystack, but I found out. Every bug in France attacked me and I was bitten, I itched. I ran out of that haystack to the tune of all of my men doubled over in laughter. At least they had the decency to give me their flea powder, which I spread liberally—it stopped the bugs, but didn't stop the itching. So that's how we spent the night there. Actually, we did hold a meeting of our battalion and the 1st Battalion of the 116th Regiment with Colonel (Charles) Canham and General Cota together and made plans for the following day.

Those plans were very simple. The advance guard would consist of the 5th Ranger Battalion, seven tanks from the 743rd (Tank Battalion) and the provisional company of the 2nd Rangers. We took their C Company, B Company and A Company—they had so many casualties, we barely made a Ranger company out of them (combined). So that was the advance guard, the 5th Rangers plus that. After that, the regular forces would come, the 2nd Battalion of the 116th and then the 3rd Battalion with scatter tanks, engineers, things like that.

So the next morning, bright and early, I got up and there was a German counter-attack. It was not more than 200 yards from me, probably down where the engineers were positioned. Suddenly I saw our tanks were sitting there on the road doing nothing and yet 250 yards away, there was a major counter-attack, probably company size. So I banged on the turret with my rifle until the commander came out and I pointed out this little counter-attack and said, "Don't you think you should take them under fire?" And he said, "Oh sure!" And he turned around, gave orders and they took them under fire, but with the coaxial machine guns, not with the cannons. I said, "Why don't you use your cannon?" He said, "Overkill."

Sullivan gave me orders to take a four-man patrol out toward the north seaside of the road that runs through Vierville. And so I took the battalion sergeant major and the battalion supply sergeant and the corporal and we made ourselves a nice little diamond formation. We patrolled to 100 yards south of that road, flashed two Germans, chased them across the main road from Vierville to the beach and pursued them beyond the military crest, where I was able to find a *feldgrau* (German) overseas cap with one bullet hole. We came back to the road and we heard the grinding of motors. This battalion master sergeant says, "I have to be with the battalion captain." So the two master sergeants left me and I was with Corporal (Jack) Sharp and proceeded back down to where I knew the 29th Division would be, back down to the beach.

I had to run through a gauntlet of MPs to get to their G3 (operations officer) tent. General (Charles) Gerhardt (commanding officer, 29th Division) heard that I was there and made me come in so I was able to give my report to him, and then he said, "What can we do for you, Rangers?" And I said, "Well, we are out of ammunition. We need mortar and we need machine-gun ammunition, not so much rifle ammunition." So he told the aide de camp, "Take them down to the beach, get them a jeep, and we'll load it up with ammunition." So that's what they did. With Sharp driving it, we went back up to Vierville—and it was spooky, all the troops (appeared to have) left town. So I proceeded toward Pointe du Hoc on an empty road and I could tell where (other troops) had been because when tanks pass a place, if they've used their guns, there's big brass. If they've used their machine guns there's little brass. And of course, if infantry is there, there is always little brass. And there's usually blood and some damaged things.

So I could tell I was on the right track. But it was awfully lonely during that trip and I was shot at three or four times at least, including one where my helmet was hit, spun off my head and into my lap. I finally got to a spot where I was no longer on the road, no longer protected by hedgerows right and left. There was just a great big gap and we couldn't take the jeep across there (vulnerable to enemy fire). So what we did was, we drove to the edge of that visible area and Sharp and I got under the jeep— believe it or not—and muscled it over our heads for a full 50 yards until we got past the open area. We got back in the jeep. The jeep was hit several times by rifle fire or machine-gun fire, we never knew which. And a short time later we ran into the rear end of the advance guard. We distributed the ammunition and the jeep ran out of gas, probably because the gas tank was hit by one of those sniper rounds. So we disposed of the jeep and I went in, finally found Sullivan and reported to him. He said, "You are an armored officer, or were," and he said, "Go check the tank positions and see if they're properly placed for defense for the night, because we are probably going to end up here."

So I went and checked where the tanks were. They were all good tankers, had gotten in the right kind of place, behind good walls and things like that. And I reported back to Sullivan and he said, "Raaen, we just got word from the 29th Division. They need the tanks and us—me and Metcalf—back there at the beach as soon as we can get there. So the monkey's on your back, fellow." And the tanks took off and so did the two commanders, leaving me in command. So I called the company commanders in. We worked out a plan for the defense of the place for the night, knowing each company's position and knowing the password and the countersign. Also I sent out a patrol of two men to Pointe du Hoc to find it because we were at Saint-Pierre-du-Mont and we were no more than 1,000 yards from Pointe du Hoc. It was on a northwest course from where we were.

So we went into night fighting positions and in the morning I got up, went down and said, "Are (Willie) Moody and (Howard) McKissick back?" They were the two men I sent on patrol. "Yes, sir, they are back." I went over there to Sergeant Moody and I said, "Did you see Rudder?" He says, "Yes, sir, I saw Rudder, gave him the full situation, told him we would attack this morning. And I laid a wire so you can talk to Colonel Rudder." I picked up the phone and there I was, talking with Colonel Rudder. Well, I had made plans for the relief with my force. All I had was C Company of the 116th, the provisional company of the 2nd (Ranger) Battalion, and I had D Company and C Company of the 5th (Ranger) Battalion, plus a few hangers-on from battalion headquarters.

But before we could jump off on our attack, up comes the 5th Ranger Battalion from Vierville. And so their plan took over—which was essentially to execute our plan and they would follow. And that's the way we would leave for Pointe du Hoc— we just went across country on a diagonal path; we didn't go down the way the road runs to Pointe du Hoc. It was a very nice homecoming (with fellow Rangers). There were approximately 100 of them left of the 2nd Battalion—they started with about 225. Their casualties were very high. Now of these 100, many of them were walking wounded.

I was sitting on a turret, one of the big, big gun turrets, talking with a 2nd Battalion officer when suddenly the tanks of the 743rd burst out of the underbrush and started shooting at us. We had a flag but they kept shooting. What I remember is the motor

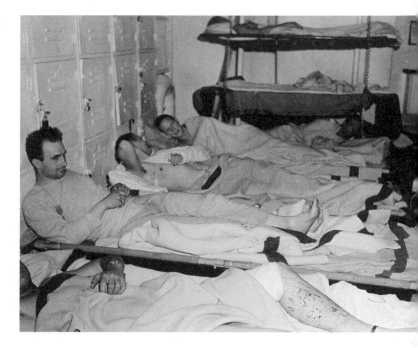

Wounded Rangers aboard USS *Texas*.

officer of the 2nd Ranger Battalion ran about 50 yards from cover to the lead tank, jumped on the tank, banged on the turret until he got the attention of the commander and said, "You are attacking the wrong people!" So they stopped firing. I think we took a kill in that, which was a very unfortunate incident. Well, we reorganized a little bit and then started toward Grandcamp and later toward Maisy.

From what I have seen (results from 5th Ranger actions during the invasion), we met with nothing but military success. We did in fact relieve the 2nd Battalion, and we did in fact get all the way through to Maisy and captured the artillery batteries they had there. It certainly was a giant step towards unseating Hitler. It all depended upon the fact that the 5th Ranger Battalion landed intact. We were a major fighting force. We had help from the tanks, we had help from artillery; don't kid yourself, we had lots of help. But still, the main thing was that our Ranger battalion, well trained, was intact. We just brushed by the enemy opposition.

John Raaen, who retired as a Major General in the army, is one of the last surviving officers from the D-Day invasion. He has written extensively about the invasion and advised historians at The National WWII Museum.

James Earl Rudder

Commanding Officer, 2nd Ranger Battalion

Selected personal communications from the D-Day period have been shared for use in this work by James Earl Rudder's daughter, Anne Rudder Erdman. Chick, Sis and Bud were Rudder's nicknames, respectively, for his wife, daughter and son. Other named references are to relatives or friends, and to other Rangers.

Letter to Lieutenant Colonel James Earl Rudder, Commanding Officer, 2nd Ranger Battalion, from wife
Margaret, June 12, 1944, as Margaret absorbed reports of the successful Ranger assault at Pointe du Hoc.

Mon. – June 12th

Our anniversary!

Earl—my darling—

Honey, I'm so excited I can't even breathe normally. We are at Pat's—and Jewell called me this A.M. to tell me there was a picture of you and a write-up about you & the Rangers on the front page of the San Angelo paper. Joe Aycock of Menard had called her about it. So I called Joe and he read it to me over the telephone Honey. There must have been some awfully tough going, but I'm oh so proud of you. Darling, I married you seven years ago today and I really married you for the man you were. Not dreaming that you would turn out to be my hero too! Derie called me from Brady to tell me about it too. I can hardly wait to see the paper for myself but the mail won't get here till about noon. Alice is taking the news calmly but I know she must be worried about Jerry. She is almost as proud of you as I am—and that's saying an awful lot. Honey, I think I'm just going to pop if I don't hear from you soon. What I want is a letter written after the invasion started. I know in my own heart that you're going to be all right, but a letter now and then confirming the fact will mean the world to me. Darling, I wish that someone had the power to end all wars, they are such terrible things. We will try to make up for everything you've missed when you come home.

Must rush this out to the box so it won't miss the mail. Your two darling youngsters are having a big time out here. Will write you more tomorrow—and in the meantime will be praying for your continued success and safety.

All our love—Sis, Bud and Chick

Left: Margaret, James "Bud" and Anne Rudder.

Below: Telegram to Rudder from his wife Margaret.

Bottom: Rangers receive the Distinguished Service Cross for gallantry and heroism in action during the Normandy invasion.

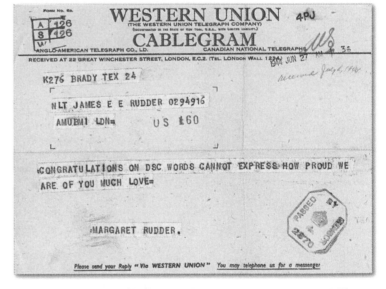

Letter from Lieutenant Colonel Rudder to wife Margaret and children
more than a week after the Rangers secured Pointe du Hoc.

Somewhere in France

June 15, 1944

My dear wife, son and daughter,

No doubt you have had many anxious hours during the past few days, but I'm hoping you have had word that I am ok from Maj. Jack Street as he promised me he would write you an air mail letter for me several days ago. As you probably have read in the news paper everything is going very good with us. The German is a good fighter but he is no match for the Rangers—they are a crew to really be proud of. I guess you and Alice had a fine visit in San Antonio, be sure to tell me all about it. We are very anxious for mail as we haven't had any since we arrived here. You are eager for war news and we are eager for home news. Bud, did you and Sis have a good visit with Bill and Lucille? I know you must have—Darling—I will send you more about things as soon as I have time. Don't worry about me—just keep the home fires burning and I'll be home before so very long. Tell mother, I'll write her soon. God bless and keep you my darlings for my return.

All my love,

Earl

Rudder's letter to his wife and children, June 15, 1944.

Lieutenant Colonel Rudder sent a personal condolence letter to Lorraine Goudey of Lyndhurst, New Jersey, widow of one of his Rangers killed in Normandy. Still reeling from her loss, she responded immediately.

July 28, 1944

Dear Colonel Rudder,

Your letter arrived just a few minutes ago, and I think it was most kind of you to take time from your numerous duties to send me those comforting words. I cried as I read it, but then, I think you knew I would.

The news of David's death came as a very great shock, sir, and I still have not recovered from it completely. I thought I was all ready for it if it should come. I was sure I would be brave, and be as good a soldier as David was, but I wasn't, Colonel Rudder. I broke down completely. Everywhere I go, almost every song I hear brings back memories of him, things we did together. Memories that will never leave me.

We were married only a year, David and me—a year in April, April third. Out of that whole year we had only about two months altogether, but I feel that the little happiness that we did have together was worth the heartache I have to now suffer alone.

I loved David very much, Colonel Rudder, and no one will ever be able to take his place, but life goes on, they tell me, and I shall try to make the best of things.

You see, sir, I've been hoping against hope that it may have been a mistake—that I'd receive word from David telling me he was all right and not to worry. When I received the Purple Heart, I began to lose hope, but now your letter confirms what I prayed wasn't true—that David is dead. I hope he knows, somehow, how terribly I miss him, and how very proud I am of him.

May I ask a favor of you Colonel Rudder? If you have any information at all as to how he died, or what his last words were, I shall be forever grateful if you would forward the information to me. At Camp Shanks, I met two of his ranger buddies, one named O'Connor, the other, Slagel. Perhaps they would know something if they are among the survivors, which I hope they are.

Thank you again, with all my heart, for your kind sympathy.

Lorraine Goudey

CONCLUSION

The actions of US Army Rangers at Pointe du Hoc attracted immediate and enduring attention, and would become iconic in the history of World War II and the US Army alike. "Rudder's Rangers" suffered a casualty rate of more than 60 percent during the fighting of June 6–8, with fewer than 90 of the original 225 assigned to the main assault still fit for combat duty. Rudder himself, the tenacious leader of the main assault group, was wounded twice; he and thirteen of his men received the Distinguished Service Cross and the 2nd Ranger Battalion was awarded a Presidential Unit Citation in recognition of their success and heroism.

The Rangers would take part in clean-up operations near the Normandy coast as Allied forces drove back the German defenders. They supported various American infantry units in the campaign to liberate Europe, but their continuing combat roles were overshadowed by the daring and costly raid on the feared coastal artillery battery. A decade after D-Day, Rudder traveled back to the Pointe to show his son Bud, fourteen years old, how the battle had played out, where the commander had set up his command post amid the rubble, and how the Rangers fought and prevailed over the course of three bitter days.

Decades later, on the 40th anniversary of the battle, President Ronald Reagan visited the site and paid tribute to the veterans of the raid: "These are the boys of Pointe Du Hoc," he declared to the nation and to the world. Then, turning directly to the veterans, he put their long-ago exploits into perspective:

> You were young the day you took these cliffs; some of you were hardly more than boys, with the deepest joys of life before you. Yet, you risked everything here. Why? Why did you do it? What impelled you to put aside the instinct for self-preservation and risk your lives to take these cliffs? ... We look at you, and somehow we know the answer. It was faith and belief; it was loyalty and love.

In doing what seemed impossible, in scaling the cliffs and taking Pointe du Hoc, Reagan said, the Rangers had struck a resounding blow for democracy and liberty.

OTHER PERSPECTIVES

CHAPTER FIVE

6.6.44

The climactic struggle at the Normandy beaches and beyond directly impacted the lives of many thousands of individuals who did not trade fire at the shoreline, drop behind enemy lines or man perilous stations on naval vessels. A diverse collection of participants and witnesses bring other distinct vantage points to the collective memory of D-Day, essential to anyone seeking the complete picture.

The archive of The National WWII Museum is seasoned with "other" vivid narratives. Excerpts from six of the accounts follow. They take the reader through the experiences of two fighter pilots who were itching to get into the long-awaited battle; a young French girl transfixed by the arrival of Americans bearing candies; a combat cameraman who was instructed not to pause to help wounded comrades; a hospital nurse determined to hold her composure in a sea of agony; and a German soldier facing a hopeless assignment in low-grade shoes. Their stories resonate along with more high-profile American D-Day accounts, helping to illustrate the far reach of this pivotal episode in world history.

Previous page: Rows of stretchers bearing wounded American and British soldiers cover the deck of a Coast Guard LCT bound for England after the D-Day invasion.

Above: Not all members of the German Army in Normandy were German. These men, forced into service, are Mongolians. They were some of the first men taken prisoner in Normandy.

Left: US Army nurses Barbara Forrester (right) and Elizabeth Mecomber.

Below: The *Marschstiefel*, commonly known as the jack boot, was the traditional calf-length leather boot of the German Army. On June 6, 1944, Franz Gockel, of the 726th Infantry Regiment, 352nd Infantry Division, German Army, wore these boots while defending *Widerstandsnest* 62 (Resistance Nest 62) at Colleville-sur-Mer, Omaha Beach.

OTHER PERSPECTIVES

Clayton Kelly Gross

First Lieutenant, P-51 Pilot, 355th Fighter Squadron,

354th Fighter Group, Ninth Air Force

Born in 1920 in Walla Walla, Washington, Clayton Kelly Gross learned to fly before the war. In 1941 he applied to the Army Air Forces and US Navy flying programs. Approved by both, he selected the Army Air Forces, and reported to the first Aviation Cadet class to assemble after the bombing of Pearl Harbor. Gross was trained as a fighter pilot and assigned to the 355th Fighter Squadron, which shipped out to England in late 1943. By D-Day, Gross had four aerial kills flying his P-51 Mustang nicknamed "Live Bait." Gross flew two missions on June 6 to escort C-47s towing gliders to France.

Above: Clayton Kelly Gross in front of "Live Bait."

D-Day was a big day. We knew it was coming. We had been confined to the base for about two weeks, which meant that it was very difficult to sneak over the fence to the pub [laughs]. I think the statute of limitations is gone, but I know that we did go to the pub every now and then. They had us put planes on the end of the runway with pilots in the cockpit, with the engine warmed up for immediate takeoff. So, the first few days they did that, we had all the veteran pilots in those planes because we didn't want to miss the action. But after several days just sitting there and nothing happening, we started putting the rookies in the cockpit.

On the night of June 5, we finished dinner and went to the club, which was very normal, and I ordered a beer. And we're drinking beer when Bowers Espy, the executive officer of the group, came in and hollered, "Close the bar, close the bar." "What do you mean, close the bar?" "I mean, close it, we're going to fly." I said, "You've got to be out of your mind, the weather is terrible." There was about a 1500-foot, 2000-foot maximum ceiling, and you couldn't see your hand in front of your face in there (clouds).

We were ordered to a briefing, and at the briefing they told us, "You're going to escort gliders in with the Airborne troops," so we got ready. We had three squadrons of, I think, twelve planes each, and we took off and we met the bunch of C-47s towing gliders. The only way we can see people is by the exhaust stacks on the engine. It was absolutely brutal, but we made it to the French coast. And on the French coast, at the Omaha Beach area, we saw a wall of fire coming up—an absolute wall of fire, and those poor guys had to fly right through that. They don't have any armor plate in those things. How many made it, I don't know. I know it was absolutely brutal but they did get there. We turned around and came back.

Now, our base was closed in, the weather was so bad, we could not get back to the base, and so we landed at an empty RAF base. Colonel (George) Bickell was leading the group, and he got on the phone to find out what we were going to do, and then he came back and by this time it's one o'clock in the morning on June 6 and he says, "We're going to take off and escort a second mission," because we can't get the planes back (to the regular base) for the replacement pilots. So we tried to sleep for a couple hours and then about 3:30 we had a briefing again. We took off at four o'clock maybe and we met more gliders, and more C-47s. This time it was a sight I will never forget. Down below us on the Channel dawn was coming up and there were so many ships. You cannot imagine it, and we were over them and watched them.

We watched the gliders go in, again, and in the meantime the ships were trying to escort their (forces headed to) the beach, and we could do nothing except see that no enemy aircraft came in to disrupt it. I mean, it was so exciting to think that this is just started. This time we were able to get back to our base—and when we got back, King Peter of Yugoslavia was in our briefing room to congratulate us, because eventually his country was going to be freed again, so a great mission. I remember saying to the guys, "If you have to go down in the Channel, don't worry about it, you could walk back to England on the ships," there were that many of them—an unbelievable number. What a job that was to put together.

Gross stayed with the 355th Fighter Squadron for the duration of the war, eventually becoming an Ace with a total of six kills. In the spring of 1945 Gross shot down a rare Messerschmitt Me 262, an early jet fighter.

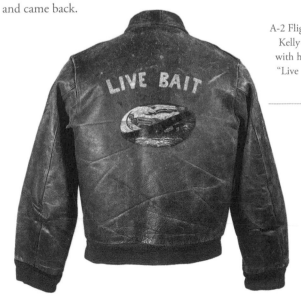

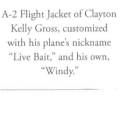

A-2 Flight Jacket of Clayton Kelly Gross, customized with his plane's nickname "Live Bait," and his own, "Windy."

OTHER PERSPECTIVES

Clyde Bennett East

Captain, P-51 Pilot, 15th Tactical Reconnaissance Squadron,

10th Photographic Group, 9th Air Force

Clyde East was born on a tobacco farm in Virginia in 1921 and even as a young boy was fascinated with aircraft. Unable to meet qualifications for joining the Army Air Forces, East hitchhiked to Canada and joined the Royal Canadian Air Force in 1941. He was elevated to the officer ranks in November 1942 and assigned to duty in England. Trained to fly P-51 Mustangs, East successfully applied to the US Army Air Forces and joined its 15th Tactical Reconnaissance Squadron. Tasked with flying reconnaissance missions to photograph behind German lines, East also had permission to engage enemy targets.

Allied planners feared attacks by the deadly the German Luftwaffe on June 6. While some fighter groups were assigned to cover C-47s towing gliders to France, other Army Air Forces units were assigned patrol duties along the coast or over interior transportation corridors. Experienced pilots in P-51 Mustangs took to the skies to carry out reconnaissance duties and hunt for enemy planes.

The onset of June 6th came on the night of the 5th when all of the pilots and the intelligence officers were called into the officers' club and the doors were locked and the commander announced, "Tomorrow's D-Day. The fight we've been waiting for is going to take place and even as we speak the paratroopers and the ships are on the way. Tomorrow's going to be a big day. I can't tell you exactly where the landing is going to be, but we will be involved and they're within good range of Middle Wallop (airfield) so we can expect to have a very active day."

So we all went to our respective squadrons where the commanders elaborated quite a bit on what kind of activities we expected, what we were supposed to do, how we were supposed to act, and the fact that we would be flying as many missions as we could schedule for the next day. The only thing that interrupted (the mission) was the early morning fog that we had over the airbase, which made all of our airplanes late in getting off. It was just too thick. But by ten, eleven o'clock in the morning everything was clear.

I flew around three o'clock in the afternoon because I had been on runway alert. Just in case the German air force decided to attack our base, they put four airplanes on runway alert to intercept them. They of course didn't show up and I was able to fly with my regular wingman, one that I had flown with several times before.

About two o'clock, three o'clock in the afternoon (I took off). You have to remember we were on daylight savings time so consequently, there was lots of daylight left at three o'clock in

---

Opposite: Clyde East, center. On the right breast of East's jacket are his Royal Canadian Air Force wings.

Above: Captain East's P51 F-6D at the end of the war, showing crosses for each of his 13 aerial victories.

Above: Allied planners gained valuable intelligence on beach obstacles from photographs like this one, taken by 10th Photo Reconnaissance Group pilot First Lieutenant Albert Lanker in May 1944.

the afternoon. My flight was around two hours and it was about 125 miles to the invasion beach. I was supposed to look for traffic on the roadways and rail lines between two of the important transportation centers in France.

I did this and saw practically nothing in the way of moving traffic that wasn't obviously civilian. They (Germans) just did not react the way it was expected that they would. It was after I had been almost an hour on my recon route and just ready to turn and head north to go back to England that we ran across the four German fighters.

We were flying along the road and railroad net that I was scheduled to follow and my wingman called out the fact that there were four fighters just ahead of us. My response to that was "They're probably ours" or words to that effect because we had not seen any German fighters at that time, and keeping up with

the daily developments from our intelligence people, there was no indication of any heavy German resistance.

Now we did have one of our pilots that morning that caught a Messerschmitt 109 on a final approach to landing at one of the small bases in France. He attacked it right away and shot it down just before it touched down. His was the first airplane that was destroyed on D-Day. Mine was the second and my wingman's was the third, and there was another encounter by a Typhoon somewhere in the British sector that shot down an airplane. So there were only four airplanes destroyed that day and my squadron destroyed three of them—and we were rather proud of that.

Well, it was something that was really a thrill, something that I just couldn't really believe happened. It turned out that here I was facing a German airplane and after a very short encounter—he obviously was more surprised than I was—I shot him down without any serious difficulties and so did my wingman, shot down his one airplane. It was a real thrill because I'd been working toward this for months and months and it just seemed incredible.

The most interesting portion of that flight was seeing the invasion fleet and flying across the Utah and Omaha beaches. Seeing all of the activity that was taking place on the ground while we were flying just 3000-feet above them was a very, very interesting thing. It's something I'll never forget and will probably never happen again.

....

East scored his first aerial victory on D-Day and the second Allied aerial victory of the day. By the end of the war, East had flown approximately 250 missions. He became a Double Ace with a total of 13 aerial victories. East remained in the US Air Force after the war, retiring in 1965.

This Royal Air Force Type C flight helmet was worn by American 10th Photo Reconnaissance Group pilot James F. Frakes on D-Day. Frakes flew an F-5 (the photo reconnaissance version of the P-38 Lighting) with the 34th Photo Reconnaissance Squadron. The helmet is fitted with American headset receivers and RAF Mk. VIII flying goggles.

OTHER PERSPECTIVES

Eveline Peardon

French Civilian living near Omaha Beach

Eveline Peardon was three and a half years old in the summer of 1944. She lived with her mother, grandparents, and three siblings in the French village of Saint-Honorine-des-Pertes, where her grandfather was mayor. The family lived just east of Omaha Beach and, as German batteries inland exchanged fire with Allied ships at sea, Peardon and her family were awakened by the deafening roar.

As Allied forces began the assault on the Normandy coast French civilians were caught in the crossfire. There had been no mass evacuation. Although the French welcomed the Allied invasion, desperate for an end to the German occupation, the non-combatants suffered terribly.

Our property was surrounded by a park of trees and four kilometers inland there was a German battery—and from the Channel, the Americans and the Allies were sending shells. We were like a sandwich. We were extremely lucky, really. The reason for the noise was the back and forth of the shells going above us.

French Resistance member Marie Louise Lévi-Ménard took notes on BBC broadcasts and distributed to neighbors pamphlets she typed up on this stolen German typewriter.

Above: Liberated French citizens greet American GIs.

At that time my maternal grandparents were alive and we were living with them. My mother being alone with her four children and her parents, got up from her bed and took us like a hen and her chicks [laughs] in her bed. That I remember. And she checked on her parents and we were kind of waiting—if I may say, waiting to see if life was going on or not, I suppose, because I was not told. I remember at one point the vibration of the back and forth shelling from the windows. They were big windows,

A young French girl is pulled from her hiding place.

tall windows. My mother got up and she said, "I'm going to open the windows to avoid that." I remember the picture of her going to the window and the window burst into her face. She didn't get hurt or whatever, but that is an image that I can't forget.

And then she decided we're not going to stay upstairs. In the area where we are there are no cellars. The house is built on the ground. It's a big house and there is a wing which is much older than the other part of the house—sixteenth century—and the walls are a meter thick. So my mother decided to bring everybody down in the kitchen. I remember a detail, a child detail. In those days we had maids, and they carried mattresses from upstairs down for everybody to be a little more comfortable. The shelling was still going and at that time my older brother was scared of course, and he went under the kitchen table which is a big oak table and he prayed for his birthday [laughs].

(We learned of the invasion) the day after only. My mother found out because we obviously were the first liberated. She ventured not too far in the park. She faced an American soldier. He had his knife across his mouth—on the defensive, you know. So she understood. But the house has a farm next door, so the farmers came in to the kitchen also with their dog [laughs]. It was a lot of people in that kitchen, but on that very morning, there was nothing to do. Just to wait.

(Bombs landed nearby), oh yes, a hundred yards from the house in the corner of the park and, in fact, for years you could see the crater. We were lucky. Two years ago another bomb was discovered about fifty yards from the house, unexploded.

There is a long avenue to come to the property and a lot of (Allied) soldiers camped in there and we would visit them.

They were very happy to see kids. They spoiled us with candies. I remember the rolls of Lifesaver. I would put the whole thing in my mouth. I didn't want to share. That's a child detail. I remember that probably was not even a week after an American officer came to the house and introduced himself. He was from Philadelphia; he stayed in the area until Christmas and then he went to Germany. But during those months and all summer he came every night with an amphibious vehicle. Oh, that was a lot of fun. They would (visit) because there is huge turn-around on the property and we were allowed to go and go around [laughs]. Also, talking about the candies, every day they would give us candies. I'd never had candies anyway, and chewing gum—I didn't know what it was.

_____

Peardon and her family considered the Americans the "saviors of the country." Her family kept in touch with the officer from Philadelphia until his death. At 26, Peardon went to America to work and married a young man, settling permanently in Connecticut.

By the end of August, towns and villages all over northern France had been reduced to rubble in the Allied drive toward Paris. More than 19,000 French civilians were killed in the fighting in Normandy, but citizens of the region would be forever grateful to the Allied soldiers.

Many French citizens risked their lives to participate in the resistance movement. This homemade radio receiver was used by Marie Louise Lévi-Ménard to listen to BBC broadcasts, although listening to the BBC was illegal.

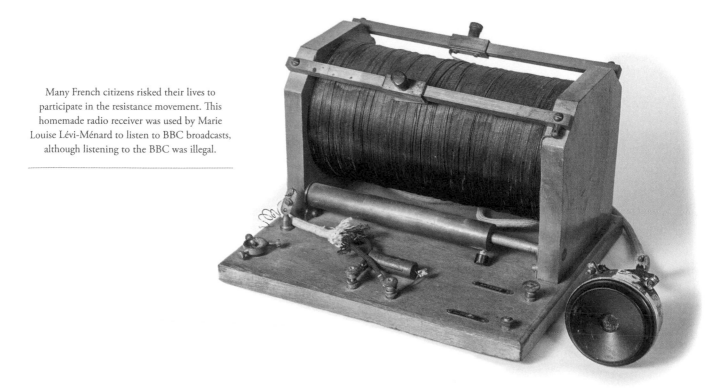

Walter Touhy Halloran

Technician, Fifth Grade, 165th Signal Photographic Company

Omaha Beach

Born in 1923, Walter Halloran grew up on a farm in Chatfield, Minnesota, where he rode a horse to high school. He was encouraged by family friends to move to Hollywood to find work and was hired by Max Factor Cosmetics as a photographer. Army recruiters visited the studio, seeking to fill slots in Signal Corps photographic units. Halloran signed up and, after initial training at Paramount Studios, was assigned to the 165th Signal Photographic Company as a combat cameraman. His mission on June 6 was to film the landings at Omaha Beach while trying to stay alive.

Members of the 165th Signal Photographic Company at Fort Polk, Louisiana in 1943. Halloran is bottom row, third from left.

Not every soldier who landed on Norman beaches on June 6 to liberate Europe was prepared to use a weapon. Army Signal Corps cameramen and photographers were armed with cameras to capture the "day of days."

Well, I just ran and got out of that thing (Higgins boat) as fast as I could. I dropped into a hole in the water, and I'm not very tall, so I got pretty wet. I just ran as hard as I could to get to the protection of a little bit of a bump in the shore. And I had something else that I guess we've not mentioned before. Prior to leaving England, we were surprised by some officers coming down with carrier pigeons for us to take with us. They had come up with real tiny little Minox cameras that could be put in a little garment they made for the pigeons, if you will. So

the last thing they did to us— and this was a total surprise—was take a couple of pigeons in a nice, lightweight, tiny crate, and they snapped it on your backpack. By the time I got to shore one of my pigeons was already drowned, so 50 percent of my capacity was gone. Even though I was a movie man, the idea we were given with the pigeons was that you can never tell, you might grab an opportunity of some kind with this little tiny film, and you put it in the saddle and send them off. Can you imagine that?

On the gear he carried: Oh, heavens, we were loaded. We had very heavy backpacks with ammunition and guns, a thousand feet of motion picture film, and then our socks and, you know, a basic pack. We were loaded with heavy stuff. You've seen pictures of these guys, their backpacks just full of stuff. And film is heavy. We had a thousand feet of motion picture film. That was kind of heavy. The camera was wrapped in plastic, and it had a wrist strap, and we just put that around our wrist so that if it got wet it wouldn't hurt anything to get the camera ashore. I don't know what I remember seeing—that's so long ago. All I can remember is running as hard as I could. I could hardly get to the protection of these bunkers.

Halloran's assignment once he hit the beach: Well, you had freedom of choice. The assignment was to cover anything you can on the activities of troops landing. I mean, nobody said do this or get that. Usually the only comments then on photographing was men getting killed, and I did shoot one scene that I know you've seen. Everybody has. Those four soldiers alive—they align. They're marching towards the camera, and the guy on the left-hand side got shot and killed, that was the first film I took. I was laying down on the sand to get as low as possible out of the machine-gun fire, and I happened to look, and here comes four soldiers abreast coming right towards me and as the camera was going one of them got shot and fell over. So that meant, well, at least the camera's working.

I've often been asked was I afraid as we approached the shore on D-Day, and I've said, "No, I don't think so." We were overwhelmed by seasickness. We were so sick. You just can't imagine how filthy you were, top to bottom, sick, weak. Most of us, myself included, my only objective in the world was get off this damn boat and get me on land. I'll worry about it once I get there. It was terrible.

I remember there was just a lot of chaos. People were coming ashore, people were getting killed, and wounded, and shot, medics in there with their litters trying to get people back. They wanted to get them back to the barges, put them in the barge to go to England. A lot of yelling. A lot of hollering. Confusion. A lot of confusion. Complete chaos. Barges were coming in, taking wounded persons back out. The sense of order was accomplished by some wonderful navy officers. They were called beach masters. They were a traffic control cop. It's what they do, and they're good, and they controlled the ships and the boats—the Higgins

boat and everything else—in and out, to keep some sort of order. But the main thing on that beach was really just the chaos. People trying to join up with each other.

The person that got shot—I captured it. I was laying down on my belly, wet and sloppy and dirty, to check my camera out, and I saw these four men coming towards the beach. I'm on the beach shooting out to the water, and it was just luck. I shouldn't say luck, the guy died, but these four guys gaze in. You could see it, he was right there in the camera, gets shot and falls over. So then you kind of gradually wiggle back till you get to the sand that's higher, and then you get up and run, get out of there. You get away from the beach. That's where the enemy was obviously, they were aiming on the beach. You got to get away from this doggone beach and get out of there. Good thing I was young, a teenager.

Bell and Howell 35mm Eyemo camera, similar to the one used by Halloran.

Opposite: Walter Halloran

Sharply mixed sentiments on not helping the wounded: Interestingly enough, that didn't bother me a bit. You'd say how can that be, you're an animal. I'd suggest that you go see *Saving Private Ryan*, because they show pictures of pushing bodies out of the way. You had to. You had to. I remember the little navy boats that were coming in and out and so forth. I still remember a navy officer, I have no idea what rank he was. He was still on the ship yelling at the people getting off the Higgins boat, "Keep going, keep going," you know, got some choice language, "Get out of that. You're blocking the whole thing up there." It was well executed. Did some men die? Yep, sure did. Sure did. And another thing that was really bad. Some of the guys in the water were screaming for help. "Help me! Help me! Help me!" That's kind of hard to just ignore them. Bad. That's a lot to put on a teenager. That's why I'm having trouble today.

On the end of the day: As I recall vividly, we ended up in an apple orchard, and we seemed to have gathered some sense of security or safety—I can't imagine why—amongst all the trees in the apple orchard. On our first night we put up our little tents and, oh, yeah, the next thing was the heavy artillery moved into the area, and they fired all night. It just rattled your head, the concussion. But I still recall feeling sort of a sense of not wellbeing, but a sense of satisfaction that we got this far and are still alive in the safety of an apple orchard.

Halloran remained in Europe, capturing pivotal moments in both video and photographs including the Battle of the Bulge. He filmed the liberation of Buchenwald before becoming a prisoner of war for a brief period. Halloran stayed in the army, receiving a field commission during the Korean War. He retired in 1970 as a colonel.

OTHER PERSPECTIVES

Opal Grapes

Lieutenant, US Army Nurse, Station Hospital, England

Opal Grapes was born in Franklin Country, Virginia in 1920. Raised on a farm, she was one of six children. Grapes' mother worked with the family doctor, and an older sister became a nurse. After a year of college, Grapes followed in their footsteps and went to nursing school, becoming a registered nurse before the bombing of Pearl Harbor. She joined the army after the December attack, and reported to an army hospital near Axminster, England, where she worked as a ward nurse.

While military cameramen captured images that would tell the story of the war for decades to come, those who treated wounded and dying soldiers had searing experiences of their own to pass on. Wounded soldiers and sailors were shipped to England as quickly as possible. At army hospitals, they were cared for by female nurses who were specially trained to deal with combat injuries.

I suppose there were rumors (of the invasion) from time to time, but we were just so involved in seeing that our hospital was in order. And of course we were drilling, we were hiking, and we were doing calisthenics all this time. We were told to keep in shape. If we had a lull in getting patients, we were out doing calisthenics and this sort of thing. So I didn't really pay much attention to rumors. But we knew at midnight, on June 5th/6th, that something was happening. When we saw the sky filled with planes, we knew it had to be D-Day.

By morning, by the break of day, we could hear guns, and of course, we were alerted to the fact that we could be getting inpatients, so we were on the wards and we had things set up—we were ready for them when they arrived. I don't remember exactly what time patients started arriving, but sometime probably about mid-morning or noon, around that area. That soon, yeah.

(It was) mostly Americans at that time. A little later, we got in Germans. I don't remember if we got French at all, but I don't imagine we did. But we did get Germans from time to time and we treated them just like anybody else. (Regarding whether the Germans were

guarded), not really, they were just there [laughs] because probably they got through without anybody actually knowing that they were Germans. But we knew that when we got them, when we were taking care of them. And they were nice, they were just as nice as could be. They treated the nurses with much respect and we took care of them just like we took care of our own soldiers.

Well, we worked sixteen and eighteen hours when we had a big surge of wounded in, and then when things slowed down a bit, we worked regular hours. We worked until we had taken care of all of them, with first aid, and baths, and feeding and so forth.

There were a lot of abdominal wounds. There were a lot of face wounds and legs—mostly facial and limbs, but quite a few abdominal wounds.

We simply had to keep our emotions under control. It was extremely upsetting at first to see so many wounded at one time, and I did see patients with faces half shot off or limbs shot off—I mean, you just simply had to keep your emotions under control. I don't get real emotional now—this is just a hangover from that time. One of the worst things for me, if you don't mind my telling about one particular person: this young, young soldier—he was nineteen. He was wounded very, very badly. He had an abdominal wound. We expected him to die that night. But he didn't. I stood with him all night. He simply was crying and screaming and praying all night. And I stood there praying and crying with him all night. And that is the worst thing that I really went through. I mean, it was just a very hard thing. And then in the morning, early in the morning, he died. At that time, I felt a great relief. I thought, he is now at rest, not in pain anymore. That is a vivid, vivid thing in my mind to this day.

But that's the most emotional that I ever got. After that—this was early, early in the war—I thought, I have to keep myself in control. I can't get so emotional over things, I have to keep it under control. And I did. And we did. We just had to.

Opal Grapes worked as an army nurse in England for two and a half years before returning to the United States. She was training to go to the Pacific Theater when the war ended.

Above: A Red Cross member tends to a wounded sailor after D-Day. Women served as nurses in several organizations, including the Red Cross, US Army and US Navy.

OTHER PERSPECTIVES

Gerhard Winnecken

Platoon Leader, 1057th Grenadier Regiment, German Army

Gerhard Winnecken grew up in Bonn, Germany, where he was a member of the Hitler Youth. At eighteen he joined the Wehrmacht and was sent east to fight in Russia, where he served as a dispatch rider. Winnecken was sent to France in 1944 and was in command of a platoon in the 1057th Grenadier Regiment on June 6.

As wounded American soldiers were being treated in England, their fellow soldiers in Normandy gained ground against a mix of expert and poorly prepared German units. Some of the Germans were veterans of the brutal struggle on the Eastern Front, and faced a new struggle for survival in France. Even as they rallied against the invading forces, many concluded they could not prevail.

So, I had been in Russia. We got everything new—uniforms, vehicles, all radio equipment, shoes, socks—everything new. Now where I was in France, the uniforms were rather old, the shoes were captured from Poland—they weren't German shoes, only lace-up shoes—and then some short leggings. But our weapons were all new.

We arrived in Normandy on May 20th approximately, and our work consisted mostly of planting Rommel's asparagus. Tree trunks—they must have been five meters long and at the top 15-20 centimeters (wide) at the least. They were embedded on large flat areas and meadows, and we surmised these were possible landing (zones). And in some places we strung barbed wire between the columns at the top. On June 6th, in the morning, we heard firing from the coast, the rolling from the bombs that were falling on the coast. Then two gliders flew over us. We already had an order to shoot—I was a sergeant, I had a platoon, that was 30 men. We had 30 machine guns mounted in stands high up, with a different sight for moving targets. After the two gliders flew over us, a third one came and we fired at it, and it made a funny movement and turned. It was still dark; it hadn't become completely light. Then we had to get in the vehicle quickly and take off.

On the next day we were (scheduled) to have target practice. We had a lot of ammunition for our mortars—practice rounds, already loaded on our vehicle—we had a kind of little wagon with bicycle wheels. It was pulled either by the mule or by us. We had to unload it again, the practice ammunition, and then had to load the live ammunition. And then we were through Saint-Sauveur-le-Vicomte and in Saint Sauveur we had the first attack from the air, from the Jabo (German nickname for American fighter-bomber aircraft)—but with no injuries.

Then, with the whole baggage train—all the baggage, the ammunition, the field kitchen which was so important—we all had to leave Saint Sauveur and we, who were only on foot, had to cross the bridge. On the other side there were trucks. We were loaded up on them, and transported in the direction of Sainte-Mère-Église/Amfreville. After we got down off the truck there were parachutes lying all around, so we knew they were mostly American. It wasn't only the Americans who came down—also supplies. Sacks with ammunition, weapons, clothing for the Americans and food above all. That interested us, naturally. We have then cigarettes and chocolate for us, right?

Then we were on a broad front in the direction of the Merderet River. On the third day we are in a trench in Cauquigny. We were dug in and I had the order to stop them by any means. The Americans came with amphibious tanks, and it was all over. We had only machine guns. I couldn't go up against a tank with a machine gun. We had no *Panzerfausts* or bazookas. When the tanks came, I had—enough! Then we were seven men of the thirty. (After being captured by American forces) we came to the coast, one night spent in a sheep pen, and a few days later the Americans interrogated us. And there on the coast I saw how much materiel came in. I said to my friend, "Look here. We have lost the war."

After being shipped to the United States with other prisoners aboard the RMS *Queen Mary*, Winnecken spent the rest of the war in prisoner of war camps. As a POW, he was assigned to work on tobacco and sweet potato farms. After the war Winnecken was shipped back to Germany.

Prisoner of War enclosure on Utah Beach. Prisoners were kept in barbed wire enclosures on the beach until they boarded ships to England. Their final destinations were POW camps in the United States.

CONCLUSION

CHAPTER SIX

6 . 6 . 44

On June 6, 1944, D-Day, nearly 160,000 Allied boys leaped from landing craft and planes to do battle with the armed forces of Hitler's Third Reich and liberate Europe from tyranny. Those Americans who fought on the beaches and fields of Normandy, flew the planes and manned the ships, gave all they had—many gave their very lives—for our freedom and democracy. On that riveting day the end of a terrible world war became possible. The fortified perimeter of Germany's defense system was shattered. But victory came at great cost for the young Americans and their allies. Some 9,000 who died in the Normandy campaign are buried in the Normandy American Cemetery above Omaha Beach and many more lie in graves in the towns and countryside of the United States. Estimates vary, but roughly 2,500 Americans lost their lives on D-Day alone. Dozens of selected accounts from individuals who survived the day are shared in this book, and these stories open a window into poignant experiences.

When President Ronald Reagan returned to Normandy in 1984 on the 40th Anniversary of D-Day, he spoke of the dedication and sacrifice of those who rallied for their country:

"We're here to mark that day in history when the Allied armies joined in the battle to reclaim this continent for liberty. For four long years, much of Europe had been under a terrible shadow. Free nations had fallen, Jews cried out in the camps, millions cried for its rescue. Here in Normandy the rescue began. Here the Allies stood and fought against tyranny in a giant undertaking unparalleled in human history."

Indeed, D-Day will always stand out as a pivotal episode. A growing number of scholarly accounts, memoirs, film, memorials and museums preserve memories of that day. While every amphibious landing of World War II had its own D-Day, for most, the Operation Overlord campaign of June 6, 1944, executed principally by American, British and Canadian forces, will remain *the* D-Day. The story of this day will be told for thousands of years, just as the epic battles of Marathon, Thermopylae, Hastings, Yorktown and Gettysburg still resonate in our collective memory. These all were decisive moments, when war tested warriors and their values. The Normandy Allied assault required extraordinary courage and character among the citizen soldiers who determined the outcome.

Opposite: American GIs leave an LCVP at Omaha Beach.

Above: A GI helps a fellow soldier by removing small bits of shrapnel embedded in his face during the Normandy invasion.

A young French girl places a flower on the grave of an American soldier.

Everything We Have focuses on rank and file soldiers and other armed service members, conveying their experiences and feelings, details of their actions and motivations. In their words, one senses their great pride in being a part of that day. You also understand their sadness, their good fortune, and sometimes their survivor's guilt. In many of these accounts it becomes clear how discipline, motivation, toughness and training overcame fatigue and fear amid the heat of the battle. There is an overwhelming sense of determination in the face of the uncertainty about whether one would live to see another day and to return home.

The story of D-Day enables the reader to understand the deeds of these men as we stand in awe of how they fought and why. In this book we find a diverse mix of remembrances drawn from The National WWII Museum's collection of more than 10,000 curated accounts. At the Museum's campus in New Orleans, or through its online offerings, visitors can see many of these veterans' recorded videos, gain a better sense of their pain, their modesty and their courage. In these pages you have read excerpts from their recollections supported by photos, maps and images of artifacts and weapons that weave into the tapestry of D-Day memories. Whether in print or video, these voices are authentic. There is no pretense. They speak to the best in all of us and to the American Spirit. As we learned from two modern chroniclers of

those veterans, Stephen Ambrose and Tom Brokaw, these young Americans generally did not relish talking about themselves and what they did on the battlefield. It took others to draw out stories that, in many cases, had never been shared previously with anyone. We are privileged to learn from them now. While some may challenge Brokaw's *Greatest Generation* depiction, most Americans agree that veterans of D-Day and other WWII conflicts deserve special credit for their devoted service and for what they contributed to our country after returning home.

In reading their recollections or hearing their stories, many marvel at their actions during a time of crisis and danger in the world, and ask the question: "Could I do what they did?" And if you are inspired by their love of country, by their quiet strength and courage, you will likely answer, "Yes, I would do this if my country needed me." What strikes us most are their qualities of commitment, initiative, optimism and determination in the face of obstacles, their sense of duty. Their values were forged from experiences on the home front and the war front. All of us are the beneficiaries of those who gave everything they had in the fight for our freedom. They would want the memory of their fight to give greater meaning to our lives. These individuals answered the big questions for their generation, and they leave us with questions for today.

What does World War II mean to us? Did the sacrifices of the boys of D-Day, as well as the millions who sustained them, make a lasting difference? Was this just another military victory? Did victory make the world better? Was the battle really about freedom and the destruction of tyranny? Did the American Spirit make a difference then, and does it still?

While the American spirit is difficult to define, many would say—as Stephen Ambrose often did—*you know it when you see it*. Look for the bright threads of that spirit in the reflections of D-Day veterans. This spirit and the values it engenders should be honored by every generation.

In times of peace, problems at home and abroad often cloud our memories and vision, shifting attention away from what is important to our communities and our nation. But our troubles usually pale in contrast to the challenges and sacrifices of the soldiers, sailors and airmen of World War II. They remind us to think about what we believe in and what we will fight to defend. At The National WWII Museum, we recall the sentiments of President Franklin Roosevelt

and other leaders who were devoted to keeping the beacon of freedom burning for Americans and others around the globe.

Roosevelt, as he rallied the nation for war, emphasized that four freedoms—freedom of speech, freedom of worship, freedom from fear and freedom from want—were among fundamental human rights, and should be secured for all peoples of the world. At Dwight Eisenhower's presidential inauguration in 1953, the former Allied Supreme Commander proclaimed that "freedom has its life in the hearts, the actions, the spirit of men, and so it must be daily earned and refreshed—else like a flower cut from its life-giving roots, it will wither and die."

In 1962, President John F. Kennedy, a PT boat commander in the Pacific during World War II, called fresh attention to FDR's "four freedoms" message and warned that these liberties "have been under harsh and insistent attack from another totalitarian faith" in the postwar era. "Let the word go forth from this time and place, to friend and foe alike, that the torch has been passed to a

Normandy American Cemetery. "You can manufacture weapons and you can purchase ammunition, but you can't buy valor and you can't pull heroes off an assembly line."—Sergeant John B. Ellery, 1st Infantry Division, quoted on a wall at the cemetery.

Walt, Marie and Roland Ehlers (L-R) in
1941.

new generation of Americans—born in this century, tempered by war, disciplined by a hard and bitter peace, proud of our ancient heritage—and unwilling to witness the slow undoing of those human rights to which this nation has always been committed, and to which we are committed today at home and around the world. The cost of freedom is always high, but Americans have always paid it."

The measurable legacies of the Allied victory in World War II were great. First came the gift of democracy to Japan and to West Germany (although East Germany and other Soviet bloc states would face a different fate), as well as the war's impact on reducing colonialism around the world. Second was the Marshall

Plan which rebuilt the economies of nations and cities we had just destroyed, and was described by Winston Churchill as "the most generous act in human history." No one doubts the powerful repercussions of the Marshall Plan in restoring economic life and hope across much of Europe, with similar assistance given to Japan.

We know of the peace and prosperity ultimately made possible by victory on D-Day. We are inspired by the words and actions of our leaders who advanced the cause of freedom. But in the end, we pay special tribute to those who stormed into Normandy, risking everything.

Among those were three soldiers who went ashore at "Bloody Omaha."

Private Felix Branham, whose K Company, 116th Infantry Regiment, took heavy casualties, said D-Day "will live with me till the day I die, and I'll take it to heaven with me. It was the longest, most miserable, horrible day that I or anyone else ever went through."

Walt Ehlers, an Army sergeant who received the Medal of Honor for his exploits in Normandy, long suffered nightmares and guilt over the loss of his older brother Roland at Omaha. "I felt like if we'd been together, that wouldn't have happened. But God sent us in different ways. He was a great soldier, a fantastic soldier … He was my hero until the day he died. He still is."

Dr. Harold Baumgarten, a rifleman wounded five times over two days, described a horrific scene on Omaha as fellow soldiers were torn apart by German gunfire. In recalling the battle, he always paused to identify comrades who went down – "Private Robert Dittmar, Fairfield, Connecticut … Sergeant Clarence Roberson of Lynchburg, Virginia." He explained, "I always mention their names and where they came from. I don't want people to forget about them."

The distinguished British poet Stephen Spender framed the sacrifices of such individuals with these timeless words:

The names of those who in their lives fought for life,
Who were at their hearts the fire's center
Borne of the sun, they travelled a short way toward the sun
And left the vivid air signed with their honor.

American soldiers who gave everything they had on a beach in Normandy.

RESEARCH SOURCES

The author relied on The National WWII Museum's artifact collections, oral histories, memoirs and many of the best secondary works on the events of D-Day covered in this book. At the heart of this work are the eyewitness testimonies of those who experienced these decisive hours and days. Their full accounts are preserved in the Museum's archives, and many are accessible online at ww2online.org. Readers are encouraged to explore the outstanding D-Day histories below.

Ambrose, Stephen. *D-Day: June 6, 1944: The Climactic Battle of World War II*. New York: Simon & Schuster, 1994.

Ambrose, Stephen. *Band of Brothers: E Company 506th Regiment, 101st Airborne From Normandy to Hitler's Eagle's Nest*. New York: Simon & Schuster, 1992.

Astor, Gerald. *June 6, 1944: The Voices of D-Day*. New York: Dell, 2002.

Atkinson, Rick. *Guns at Last Light: The War in Western Europe, 1944–1945*. New York: Henry Holt and Co., 2013.

Balkoski, Joseph. *Omaha Beach: D-day, June 6, 1944*. Mechanicsburg: Stackpole Books, 2006.

Balkoski, Joseph. *Utah Beach: D-Day, June 6, 1944*. Mechanicsburg: Stackpole Books, 2005.

Baumgarten, Dr. Harold. *D-Day Survivor: An Autobiography*. Gretna: Pelican Publishing, 2006

Beevor, Antony. *D-Day: The Battle for Normandy*. New York: Viking/Penguin, 2009.

Brinkley, Douglas. *The Boys of Pointe du Hoc: Ronald Reagan, D-Day, and the US Army 2nd Ranger Battalion*. New York: Harper Perennial, 2005.

Capa, Robert. *Slightly Out of Focus*. New York: Modern Library, 2001.

Eisenhower, Dwight. *Crusade in Europe*. Baltimore: Johns Hopkins University Press, 1948.

Gross, Dr. Clayton Kelly. *Live Bait: WWII Memoirs of an Undefeated Fighter Ace*. Portland: Inkwater Press, 2006.

Hastings, Max. *Overlord: D-Day and the Battle for Normandy*. New York: Vintage, 1984.

Hatfield, Thomas M. *Rudder: From Leader to Legend*. College Station: Texas A & M University Press, 2011.

Keegan, John. *The Second World War*. London: Penguin Books, 1989.

Koskimaki, George. *D-Day with the Screaming Eagles*. Novato: Presidio Press, 2006.

Malarkey, Don. *Easy Company Soldier: The Legendary Battles of a Sergeant from World War II's "Band of Brothers."* New York: St. Martin's Press, 2008.

Matthews, Anne, Nancy Caldwell Sorel, and Roger J. Spiller, compilers. *Reporting World War II*. New York: The Library of America, 1995.

McManus, John C. *The Americans at D-Day, The American Experience at the Normandy Invasion*, New York: Forge Books, 2005.

Murphy, Robert. *No Better Place to Die: Ste. Mere-Eglise, June 1944: The Battle for La Fière Bridge*. Philadelphia: Casemate, 2000.

Nordyke, Phil. *All American, All the Way: The Combat History of the 82nd Airborne Division in World War II*. Minneapolis: Zenith Press, 2005.

O'Donnell, Patrick K. *Dog Company: The Boys of Pointe du Hoc*. Cambridge: De Capo Press, 2012.

Pogue, Forrest C. *Pogue's War: Diaries of a WWII Combat Historian*. Lexington: The University Press of Kentucky, 2001.

Pyle, Ernie. *Brave Men*. New York: Henry Holt, 1944.

Raaen, General John C. *Intact: A First-hand Account of the D-day Invasion from a 5ᵗʰ Rangers Company Commander*. St. Louis: Reedy Press, 2012.

Ryan, Cornelius Ryan. *The Longest Day*. New York: Simon and Schuster, 1959.

Sheeran, James J. *No Surrender: A World War II Memoir*. New York: The Berkley Publishing Group, 2011.

Smith, William C. Jr. *The First Man on Omaha Red: D-Day H-Hour – 2:00: The War Memoirs of Capt. William C. Smith Jr.* Scotts Valley: CreateSpace Independent Publishing Platform, 2014.

Symonds, Craig. *Operation Neptune: The D-Day Landings and the Allied Invasion of Europe*. Oxford: Oxford University Press, 2014.

Tedder, Lord Arthur William. *With Prejudice: The War Memoirs of Marshal of the Royal Air Force, Lord Tedder*. Boston: Little, Brown and Company, 1966.

Taylor, Thomas. *Behind Hitler's Lines: The True Story of the Only Soldier to Fight for both America and the Soviet Union in World War II*. Novato: Presidio Press, 2004.

Von Luck, Hans. *Panzer Commander: the Memoirs of Colonel Hans von Luck*. New York: Dell Publishing Company, 1999.

Webster, Daniel. *Parachute Infantry: An American Paratrooper's Memoir of D-Day and the Fall of the Third Reich*. New York: Bantam Dell, 2002.

Wilson, George. *If You Survive: From Normandy to the Battle of the Bulge to the End of World War II, One American Officer's Riveting True Story*. New York: Ballantine Books, 1987.

Winters, Dick. *Beyond Band of Brothers: The War Memoirs of Major Dick Winters*. New York: The Berkley Publishing Group, 2006.

PICTURE CREDITS

All images and maps are from the collections of The National WWII Museum, unless otherwise stated.

Note the abbreviation:

NARA—The United States National Archives and Records Administration

2 NARA/US Army Air Forces, A16034, **6** Official U.S. Coast Guard Photograph, Gift of Jeffrey and Mary Cole, 2002.119.036, **9, 11, 12-13** NARA/US Navy, 80-G-252146, **14** Gift in Memory of Allan Voluck, 2015.111.160, **15** Gift of Grace A. Forsch Bagg, 2010.161.211, **17** NARA/US Army Signal Corps, 111-C-1135, **18** NARA/US Army Signal Corps, 111-C-1232, **19** Courtesy of the Dwight D. Eisenhower Presidential Library, **20** Gift of C. Ed Nelson, 1999.014.007, **20-21** NARA/US Navy, 80-G-252146, **26-27** NARA/US Army Signal Corps, 111-SC-222749, **28c** Gift in Memory of Wallace C. Strobel, 2016.189.001, **28b** US Army Signal Corp Photograph, Gift of Maude Hayman, 2004.311.106, **29** NARA/US Army Signal Corps, **30** NARA/US Army Signal Corps, 111-SC-190367, **33t** NARA/US Army Air Forces, A17145, **33b** The National WWII Museum, 2006.181.001, **34** The Charles L. Moore Collection, OH.3358, **35** Gift of Musée Airborne, Sainte-Mère-Église, 2007.337.002, **36t** US Army Signal Corps Photograph, Gift in Memory of Maurice T. White, 2011.065.1313, **36b** Gift of Voorhies P. Dewailly, 2000.117.004, **37** NARA/US Army Signal Corps, 111-C-1050, **37 inset** Gift of the Bornio Family, 2010.299.077, **38** The Robert L. Williams Collection, OH.2828, **39** Gift of Ford McKenzie, 2003.001.001, **40** NARA/US Army Signal Corps, 111-SC-222749, **41** The Robert L. Williams Collection, OH.2828, **42** The John W. Marr Collection, OH.1657, **43** The John W. Marr Collection, OH.1657, **44t** U.S. Army Heritage and Education Center, Carlisle, PA, **45** U.S. Army Heritage and Education Center, Carlisle, PA, **46** US Army Signal Corp Photograph, Gift of Maude Hayman, 2004.311.134, **47t** The John W. Marr Collection, OH.1657, **47b** The St. Lô Collection, 1994.001.0578.004, **48** The Robert Murphy Collection, OH.1826, **49** The Robert Murphy Collection, OH.1826, **50** Gift of Kenneth Rendell, 1999.037.014, **51t** The National WWII Museum, 2007.070.004, **51b** Gift of Kenneth Rendell, 1999.021.001, **52** NARA/US Army Signal Corps, **53l&r** Courtesy of the Czekanski Family, **54** The Elmo Bell Collection, OH.0129, **55t** The National WWII Museum, 2008.179.001, **55b** Gift of Tom Blakey, 2004.241.042, **56** Gift in Memory of John H. "Johnny" Capehart, 2003.147.001, **57** The St. Lô Collection, 1994.001.1103, **58** The Clinton Riddle Collection, OH.1547, **59l** Gift of Paul Rogers, 1999.098.001, **59r** Gift of George H. Leidenheimer, 2004.096.001, **60** The Wayne Pierce Collection, OH.1984, **61** NARA, **61 inset** Gift of Colonel Keith Schmedemann, 2009.384.186, **62** Gift of Linda Sabo Peck, 2003.352.001, **63** Gift of

James Peninger, 2002.451.004, **64** Hershey Derry Township Historical Society Collection/ P-1285-10, **65** NARA/US Army Signal Corps, 111-SC-192441, **66** Hershey Derry Township Historical Society Collection/ P-1285-11, **68** NARA/US Army Signal Corps, 111-SC-320862, **69** Loan Courtesy of Curt Schilling, L2007.005.001, **71** NARA/US Army Signal Corps, 111-SC-320864, **72** Gift in Memory of Arthur "Dutch" Schultz, 1998.001.001, **73** (from top) Gift in Memory of Wallace C. Strobel, 2016.189.002, 004 & 003, **74-75** Gift of Robert E. Bedford, 2012.541.018, **76** Official US Coast Guard Photograph, Gift of Jeffrey and Mary Cole, 2002.119.014, **77** NARA/US Navy, 80-G-302423, **78** Gift of Robert E. Bedford, 2012.541.018, **79t** Gift of Stuart Mahlin, 1999.047, **79b** Gift of Asa Clark, 1999.012.001, **80** Gift of Asa Clark, 1999.012.001, **83** Gift in Memory of Robert D. Maidlow, 2013.615.008, **84l** Gift of Robert E. Bedford, 2012.541.030, **84r** Gift in Memory of Robert D. Maidlow, 2013.615.029, **85** Gift of Stuart Mahlin, 1999.047, **87** NARA/US Navy, 80-G-231647, **88** NARA/US Navy, 80-G-252288, **89** U.S. Navy Official Photograph, Gift of Charles Ives, 2011.102.478, **90** Courtesy of Gregg Gullickson, **91** NARA/US Navy, 80-G-231649, **92l** NARA/US Navy, 80-G-229310, **92r** Gift of Barbara Thompson, 2013.067.010, **95** The United States Naval History and Heritage Command/NH 82516, **96** NARA/US Army Signal Corps, 111-SC-190276, **97** U.S. Navy Official Photograph, Gift of Charles Ives, 2011.102.483, **98** The Marvin Perrett Collection, OH.1973, **99** NARA/US Navy, 80-G-252377, **100** The National WWII Museum, 2006.129.001, **101** NARA/US Coast Guard, 26-G-2410, **103** NARA/US Army Air Forces, A16065, **104** US Navy Official Photograph, Gift of Charles Ives, 2011.102.465, **105t** Gift of Edward Gilleran, 1999.020.001, **105b** Gift of Charles W. Hostler, 2001.118.001, **106** Gift of Stuart Mahlin, 1999.047.002, **107** NARA/US Army Signal Corps, 111-SC-275831, **108l** The St. Lô Collection, 1994.001.0590.1, **108r** Gift of Morris Self, 2004.133.002, **109** Gift of Stuart Mahlin, 1999.047, **110** Gift of Herbert Davis, 1999.045.001 & .002, **111** NARA/US Navy, 80-GK-13347, **112t** Gift of C. Ed Nelson, 1999.014.004, **112c** Gift of C. Ed Nelson, 1999.014.003, **113t** Gift of Robert E. Bedford, 2012.541.013, **113b** Gift of Robert E. Bedford, 2012.541.007, **115** Gift of Robert E. Bedford, 2012.541.019, **116** Gift of Robert E. Bedford, 2012.541.023, **117** Gift of Grace A. Forsch Bagg, 2010.161.120, **118** The David Roderick Collection, OH.2167, **119l** NARA/US Army Signal Corps, 111-SC-275765, **119r** Gift of Grace A. Forsch Bagg, 2010.161.065, **120t** NARA/US Army Signal Corps, 111-SC-275936, **120b** The National WWII Museum, 2002.467.001, **122-123** NARA/US Navy, 80-G-254279, **124** Official U.S. Coast Guard Photograph, Gift of Jeffrey and Mary Cole, 2002.119.036, **125t** Gift of Joyce H. Lamont, 1999.049.001, **125b** US Navy Official Photograph, Gift of Charles Ives, 2011.102.486, **126l** Gift of Colonel Keith Schmedemann, 2009.384.001, **126r** Gift of Robert P. Stoddard,

Every effort has been made to acknowledge correctly and contact the source and/or copyright holder of each picture and Carlton Publishing Group apologises for any unintentional errors or omissions, which will be corrected in future editions of this book.

THE NATIONAL WORLD WAR II MUSEUM ORAL HISTORY COLLECTION

Available online at http://ww2online.org

The Harold Baumgarten Collection, OH.0114.
Interviewed in 2007 by Thomas Lofton.

The Elmo Bell Collection, OH.0129.
Interviewed in 2006 by Steve Droter.

The William Dabney Collection, OH.0523.
Interviewed in 2005 by Betsy Plumb.

The Frank Denius Collection, OH.3008.
Interviewed in 2013 by Hugh Ambrose, Joey Balfour.

The Clyde East Collection, OH.0667.
Interviewed in 2010 by Thomas Lofton.

The Walter Ehlers Collection, OH.0677.
Interviewed in 2006 by Steve Droter.

The Bernard Friedenberg Collection, OH.4373.
Interviewed in 2016 by Larry Miller.

The Opal Grapes Collection, OH.0933.
Interviewed in 2010 by Thomas Naquin.

The Clayton Kelly Gross Collection, OH.0961.
Interviewed in 2010 by Thomas Lofton.

The Walter Touhy Halloran Collection, OH.5207.
Interviewed in 2018 by Hannah Dailey.

The Lucien Laborde Collection, OH.1453.
Interviewed in 2013 by Thomas Lofton.

The Leonard Lomell Collection, OH.1552.
Interviewed in 2006 by Steve Droter.

The John W. Marr Collection, OH.1657.
Interviewed in 2007 by Steve Droter.

The Robert Miksa Collection, OH.3164.
Interviewed in 2014 by Seth Paridon.

The Charles L. Moore Collection, OH.3358.
Interviewed in 2014 by Dan Olmsted.

The George Morgan Collection, OH.4832.
Interviewed in 2017 by Patrick Stephen.

The Robert Murphy Collection, OH.1826.
Interviewed in 2007 by Steve Droter.

The Eveline Peardon Collection, OH.4982.
Interviewed in 2017 by Joey Balfour.

The Marvin J. Perrett Collection, OH.1973.
Interviewed in 2006 by Thomas Naquin.

The Wayne Pierce Collection, OH.1984.
Interviewed in 2007 by Steve Droter.

The John Raaen Collection, OH.3261.
Interviewed in 2017 by Seth Paridon.

The John Raaen Collection, OH.5205.
Interviewed in 2018 by Nick Mueller.

The David Roderick Collection, OH.2167.
Interviewed in 2008 by Thomas Lofton.

The Arthur Seltzer Collection, OH.2296.
Interviewed in 2010 by Thomas Naquin.

The Edward Tipper Collection, OH.3482.
Interviewed in 2014 by Joey Balfour.

The Robert L. Williams Collection, OH.2828.
Interviewed in 2007 by Thomas Lofton.

The Gerhard Winnecken Collection, OH.2924.
Interviewed in 2007 by Seth Paridon.
Translated from German by Bob Wolf.

The Eisenhower Center Peter Kalikow World War II Collection, University of New Orleans

John Ahearn, account provided circa 1992.

John Richard Blackburn, account provided circa 1993.

Joseph Louis Camera, account provided circa 1992.

Clair Galdonik, account provided circa 1992.

Grant Gullickson, account provided circa 1991.

Leonard Lomell, interviewed in 1993 by Ronald Drez.

Ross Olsen, account provided circa 1994.

Frank South, account provided circa 1992.

Howard Vander Beek, account provided circa 1993.

Elmer Vermeer, account provided circa 1986.

Orval Woodrow Wakefield, account provided circa 1992.

Richard Winters, Interviewed in 1990 by Stephen Ambrose.

Other Sources

The Gordon Osland Collection, 2013.174. Gift of Lynn Tepper, the collection of The National WWII Museum.

Personal letters of James Rudder provided by the Rudder family.

Other Credits

DEAR MOM
By Maury Harris
Copyright © 1941 (Renewed) by Embassy Music Corporation (BMI)
International Copyright Secured. All Rights Reserved.
Reprinted by Permission

INDEX

THIS IS AN ANDRE DEUTSCH BOOK

The National WWII Museum
New Orleans

Published in 2019 by André Deutsch Limited
A division of the Carlton Publishing Group
20 Mortimer Street
London W1T 3JW

Text and maps © The National WWII Museum 2019
Design © André Deutsch 2019

A CIP catalogue for this book is available from the British Library.

ISBN: 978 0 233 00581 2

Printed in Dubai

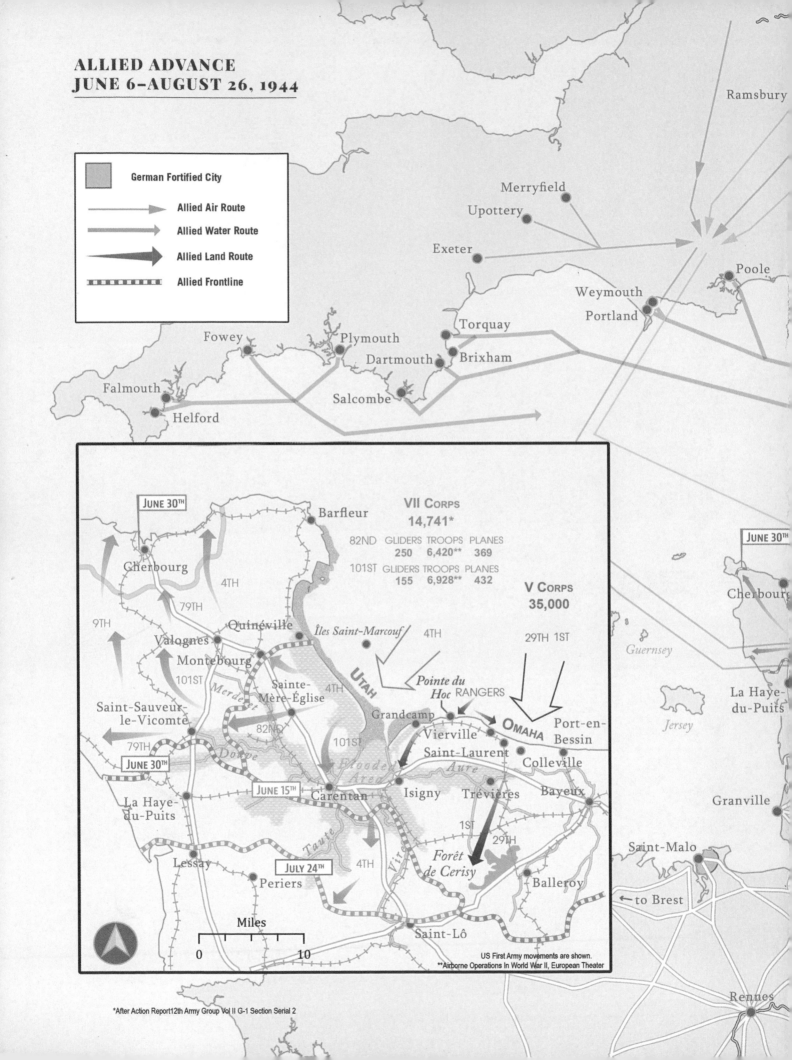

ALLIED ADVANCE
JUNE 6–AUGUST 26, 1944

Ramsbury

Merryfield

Upottery

Exeter

Poole

Weymouth
Portland

Fowey

Plymouth

Torquay

Dartmouth   Brixham

Falmouth

Salcombe

Helford

Legend
- **German Fortified City**
- **Allied Air Route**
- **Allied Water Route**
- **Allied Land Route**
- **Allied Frontline**

JUNE 30TH

Barfleur

VII CORPS
14,741*

	GLIDERS	TROOPS	PLANES
82ND	250	6,420**	369
101ST	155	6,928**	432

V CORPS
35,000

JUNE 30TH

Cherbourg

4TH

Cherbourg

79TH

9TH

Quinéville

Îles Saint-Marcouf

4TH

29TH 1ST

Guernsey

Valognes

Montebourg

101ST

UTAH

Pointe du
Hoc RANGERS

La Haye-
du-Puits

Sainte-
Mère-Église

Merderet

4TH

Grandcamp

OMAHA

Port-en-
Bessin

Jersey

Saint-Sauveur-
le-Vicomte

82ND

Vierville

Saint-Laurent

Colleville

79TH

Douve

101ST

Flooded
Area

Aure

Trévières

Bayeux

Granville

JUNE 30TH

JUNE 15TH

Carentan

Isigny

La Haye-
du-Puits

1ST

29TH

Saint-Malo

Taute

Forêt
de Cerisy

Lessay

JULY 24TH

4TH

Vire

Balleroy

← to Brest

Periers

Miles

0   10

Saint-Lô

US First Army movements are shown.
**Airborne Operations In World War II, European Theater

Rennes

*After Action Report12th Army Group Vol II G-1 Section Serial 2